INVESTING
IN YOUR
FUTURE

NATIONAL ASSOCIATION
OF INVESTORS CORPORATION

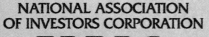

INVESTMENT EDUCATION
FOR INDIVIDUALS AND CLUBS
SINCE 1951

South-Western
EDUCATIONAL PUBLISHING
Thomson Learning™

Australia • Canada • Denmark • Japan • Mexico • New Zealand • Phillipines
Puerto Rico • Singapore • South Africa • Spain • United Kingdom • United States

Business Unit Director	Peter D. McBride
Executive Editor	Eve Lewis
Project Manager	Enid Nagel
Editor/Production Coordinator	Nicole Christopher Toms
Production Manager	Patricia Matthews Boies
Manufacturing Coordinator	Gordon Woodside
Marketing Manager	Nancy A. Long
Marketing Coordinator	Christian L. McNamee
Art & Design Coordinator	Bill Spencer
Electronic Prepress Services	A. W. Kingston Publishing Services, LLC

ISBN: 0-538-68607-3

3 4 5 6 7 8 9   VH   07 06 05 04 03 02

Printed in the United States of America

For permission to use material from this text, contact us by
- Web: *www.thomsonrights.com*
- Phone: 1-800-730-2214
- Fax: 1-800-730-2215

Reviewers

Kathryn L. Baas
Teacher
Kenosha Unified School District
Kenosha, WI

Robert Blailock
Director
National Association of Investors Corporation
Belen, NM

Jeanne E. Budig, Ph. D.
Director of Institutional Research
Vincennes University
Vincennes, IN

Bob Burns
Teacher, Business Education Department
Dixie Heights High School
Edgewood, KY

Kaye Corrigan
Department Coordinator of Business,
Technology Education, and Family &
Consumer Science Departments
Naperville Central High School
Naperville, IL

Eileen Dittmar
Business Technologies Instructor
Kent Career/Technical Center
Grand Rapids, MI

Lynn Dyer
Business Teacher
Lincoln High School
Thief River Falls, MN

Donna R. Jones
Director
National Association of Investors Corporation
Dayton, OH

Kelvin M. Meeks
Business and Technology Instructor
Raleigh Egypt High School
Memphis, TN

Kenneth Reed
Teacher, Business Department
Oakland High School
Murfreesboro, TN

Margaret Susan Short
Technology Director
Hebrew Academy
Huntington Beach, CA

Linda Simpson
Teacher
Anaheim Union High School District
Anaheim, CA

A. Ray Simms III
Certified Financial Planner
Cincinnati, OH

John Sternberg
Business Education Department Chairperson
Newton Senior High School
Newton, IA

Al J. Tieken
Former Superintendent
Diocese of Evansville
Evansville, IN

Julie Werner
Instructor
National Association of Investors Corporation
Warner Robins, GA

Saundra Wall Williams, Ed. D.
Assistant Professor, Adult Education
North Carolina State University
Raleigh, NC

Gail Yax
Teacher
Troy High School
Troy, MI

Contents

Contents

Chapter 7   PROJECTING THE FUTURE

Chapter 8   THE BOTTOM LINE

See next page for Appendices listing ▶

Appendices

PHOTO CREDITS and PERMISSIONS

Page 26, 37, 40, 47, 224, 225 EyeWire.

Page 236 Digital Vision Photography.

All other photos copyright PhotoDisc Inc. 1997-1999.

Pages 165, 174, 180, 193, 250 *Value Line Publishing, Inc.*

Pages 144, 145, 146 *Tootsie Roll Industries, Inc.*

Pages 138, 139 *Standard & Poor's*

Pages 85, 89, 90, 249 *Morningstar*

Chicago-based Morningstar, Inc. is a leading provider of investment information, research, and analysis.
For more information about Morningstar, visit *www. morningstar.com* or call 800-735-0700.

To Reach Your Goals for Tomorrow...

START LEARNING WITH NAIC

The National Association of Investors Corporation (NAIC) is a non-profit association dedicated to investment education since 1951. NAIC can help you learn more about personal finance, saving, and investing!

YOUTH MEMBERSHIPS

NAIC's Youth Membership Includes five issues of NAIC's *Young Money Matters* youth newsletter, *Better Investing* magazine each month, information on how to start an investment program or a youth investment club, NAIC's Membership Catalog, a special coupon sheet, and all NAIC membership benefits.

NAIC Youth Membership DELUXE package Includes all the items in the regular membership, plus *Investing For Life* Youth Investors Guide, NAIC's *Mutual Fund Handbook*, a special NAIC baseball cap, stock ruler and button.

EDUCATIONAL BENEFITS AND SERVICES

***Better Investing* magazine** A monthly magazine providing current investment information, company news and more!

Low Cost Investment Plan A unique program that allows you to start investing with just one share of stock.

NAIC Stock Service NAIC's new discount brokerage program allowing you to start investing with only $10 a month.

NAIC Official Guide NAIC's guide book to starting a lifetime investment program on your own or with an investment club.

Investor Information Reports NAIC's stock fact sheets providing company information and data for investors.

NAIC Regional Chapters NAIC offers you support through a network of more than 110 Regional Chapters staffed by trained volunteers who provide investment education seminars, workshops, Investor Fairs and other events. For a current listing of contacts, visit the NAIC Website or see *Better Investing* magazine each month.

YOUTH EDUCATION RESOURCES

NAIC's *Young Money Matters* Newsletter A newsletter focusing on investment education for youth featuring real-life stories of young investor experiences, educational exercises and fun games to teach youth about money concepts, saving, personal finance and investing. *(5 issues per year, included with Youth Membership)*

NAIC Membership Catalog and Investor's Web Site—FREE! These resources describe all of NAIC's educational products, services and support to young and adult investors. Visit the NAIC Website Youth Education area to read interesting youth and investing articles and learn more about starting a lifetime investment program!

For more information or a FREE NAIC Investor's Kit, contact NAIC.
NAIC, P.O. Box 220, Royal Oak, MI 48098
Toll Free Tel: 1-877-ASK-NAIC (275-6242) Fax: (248) 583-4880
Website: *www.better-investing.org* Email: service@better-investing.org

Chapter 1

PLAN FOR LIFE

INDUSTRY INDICATORS
TELECOMMUNICATIONS

MCI WorldCom, Inc.
Founded in 1983

MCI WorldCom began as a small long distance reseller in Mississippi. Known as Long Distance Discount Service (LDDS) in 1983, the company gradually grew through mergers with other telecommunications companies and went public in 1989. LDDS continued to use successful mergers and acquisitions as a means of expansion throughout the 1990s, completing three multi-billion dollar mergers in 1998 with MCI Communications Corporation, Brooks Fiber Properties, Inc, and CompuServe Corporation. Now under the name MCI WorldCom, the company provides a variety of communications services to residential and business customers.

MCI WorldCom is a world leader in providing integrated long distance, Internet, and data communications services. The MCI WorldCom network links more than 38,000 buildings in the U.S. and abroad, and allows MCI to provide a variety of communication services to its customers. Clever advertising and programs such as 5 Cent Sundays, 1-800-COLLECT, 10-10-321, 10-10-220, and 10-10-9000 have attracted many new customers. The company now boasts over $30 million in revenues annually.

The strategy of MCI WorldCom has been to capitalize on the fastest growing segments of the communications industry: Internet, data, and phone services. In accordance with this strategy, MCI announced a merger with Sprint in 1999. Sprint, also a global communications company, built the first nationwide fiberoptic network and the first all-digital, nationwide PCS wireless system. The company formed by this $129 billion merger will be known as WorldCom, and will be able to provide "all-distance" services to business and residential customers, as well as nationwide digital and wireless voice and data services, making it a world leader in the telecommunications industry.

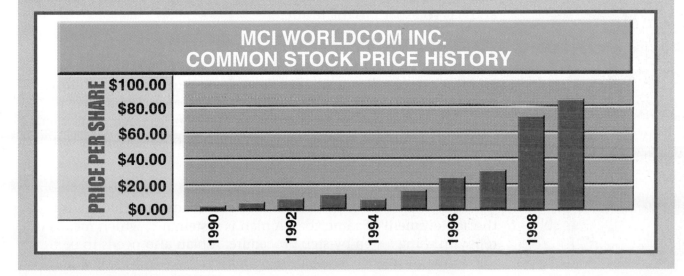

MCI WORLDCOM INC. COMMON STOCK PRICE HISTORY

LESSON 1.1

The Importance of Planning

P lanning is a process that should be applied to all aspects of life, from choosing a career to finding yourself. Financial planning works best when you understand clearly your reasons for trying to build a strong financial structure. Understanding who you are and what you want to accomplish is not easy to achieve, but it is worth looking for. As you plan you will realize the great power you have to make choices about things that affect your life.

GOALS

■ **Explain the process of planning.**

■ **Discuss planning for your life.**

■ **Describe a balance between planning and impulsiveness.**

WHAT IS PLANNING?

In the early 1900s teenagers listened to a popular recording entitled, "I Don't Know Where I'm Going, But I'm on My Way." The title may sound silly, but it seems to describe clearly how many people live their lives. Their lives show no sign of planning—they have no goal in mind and no plan to reach a goal. They live their lives by making them up as they go along.

At every age in life, you need to be looking ahead. It is important to continually set goals for yourself even for events that are likely to occur far in the future. Getting a college degree may be a distant goal for a student in the fourth grade. Yet, what that student learns at all grade levels will gradually build the academic and other skills needed to someday be accepted for college study.

Life is a journey, and if you think you can make the trip without long-range planning, you are in for a bumpy ride. You may run into detours and dead ends. No Outlet. Wrong Way. Do Not Enter. Like cryptic computer error messages, these road signs will turn you back and bar your path to the future.

PERSONAL GROWTH

Planning is part of growing up. As a child, you relied on your parents and teachers to tell you what to do and when to do it. You followed a plan others had laid out for you. But as you grow up, you have to learn to do your own planning. It is not enough to have some vague ideas about where you want to go and how you want to live. You need an active plan for getting there.

WHAT IS A PLAN?

A **plan** is a method or process worked out in advance that leads to the achievement of some goal. A plan is systematic, which means it relies on using a step-by-step procedure. A plan also needs to be flexible so that it may be adapted to gradual changes in your goal.

Rule #1 If you want to enjoy a successful and rewarding life, you have to plan for it.

Don't count on winning the lottery. Create your own success. Design a plan and follow it.

THE PLANNING PROCESS

Step 1: Set a Goal Identify something you want to achieve or obtain, your **goal**. The goal, which is usually longer term in nature, will require planning, patience, and discipline to achieve. Just living in the present moment is not a goal.

Step 2: Acquire Knowledge Gain an understanding of your goal and what it will require to achieve. Fill in the picture by research, conversation, and thought.

Step 3: Compare Alternatives Weigh your options, which are the different paths you might take to achieve your goal. Analyze the pluses and minuses of each—the costs, the demands, the likelihood of success.

Step 4: Choose a Strategy Select one option as the best plan of action. The choice is based on sound information, the experience of others, and your own interests and abilities.

Step 5: Make a Commitment Resolve to proceed step by step toward achieving your goal. Keep your eyes on the prize.

Step 6: Keep Flexible Evaluate your progress, and when necessary, revise your plan to deal with changing circumstances and new opportunities.

AN EXAMPLE OF PLANNING

To understand the planning process, see how planning works in achieving a short-term goal: the purchase of a new stereo system.

Step 1: Set a Goal Purchase a stereo system.

Step 2: Acquire Knowledge Visit friends to hear their systems. Study standards and specifications. Check on dealers, brands, models, and prices. Consult *Consumer Reports*.

Step 3: Compare Alternatives
    Alternative 1 Buy a second hand system for $250.

                Pro Affordable high-end equipment. Can buy right now.

                Con Uncertain condition of equipment. No warranty or service agreement.

DOLLAR SENSE
Unless commitment is made, there are only promises and hopes...but no plans.

Peter Drucker (1909-) economist and author

Alternative 2 Buy a compact shelf system for $325.

> *Pro* Can afford now. New equipment with warranty.
>
> *Con* Not suitable for adding extra speakers or using with television. Not the best sound quality.

Alternative 3 Buy a high-quality component system for $775.

> *Pro* Excellent sound. Greatest flexibility. New equipment with warranty.
>
> *Con* Costs more than prepared to pay now.

Step 4: Choose a Strategy Decide to buy the high-quality system, but rather than using a credit card and paying interest, will delay the purchase for six months in order to save for it.

Step 5: Make a Commitment Give up going to the movies for the six-month period, carry a lunch and stop eating out, and place the savings in a stereo fund.

Step 6: Keep Flexible Four months into the plan, a model change sale provides an opportunity to buy comparable equipment for $550. Make the purchase, paying cash.

PLANNING FOR YOUR LIFE

Using the planning process to make a buying decision is a simple exercise. Making a decision about major parts of your life is far more complex. You will see that no part of life is exempt from the need for planning. It is important to apply thought, creativity, and discipline to all the interrelated phases of our lives. These phases include:

Career Choosing a field of work and developing the knowledge and skills needed to enter and move ahead in that field.

Self Deciding who you are and what kind of person you want to be, working to develop your strengths and overcome your weaknesses, refining your values.

Lifestyle Expressing yourself in the nature and quality of your everyday life, your recreation and hobbies, how you use your time and money.

Relationships Developing friendships and learning to get along with people in a variety of contexts. Building family and community ties.

Finances Building the financial resources and the economic security needed to pursue all the other dimensions of your life.

If you plan well, your goals and plans in these different parts of your life will work together and support one another. Your life will have a sense of unity and purpose.

PLANNING AND BEING IMPULSIVE

There is a natural conflict between planning and being impulsive, between pursuing a long-range goal and doing what you feel like doing right now. If you have ever had to study while the rest of the family was in the living room watching television, you know what that conflict feels like. If you have ever been invited to go to the mall to eat pizza and hang out with friends, but stayed home to work on a class assignment, you know that sticking to a plan is not easy.

Of course, planning and being impulsive are both good. They both have a place in your life. You need to balance them. Having a plan does not mean that you can't act on the spur of the moment and do something that was not planned. Spontaneous events produce some of the happiest, most meaningful times of your life. Problems arise when you consistently substitute impulsive actions for goal-oriented planning. Success in life requires a balance between the two.

If you do not engage in long-range planning and lack the discipline for it, you may limit your opportunities to be impulsive. You are not going to take a weekend fun trip just because you need a break, if you have not saved the money to do it. In the short run, planning involves sacrifice, but in the long run, it gives you more options.

DREAMS AND PLANS

Young people are natural dreamers. In their dreams, they are movie stars, criminal lawyers, airline pilots. They are married to that certain someone. They are not simply writing an essay for an English class, they are wrapping up a column that will appear with their picture and byline in newspapers in New York, Chicago, and Los Angeles. They are not shooting baskets all alone on an otherwise deserted playground. They are playing in front of a capacity crowd in the NBA. The television-viewing public adores them.

Dreams are a source of pleasure. They are also part of making a future. If you do not have dreams or think that you are not worthy of dreaming, something very important may be missing from your life. You have a right to your dreams, and you need them—even if there is little possibility that they will ever come true.

Planning is not the same as dreaming, but it uses dreams as raw materials. It translates them into specific goals. It tests them. It lays out a course of action that moves you toward realizing these goals and sets up milestones you need to achieve. Planning brings dreams down to earth and turns them into something real and attainable.

Dream   Become a trial lawyer

Plan   Analyze skills needed and take part in activities that develop those skills.

- Debate club
- Amateur theater group
- Student government
- Essay contest

Seek more information on the profession.

- Talk to working lawyers
- Read about law in occupational manuals
- Discuss requirements with guidance counselor
- Read the autobiography of a famous lawyer

Dream   Go to Spain as an exchange student

Plan   Gather program description and application materials and discuss them with

- Parents
- Guidance counselor
- Spanish teacher

Work on improving academic and practical language skills.

- Save up for and buy language tapes
- Carry and use flash cards
- Start a daily journal in Spanish

DIRECTION FOR YOUR LIFE

One of the best things about pursuing our dreams is that, even when you fall short, the effort leads to growth, and opens a path to other opportunities. The young person who practices the piano every day may not achieve the dream of becoming a concert pianist, but may eventually put appreciation of music to work as the director of an arts organization. A young basketball player may not make it to a professional team, but may enjoy a satisfying career as a coach or a sports writer. Without a plan, dreams simply dissolve. With a plan, they give shape and direction to our lives.

Planning involves a lot of thinking and finding answers to lots of questions. The answers and even the plan will change over time as you gain more knowledge and life experience. Planning is a skill that is useful in every area of your life. It is something you have to pursue consciously and thoughtfully. When you plan, you translate your goals and dreams into step-by-step strategies, specific things you can do to test your goals and bring them to reality. You often have to revise your plans, but even when your plans are not fulfilled, planning will have a positive effect on the course of your life.

UNDERSTAND TERMS AND IDEAS

1. Pick a short-term goal that is especially important to you and design a plan for it that includes all six parts of the planning process.

   a. Set a goal _____

   b. Acquire knowledge _____

   c. Compare alternatives _____

   d. Choose a strategy _____

   e. Make a commitment _____

   f. Keep flexible _____

   _____

2. Select a long-term goal and apply the six-part planning process to it.

   a. Set a goal _____

   b. Acquire knowledge _____

   c. Compare alternatives _____

   d. Choose a strategy _____

   _____

    e. Make a commitment _____

    f. Keep flexible _____

3. Ask yourself how well you are planning. What planning are you already doing? What additional planning should you be doing?

Career _____

_____

_____

Self _____

_____

Lifestyle _____

_____

Relationships _____

_____

Finances _____

_____

4. What is the difference between a dream and a plan? Do you have dreams that should remain dreams? Dreams you should convert into plans?

_____

_____

_____

5. How would you describe the balance between spontaneity and planning in your life? Would you like to shift that balance? How?

_____

_____

_____

6. What is Rule #1? How would you explain the meaning and significance of the rule to one of your friends?

_____

_____

_____

7. How would you defend planning to someone who says that planning is a waste of time because things hardly ever work out the way you planned them?

_____

_____

Develop a Career Plan

Revolutionary changes in the job market have implications for future workers. Choosing a career early and planning how to get the training and/or education you will need is crucial to your financial success. This lesson provides some insights into choosing a career and how to make it happen.

CHOOSE A CAREER FIELD

Financial planning begins with a career strategy—a plan for weighing career options, making choices, and preparing for your own field of work. The goal is to clear a path to work that offers good opportunities, pays well, and is suited to your interests and abilities.

Career planning is demanding, but it can also be fun. It requires an honest self-appraisal and an awareness of the occupations that match your talents and interests. Aptitude tests can give you a profile of what you are good at and what you like to do. You can also get a pretty good picture by reviewing your best subjects in school, your hobbies and favorite activities, your most satisfying achievements—and then asking yourself what all these things say about you.

GOALS

■ **Describe how to choose a career field.**

■ **Explain how to obtain the education you need.**

EMPLOYEE QUALITIES CHECKLIST

WHAT EMPLOYERS SAY THEY ARE LOOKING FOR

1 **WORK ETHIC**—promptness, neatness, positive attitude
2 **BASIC SKILLS**—reading, writing, math, and reasoning
3 **COMPUTER LITERACY**—able to use computers on the job
4 **DEPENDABILITY**—able to follow instructions, trustworthy, reliable
5 **TEAMWORK**—works well with others
6 **COMMUNICATION**—adept at sharing information and ideas
7 **RESPONSIBILITY**—works well without supervision
8 **INITIATIVE**—applies knowledge in new situations
9 **OPENNESS**—eager to grow and learn on the job

Many school and community libraries have career planning sections with books, pamphlets, and tapes on careers and job opportunities. The career bible is the *Occupational Outlook Handbook* published by the U.S. Department of Labor. It contains compact summaries of every conceivable job: nature of the work, required training, job outlook, earnings, related occupations, sources of additional information.

It is tempting to sit back and let your school direct you into an academic or vocational program based on your academic record. But choosing a specific career goal as early in high school as possible has a number of important benefits. It enables you (a) to select the most appropriate high school courses, (b) to begin scouting universities, colleges, community colleges, and training programs where you can continue your preparation, and (c) to seek out part-time jobs or internships related to your field of interest. Having your eye on a career goal can give a new sense of purpose and motivation to your high school studies.

JOB FACTS

Today's job market is very different from the one that awaited your parents when they were your age. In all areas, instability and change characterize jobs. You must set career goals as early as possible, yet remain flexible and open to a variety of possibilities. You should get on a career track. Finally, you should want to back yourself up with a solid all-around education in language, math, science, and technology. Here are some of the basic facts.

Fact 1 The salary gap between low-skill and high-skill jobs is growing wider. As a rule, low-skill jobs pay poorly and offer very limited opportunities for advancement. A good job today almost always requires additional training and/or education beyond high school.

Fact 2 Education pays. The more education you have, the more you can expect to earn on every paycheck and over the course of your working life. In the table, you can see that a college graduate earns almost twice as much as a person who only has a high school diploma.

MEAN MONTHLY INCOME	
High school dropouts	$ 906
High school graduates	1,380
Some college	1,579
Vocational training	1,736
Associate degree	1,985
Bachelor's degree	2,625
Master's degree	3,411
Doctorate degree	4,326
Professional degree	5,524

Fact 3 Many of the fastest growing jobs are in technical fields that do not require a bachelor's degree, but involve a year or two of training beyond high school. At the top of the list are: paralegals, systems analysts, medical assistants, radiologic technicians, physical therapy aides, data processing equipment repairers, computer programmers, medical equipment repairers, legal secretaries, health technologists, and restaurant cooks.

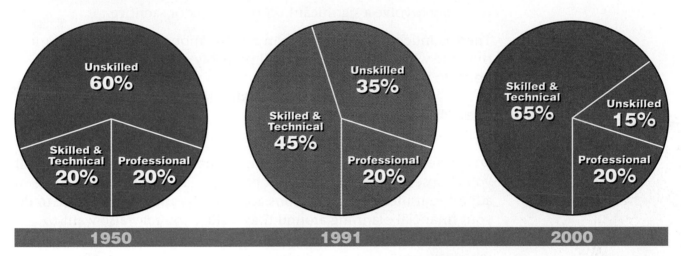

1950
- Unskilled 60%
- Skilled & Technical 20%
- Professional 20%

1991
- Unskilled 35%
- Skilled & Technical 45%
- Professional 20%

2000
- Skilled & Technical 65%
- Unskilled 15%
- Professional 20%

Fact 4 Jobs are less stable and secure than they used to be. Old jobs are being destroyed and new jobs are being created at a mind-boggling rate. Companies are attempting to keep their workforces lean and efficient. Lifetime jobs are rare. Workers can expect to change jobs six or more times, sometimes to totally different fields of work, over the course of their careers. This suggests a strategy that targets a broad career field and multiple areas of interest rather than a specific job.

Fact 5 The fastest growing group of workers in America is people who are working out of their homes. They are accountants, writers, computer experts, sales people, and many others who used to be on a company payroll, but are now selling their services to a variety of clients. Increasingly, companies employ people on a temporary or contract basis, and it is becoming more and more essential for all of us to take an entrepreneurial, self-directed approach to our careers.

A CAREER DILEMMA

Sometimes young people are caught in the middle. They know how important it is to earn a good income, but the work they would really like to do does not generally pay very well. They want to be artists or writers. They want to work with pre-school children or care for the dying. People are warning them. They are flirting with a career choice that may involve a significant economic risk or sacrifice.

There is much more to a job than making money. Between now and the time when you retire, you will probably devote more waking hours to your work than any other part of your life. The happiest people are not the ones who are making the most money, but the ones who are doing work they care about and believe in. Their work is a labor of love. For them, work is a form of wealth.

Of course, money will always be important. You have to be realistic. If you choose a career that does not pay especially well, you will have to adjust your lifestyle expectations accordingly, and you will have to do your financial planning around that reality. You may also want to plan a dual career—struggling to become an artist perhaps, but simultaneously providing a more secure economic base by teaching or some commercial application of your talents.

A good job is an important part of a personal financial plan. But a good financial plan supported by a lifelong investment strategy can also make it possible for you to do work you enjoy.

PART-TIME JOBS

Many high school students take after-school, weekend, and summer jobs. On the job, young people receive valuable workplace and money management experience. But there are also drawbacks. Most of the money is going into cars, clothing, entertainment, and personal items, which may deliver immediate gratification and status, but have little long-term value. They are the opposite of what this book is about. They are not investments in the future.

Research indicates that jobs during the school year often interfere with schoolwork and that students with jobs may not do as well as students who concentrate on school and treat school as a full-time job. Academic success increases the likelihood of winning a college scholarship and lays a foundation for success in college—and that is more valuable in the end than all the money you could possibly earn in after-school and weekend jobs.

In choosing work, it also makes sense for high school students to place more emphasis on career-related experiences, even if that means doing an internship for little or no pay. If you are interested in computers, you might want to pick up experience at a local company that does computer repairs and upgrades or offers networking services. If you are interested in television, you might want to work for a producer or television station as a production assistant. The pay may be more attractive at McDonald's or Burger King, but in terms of career development and total lifetime earnings, the career-related experience will be far more valuable.

Certainly, while in high school, you ought to be putting a lot more of your money aside to contribute to future educational expenses and to begin a lifelong investment program. As you will learn, you might want to put money into a money market mutual fund to meet college expenses which are only a few short years away. And you could also begin developing a long-term investment portfolio based on the stock market.

PLANNING FOR COLLEGE AND COLLEGE EXPENSES

Choosing a field of work goes hand in hand with selecting a college or training program, and as early as possible, you should begin exploring your educational options. Ultimately, your goal should be to develop two or more possible plans of action.

Plan A, your first choice, should involve applying to the best colleges or educational programs you think you can qualify for. Although these may be private institutions that appear to be too expensive for your family to afford, you may be surprised to discover that a combination of financial aid options may actually make it possible for you to go there. Indeed, when you factor in financial aid, the differences in cost between a private college and a public institution may be much less than you thought.

For prospective college students, there are many different financial aid programs, but most of them fall into three main categories:

Grants and Scholarships This refers to aid you do not have to repay. Grants are usually based on need while scholarships are frequently based on academic merit and other qualifying factors.

CYBER SLEUTH

Use the Internet to investigate careers that interest you. You can locate sites that provide in-depth information about a variety of professions, from accountant to zoologist. Some sites even provide an aptitude test to help you identify your abilities and skills. Enter keywords or phrases such as career or aptitude test into your favorite search engine.

Educational Loans These are usually subsidized by federal and state governments or by the colleges themselves. Generally the loans carry lower interest rates than commercial loans, and you do not have to pay them off until after graduation.

Work Aid This is financial aid you have to work for, frequently 10 or 15 hours a week on campus.

There are many cost-cutting options:

- going to a community college for the first two years and then transferring to a four-year institution
- attending a nearby college and living at home
- enrolling in one of the 1000 colleges and universities with cooperative educational programs that alternate between full-time studies and full-time employment
- taking a full time job at a company that offers free educational opportunities as a fringe benefit

To learn about college costs and financial aid, the first source to consult is *The College Board College Costs and Financial Aid Handbook*, which is probably available in the reference section of your local library. The handbook contains extensive tables outlining expenses and financial aid programs at approximately 3000 colleges and universities. It describes various kinds of financial aid, and since most financial aid is determined by need, it provides information for calculating your financial aid eligibility. It also contains bibliographical information.

WEB SITES

www.fastweb.com Fastweb has a database of more than 180,000 private sector scholarships, grants, and loans.

easi.ed.gov This is the U.S. Department of Education information site for federal aid programs.

To choose a future field of work you have to think about what you are good at and where your interests lie, and then must learn about careers that use these talents and interests. The most rewarding jobs today require at least some education or training beyond high school, and your career choice should lead to a plan for preparing for that work by continuing your education.

UNDERSTAND TERMS AND IDEAS

1. How do you make a good match between your talents and interests and a possible career?

   _____

   _____

   _____

2. Look up an occupation that interests you in the *Occupational Outlook Handbook*. What was the best thing you learned about this work? The worst?

   _____

   _____

   _____

3. Rate yourself on the nine qualities employers say they are looking for. What is your greatest strength? Weakness?

   _____

   _____

   _____

4. In your own words, explain the significance of the pie graphs on page 13 below Fact 3.

   _____

   _____

   _____

5. What balance are you trying to achieve between purpose and salary in your career thinking?

   _____

   _____

   _____

6. Using the *College Board College Costs and Financial Aid Handbook*, identify the most and least expensive colleges or universities in your state.

   _____

   _____

   _____

7. Using the *College Board College Cost and Financial Aid Handbook*, find the names of federal financial aid programs in the grants, loans, and work aid categories.

   _____

   _____

   _____

LESSON 1.3

Make a Budget

When you are young, it is especially difficult not to follow the crowd and give in to the pressure to buy now and pay later. It takes self-discipline to resist the temptation of immediate gratification. It takes an independent spirit to see through the advertising images and the celebrity testimonials of the good life. You have to know who you are and what you want. You have to have your eye on the future. You have to believe in your ability to plan and manage your life. A budget is a valuable tool for planning your spending and saving.

GOALS

■ **Discuss how to avoid pressure from advertising messages.**

■ **Prepare and use a budget.**

AVOID THE EARN AND SPEND TREADMILL

Many people are on a treadmill. They work and earn and spend their whole lives, but they never seem to get ahead. The average 50-year-old in this country has a total life savings of about $2,300. That is less than it takes to buy a reliable used car. A few of these people who have little or no savings are not earning enough to put money aside, but most of them simply spend their money as fast as it comes in. They are failing not as workers and earners, but as money managers and consumers.

ADVERTISING MESSAGES

It has been said that Americans are the most propagandized people who have ever lived on the earth. Every day from morning until night, you are bombarded with messages telling you to spend money, even money you do not have. All around you, your friends and neighbors are obeying the messages. They are writing their life stories in red ink, and they are encouraging you to do the same thing. Advertising is vital to the nation's economic welfare, but your economic health often depends on resisting the ads and making sure you buy only those things you really want and need.

BUDGETING

If you want to exercise control as a consumer and money manager, you will need to learn certain money management skills.

TRACK INCOME AND EXPENSES

The first step is to record your expenses over a period of time. By making a written account of how you have spent your money over a specific period of time, you can then use that information to give a more conscious and rational direction to future expenses. Begin by tracking your expenses for a 3-month period. Use the sample budget worksheet on page 20 or enter your expenses in a computer spreadsheet.

Record your income over the same period of time. You will probably receive income from various sources. You may have a part-time job or a relative may send you money for your birthday. Many people receive most of their income in a paycheck from a full-time job.

Some types of spending you must do. Suppose you own a car. You must make the car payments each month. This is a fixed expense. **Fixed expenses** are amounts you have committed to spend. When you set up a household, your fixed expenses may include rent or mortgage payments, utility payments, and insurance payments.

Suppose you want to estimate the amount you will budget to spend on groceries. You recorded the amounts you spent on groceries for the last 6 months. The amounts were $50.10, $45.26, $51.03, $40.95, $47.89, and $42.47.

Solution Calculate the average you spent per month on groceries.

$$
\left. \begin{array}{r} \$50.10 \\ 45.26 \\ 51.03 \\ 40.95 \\ 47.89 \\ + 42.47 \\ \hline \$277.70 \end{array} \right\} \textit{Add the amounts from the last 6 months.}
$$

Then divide this amount by the number of months, which is 6, to get the average.

$277.70 \div 6 = \$46.283333$ or $46.28 rounded to the nearest cent

You would budget $46.28 for groceries per month.

Pay yourself first. Include the amount you want to invest in your monthly budget rather than trying to save money that is "extra." It is easier to spend "extra" money than it is to save it.

You can choose to buy new clothes or to eat at a restaurant. These are flexible expenses. **Flexible expenses** are amounts that you can choose to spend or not to spend. Be sure to track both your fixed expenses and your flexible expenses.

CREATE YOUR BUDGET

A **budget** is a plan for dividing your income into spending and saving options. You can use the information you have recorded to make your budget. At the end of the tracking period, calculate one-month averages. Use the one-month average to create your ideal budget, and use it to guide future expenses.

SAMPLE BUDGET WORKSHEET

	Month 1	Month 2	Month 3	Average
Income Source				
Paycheck	_____	_____	_____	_____
Allowance	_____	_____	_____	_____
Cash Gifts	_____	_____	_____	_____
Interest on Savings	_____	_____	_____	_____
_____	_____	_____	_____	_____
Total Income	_____	_____	_____	_____
Fixed Expenses				
Housing	_____	_____	_____	_____
Utilities	_____	_____	_____	_____
Telephone	_____	_____	_____	_____
Car Payments	_____	_____	_____	_____
Car Insurance	_____	_____	_____	_____
Medical Insurance	_____	_____	_____	_____
Savings	_____	_____	_____	_____
_____	_____	_____	_____	_____
Flexible Expenses				
Groceries	_____	_____	_____	_____
Dining Out	_____	_____	_____	_____
Clothes	_____	_____	_____	_____
Laundry	_____	_____	_____	_____
Transportation	_____	_____	_____	_____
Medical	_____	_____	_____	_____
Entertainment	_____	_____	_____	_____
Personal-Care Items	_____	_____	_____	_____
_____	_____	_____	_____	_____
Total Expenses	_____	_____	_____	_____

WHAT A BUDGET SHOWS YOU

There are enormous differences between typical youth and adult budgets, but the same basic principles apply. Making a budget is the only way to get a reasonably complete picture of what is happening to your money. Often it will show that the little things are taking a surprising toll—and that your money is not going where you thought it was. The budget provides the information you need to spend your money more effectively and to bring your spending in line with your income, as well as your values and goals.

The budget enables you to compare how much you are spending on essentials and how much on discretionary items like snacks and nights at the movies. If you are interested in saving money for a major purchase, the budget will show just where you could cut back in order to do it. It will help you anticipate needs, and it will reduce the likelihood of being caught unprepared.

BUDGET SAVING AND INVESTING

Be sure to build saving and investing into your budget. Treat it as a normal expense and not, as you may find in some budget plans, something you can do with your money if there is anything left over after you have paid your bills.

Budgeting holds the key to better money management and making your money go farther. It reveals how you have allocated and spent your money in the past and what you could do to make your spending more rational and efficient. Saving and investing should be an integral part of your budget, something you do on a regular basis and not just when there is money left over. The purpose of becoming more adept at handling money is to increase your ability to achieve your long-term dreams and goals.

MAINTAIN YOUR BUDGET

Good record keeping will help you maintain your budget. Set aside an hour each week to work on your budget. Try to keep your budget relatively simple so that it works for you. Too much detail can make your budget unmanageable. Put items in a category since if you combine too many expenses under miscellaneous, you will find it difficult to plan your expenses.

UNDERSTAND TERMS AND IDEAS

1. How does advertising benefit consumers?

In nothing couse it makes you spend in unecessary things. Gives you prices where you can choose, competition, saves you time.

2. How can you avoid being overly influenced by advertising?

Making sure you know what you need and what you really want. Set your own budget

3. Your record keeping is a mess. Receipts are scattered everywhere. You did work and got paid in cash but can't remember how much you made. Explain what you would do to get organized.

I would make a budget, writ down how muche I usolly make and spend for a couple of months and divide for the many month you modo it for

4. How would you decide what to include in your budget?

Thinking of what I regulary earn and spend each month, and include the savings in my budget

5. Describe some benefits of making and maintaining a budget.

It allows us see how much you can spend in flexible expenses, It shows where your money is going. It shows usless expenses

6. Give an example of a goal you would like to accomplish by using a budget.

Buy a house

7. List the expenses you would include in your budget if you were to leave home today and had to support yourself without help from anyone. What income would you need to support yourself according to your proposed budget?

Rent 900$ Utilits 100$, servs 100$ Grocerie $100 1200$, Transportation, clothing, Credit C. Health Insurance Entretainment.

8. Give some short-term goals you may want to exchange for some long-term goals.

Buying a home theatre, buying a car of the year

Manage Your Money

*A*lthough a credit card gives the illusion of enabling you to buy more, it *actually has the opposite effect. In the long run, you get less for your money and you can afford less. This lesson describes some easy-to-understand things you can do to manage your money better and make it go further.*

GOALS

- Describe the use of credit and credit cards.

- Explain self-provider skills.

WISE USE OF CREDIT

The basic rule is simple. Reserve credit for those special purchases and expenses where it makes economic sense. Do not use it for ordinary everyday expenses such as buying food and clothing or paying for a night out. Buying these things on credit is like putting an added charge on them. As many Americans find out every year, credit card debt has a way of escalating. Before you know what has happened, all your money is going into interest payments, and you have no choice but to charge even more purchases. You are in quicksand, sinking deeper and deeper.

You should probably limit your use of credit to the following three circumstances:

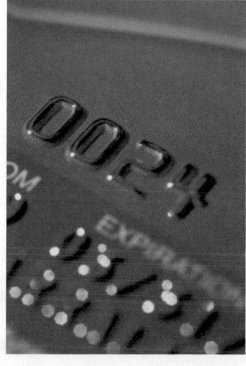

1. Major purchases such as a house, a car, or college tuition

2. An unanticipated emergency or a life-enriching opportunity

3. Purchases where a retailer is offering an interest rate that is lower than the rate you are earning on your savings or investments

USES OF CREDIT CARDS

Credit cards can be very useful, however. There are times when it makes sense to use a credit card instead of carrying a lot of cash in your purse or wallet. Credit cards come in handy when you have car trouble or some other emergency on the road, and you are caught without your checkbook or a roll of cash. If you pay the credit card bill within 30 days, there is no interest charge. Sometimes it is wise to buy with a credit card to give yourself a little time to inspect a product and make sure you like it before paying. In all of these cases you are simply using a credit card as collateral on your promise to pay cash.

DOING WITHOUT

One of the keys to achieving your goals is an ability to make sacrifices and give up, at least for the time being, some of the pleasures and luxuries others take for granted. Many of the most successful artists and scientists and people in a great variety of fields have endured tremendous sacrifices, especially early in their careers. They took these hardships in stride, hardly gave them a thought, because they were preoccupied with larger goals. In fact, they felt as if they were actually better off than their neighbors were because their riches consisted of great plans and dreams.

Doing without may mean carrying a lunch instead of eating in restaurants. It may mean buying second-hand instead of buying new—or in some cases, not buying at all. It may mean learning to appreciate public libraries, free concerts, and the simple pleasure of taking a walk. In the process you may discover that these are more wholesome and rewarding than activities which cost a lot of money. Learning to live a full and happy life on less is, in itself, a form of wealth.

The ability to do without can bring some practical benefits. It can free you from bondage to the present moment and the demands of present wants and needs—and let you look to the future. A determined pursuit of clear long-range goals and an ability to do without can be a very powerful combination.

INTELLIGENT BUYING

Knowing how to get your money's worth on the things that you buy—especially on food and other items you buy on a regular basis and on major purchases—is an important money management skill. These consumer skills include:

1. Planning your purchases and avoiding impulse buying

2. Consulting consumer reports and other product information sources and making informed product choices

3. Comparison shopping and checking prices at different locations

4. Developing the art of creative purchasing—buying generic, second-hand, flawed, wholesale, bulk, surplus, etc.

An intelligent buyer is in no hurry to have the newest product, the latest thing. The prices of many items drop significantly after they have been on the market a while, and waiting allows time for the manufacturer to work out the bugs. The latest hit movie will soon be available for two or three dollars on video. The best-seller will soon appear in paperback, and it will show up on the shelves of libraries and used book stores. Cars last a lot longer than they used to, and it makes sense to buy them used and let somebody else absorb most of the depreciation.

Excellent furniture, clothing, and household items can be bought second-hand. Wait your turn and save. The savings can be achieved with very little reduction in your quality of life.

Kelly Danko

Kelly's parents invested about $500 in stocks for Kelly when she was born. She always knew it was there for her. As she grew, she learned about the investment decisions her parents were making. Kelly learned more about investing from her parents, and gradually took a greater interest in managing her portfolio. When she turns 18, her parents will turn control of Kelly's investments over to her.

Investing is a family activity for the Dankos. Kelly's parents are both very active in NAIC activities. It is not surprising to find that Kelly has started her own IRA and has been contributing to it with money she has earned from part-time and summer jobs. She has even had contests with her father about picking the best technology stocks.

Kelly is in high school and looking forward to going to college to prepare for a career in biomedical science. She plays the French horn in the school band, runs cross country and track, is on the swim team, studies ballet, and works part-time. She plans to continue to invest to enrich her own future. She has a great head start with her average annual return of at least 10%.

SELF-PROVIDING

You can save a lot of money by **self-providing**, that is, providing in a direct hands-on way for your needs and the needs of your family. Do-it-yourself activities supplement your income, and they can be especially rewarding during periods of unemployment and under-employment which are common in today's unstable labor market.

HOME REPAIR AND REMODELING

Home repair and remodeling can really pay off. When you save the price of a carpenter, roofer, plumber, or painter, it is money in your pocket. And there are triple savings when these skills make it possible to buy a house in need of repairs at a reduced price. You not only save labor costs when you do the work yourself, you save on the price of the house and the interest that is included in the mortgage payments. In this way, self-providing can be an integral part of an overall savings and investment plan.

OTHER FORMS OF SELF-PROVIDING

There are many other useful forms of self-providing: car maintenance; yard work; clothing construction and alteration; furniture refinishing; gardening; canning, freezing, and drying food; furniture, musical instrument, and electronic kit assembly, etc. Creating your own entertainment—parties, games, jam sessions, etc.—is a form of self-providing

which should not become a lost art. Although you may not think of them in these terms, managing your own financial planning and investing and bypassing brokers and advisors is also self-providing.

Self-providing not only makes economic sense, it develops a more active and participatory involvement in the whole of your life. Financial planning goes far beyond money management. It spreads through every aspect of life. It is an important expression of who you are. It expresses a determination not just to accept your fate, but to take charge of your life and control your future.

UNDERSTAND TERMS AND IDEAS

1. Find out what the interest rates are on the credit cards your parents have. How do those interest rates compare with the interest rates you could earn on a savings account? What does that tell you about credit cards?

_____

_____

_____

_____

2. Describe a situation in which you think using credit is a good idea.

_____

_____

_____

_____

3. Describe a situation in which having a credit card handy is a good idea.

_____

_____

_____

4. Can you remember any times when you put off or avoided buying something in order to achieve a long-range goal?

_____

_____

_____

5. Why do you think having good consumer skills is important?

_____

_____

_____

6. How is your family already engaged in self-providing? If you had to pay for those services, how costly would they be?

_____

_____

_____

SUMMARY

LESSON 1.1 **THE IMPORTANCE OF PLANNING**
Planning is central to success in your financial life. Having a plan does not necessarily mean that you cannot be spontaneous. Planning can help you turn your hopes and dreams into reality.

LESSON 1.2 **DEVELOP A CAREER PLAN**
Choose a career as early as possible by learning as much as you can about your interests and abilities. Your career plan may include training or continuing education to keep your skills current.

LESSON 1.3 **MAKE A BUDGET**
Budgeting can make the difference between living within your means and getting into trouble with debt.

LESSON 1.4 **MANAGE YOUR MONEY**
Learn to manage your money well. It is a life-long process that never ends.

REVIEW INVESTING TERMS

Write the letter of the term that matches each definition. Some terms may not be used.

1. _b_ amounts of money you have committed to spend

2. _f_ reducing costs of goods and services by providing or performing them yourself

3. _a_ plan for dividing your income into spending and saving options

4. _c_ amounts of money you can choose to spend or not to spend

5. _e_ a method or process worked out in advance that leads to the achievement of some goal

a. budget

b. fixed expenses

c. flexible expenses

d. goal

e. plan

f. self-providing

UNDERSTAND TERMS AND IDEAS

6. What is the best age at which people should begin to do some serious planning about their career? Why?

   As early as possible, so you can develop two or more possible plans

7. Of the budget planning process, which part do you believe would be the most difficult to do? Why?

   Recording daily spending of unecessary things. Planning the savings

8. Many high school athletes, including the bench sitters, believe that they will get an athletic scholarship to a Division I college and also play professionally. What do you think of this dream?

   Its a good way to get into a good college but it does not give you the necessary knowledge to prepare yourself for life. A plan cannot be based on a dream.

9. Describe "self-providing" in your own words.

   Self-providing means "having money buy and doing things yourself.

SHARPEN YOUR RESEARCH SKILLS

10. Find each of the products listed below in your home or on a store. For each product, write the band name and location (city/state/country) of the product's manufacturer or distributor.

a. cereal _____

_____

b. toaster _____

_____

c. toothpaste _____

_____

d. adhesive bandages _____

_____

11. Look on the Internet, in your local library, or in your local city hall for information about your school's budget. How are budget decisions made for your school?

_____

_____

THINK CRITICALLY

12. Many of the skills and qualities that employers want in their employees cannot be taught in a classroom. How would you go about learning or developing these skills and qualities?

_____

_____

_____

13. A very nice, sincere friend of yours makes custom designed jeans. He operates a small company from the basement of his home. He offers to sell you a 5% ownership in the business for $2,000. Should you accept his offer? What is the reason behind your answer?

Need to know more information. Reserch before you do anything.

PROSPECTIVE PORTFOLIO PROJECT

In this project, which you will continue in the following chapters, you will start learning to build your prospective portfolio. Your prospective portfolio will include companies in which you might someday invest. Like any good investor, you will start at the very beginning.

There is an age-old adage that says, "invest in what you know the most about." Make a list of a few products you buy on a regular basis. Next to each product, list the company that produced it. Go to the Internet or the reference section of your school or local library for more information about this company. A reference librarian can direct you to publications for your chosen company's industry. Write your notes about these products, companies, publications, and any observations you made about the company while you were researching it.

PRODUCT	COMPANY	PUBLICATIONS	OBSERVATIONS

Keep this list handy. You will learn more in the next chapters about how to research these companies to get the information you need to decide whether or not to invest.

Chapter 2

INVESTMENT POWER

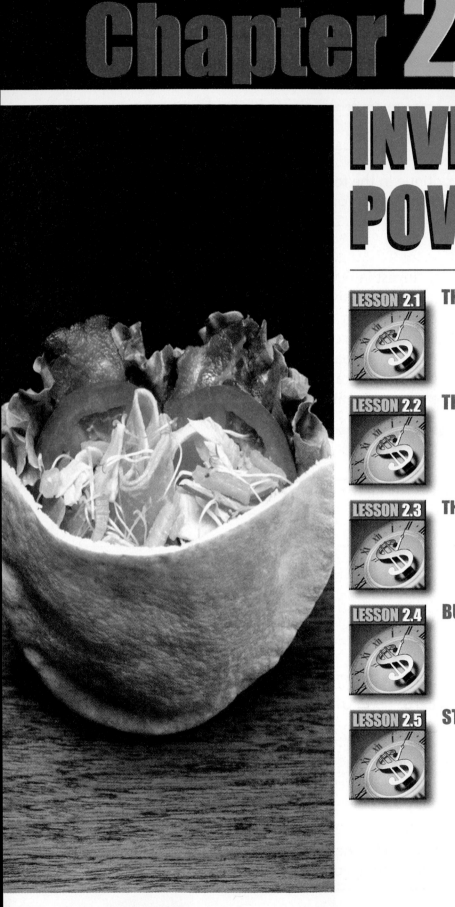

 LESSON 2.1 THE POWER OF INVESTING

 **LESSON 2.2** THE CORPORATION

 LESSON 2.3 THE INVESTMENT SUPERMARKET

 **LESSON 2.4** BUYING AND SELLING STOCK

LESSON 2.5 STOCK MARKET LITERACY

INDUSTRY INDICATORS

RESTAURANTS

Wendy's International, Inc.

Founded in 1969

Dave Thomas opened the first Wendy's Old Fashioned Hamburgers restaurant in Columbus, Ohio in 1969. Thomas had already worked in the restaurant business for 22 years, yet he had an idea to create a family restaurant with a comfortable and friendly atmosphere, made-to-order menu items, and reasonable prices. This idea turned into one of the fastest growing restaurant chains in the world.

Dave Thomas began franchising the Wendy's concept in 1973. His method of selling franchises for entire cities and parts of states, rather than single units, allowed the company to expand rapidly. The first Wendy's franchise was bought for Indianapolis in 1972 and, by 1979, there were more than 1,700 Wendy's stores worldwide. More than 750 Wendy's restaurants had opened in only 21 months—that means 1.2 new stores opened every day during that period.

Several factors have contributed to the success of the Wendy's restaurant chain. Wendy's offers a variety of made-to-order menu items at reasonable prices. The Super Value Menu was introduced in 1989, offering 9 items for 99 cents, and Wendy's was the first quick-service restaurant to carry baked potatoes and fresh-stuffed pitas. Popular advertising campaigns have helped Wendy's grow in popularity and have made Dave Thomas one of the nation's most recognizable spokespeople. Wendy's merged with Tim Horton's, a Canada-based coffee and baked goods chain, in 1995. As a result, the two restaurants are growing together, opening combination Wendy's/Tim Horton's stores in the U.S. and Canada. In 1999, Wendy's was the third largest quick-service restaurant chain in the world, with more than 7,000 stores in 32 countries.

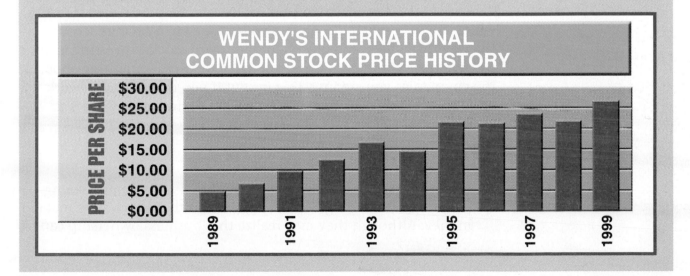

WENDY'S INTERNATIONAL
COMMON STOCK PRICE HISTORY

LESSON 2.1

The Power of Investing

*C*ongratulations! You are onto something. You have decided to learn about investing and to begin building your own investment portfolio. This is an activity very few young people even consider. In fact, most Americans do not become serious about investing until they are middle aged. Beginning young will give you a tremendous advantage, and that advantage will grow over the course of your lifetime.

GOALS

■ **Compare and contrast investing and saving.**

■ **Determine how compounding works.**

■ **Discuss four basic rules for taking advantage of the long-term power of investing.**

SAVING AND INVESTING

The term **saving** is generally used to refer to putting money aside for a rainy day, whether you stash it in a savings bank or a piggy bank. In a savings bank the money may draw a little interest, but that is not the main object. The point is to have the money on hand when you need it. Everybody should have some money in an interest-bearing account that can easily be withdrawn in a time of need.

Investing refers to something quite different from that. When you invest, you are not just putting money aside for a time when you may need it, you are taking measures to make your money grow. You are buying stocks or properties or anything you think will increase in value over a period of time. You are not worried about the immediate accessibility (liquidity) of your money. You are putting the money to work for you. You are using it to make money.

As you learn about different kinds of investments, you will see that there is no precise line between saving and investing. The investment vehicles that are available today vary from money market certificates, which are very much like having your money in a savings account, all the way to aggressive, high-risk, high-growth stocks. Investing in the stock market involves risk, and you have to know something about the companies you are investing in. But if you do your homework and invest wisely over an extended period of time, investing is a proven and powerful way of increasing your wealth.

THE REWARDS OF INVESTING

1. **Investing is a great way of making money.** Too many young people think carrying home a paycheck is the only way of making money. Although they may realize that business ownership can be

a source of income, they never consider the possibility that, by owning shares of stock, they themselves could participate in business ownership and business profits. They have yet to discover the art of using money to make money.

2. **The rewards of investing can last a lifetime.** Financial success does not consist of the stereo or the athletic shoes you can buy now. It grows out of the assets you build up over a period of time. Investing brings the deeper and more lasting rewards of security and economic power that come from the accumulation of wealth.

3. **With investing, time is on your side.** Stock prices go up and down. On Wall Street, there are good times (bull market) and bad (bear market). But over the long haul, stock prices have always gone up, and patient stockholders can profit from that trend. In addition, investors who reinvest their earnings will see their money grow at an ever increasing rate.

4. **Investing can help you beat inflation.** Prices have a tendency to rise over a period of time and we call that inflation. If your wages are rising at about the same rate as prices, inflation does not really bother you very much. You are not losing buying power.

   Inflation does hurt, however, when you are saving or investing because the dollar you get back is no longer worth as much as the dollar you invested. If you put your money in the bank, for example, and earn 3% interest, but the inflation rate is 5%, you are losing money. Your money has developed a slow leak. Intelligent investing produces a larger return on your money than the rate of inflation. In spite of the bite inflation takes out of your money, you still come out ahead.

5. **Investing is a way of owning a piece of corporate America.** The money you invest helps companies buy the facilities and equipment they need to do business. Sometimes it is the money it takes to turn a creative idea into an exciting new enterprise. If the businesses to which you have contributed make money, you have a claim to a share of the profits.

6. **Investing is fun.** Sports fans never seem to get tired of trying to predict who is going to win the big game. Investors are trying to pick winners, too, only the teams they are rooting for have names like AT&T, American Express, and General Motors. Sometimes investors, like sports fans, play a hunch. But if they are smart, they base their choices on research and reliable information. That is where this course comes in.

ROCK SOLID

Paying off debts can save you money. It is better to take the $100 a month that you usually deposit into a savings account that pays 2% interest and use it to pay off a credit card debt on which you pay 15% interest.

THE GROWING IMPORTANCE OF INVESTING

Jobs are changing rapidly. The old notion that you would work for one company all your life and then retire on a company pension is totally out of date. The world you are preparing for is not like that at all. Over the course of your career, you will probably work for at least a half dozen different employers, possibly in several different fields. Or you may work on a contract basis for a number of employers at once. With no single lifelong employer and no company pension, your long-term security will reside in your own hands. It will depend on your ability to manage and invest your money. Investing will not be a luxury, it will be a necessity.

THE MAGIC OF COMPOUNDING

One of the reasons why investing over a long period of time is so profitable is the fact that your earnings compound, and as a result, grow by larger and larger amounts. The concept of **compound interest** is simple enough. It is what happens when you earn interest not only on your initial deposit, but also earn interest on the interest. If you deposit $100 in the bank and earn 6%, you will have $106 at the end of the year.

But if your account compounds annually, in the second year you will earn 6% on $106, and you will have $112.36 at the end of the year. At the end of five years, you will have $133.82.

When you study the Growth Rate Table on page 37, you have to be impressed with the fact that, although the monetary gains created by compounding are modest in the early years, they really begin to add up after two and three decades. At the bottom of the table, the numbers generated by each dollar are growing by leaps and bounds. That is how it works. The payoff is huge for the person who starts early and keeps at it.

When you invest in the stock market, you make money in two basic ways—through the dividends which some companies pay to their stockholders and by increases in the prices of the stocks you own. Any dividends are reinvested, buying more shares of stock. Stock price increases are based on previous increases, so that the compounding effect is very real. How have stocks done through the years? Numerous studies estimate that the largest U.S. corporations (the S&P 500) have delivered an average annual return of 10% to 12% over the past seven decades!

GROWTH RATE TABLE

GROWTH RATES

YEARS	1%	3%	5%	7%	9%	11%	15%
1	1.01	1.03	1.05	1.07	1.09	1.11	1.15
2	1.02	1.06	1.10	1.14	1.19	1.23	1.32
3	1.03	1.09	1.16	1.23	1.30	1.37	1.52
4	1.04	1.13	1.22	1.31	1.41	1.52	1.75
5	1.05	1.16	1.28	1.40	1.54	1.69	2.01
6	1.06	1.19	1.34	1.50	1.68	1.87	2.31
7	1.07	1.23	1.41	1.61	1.83	2.08	2.66
8	1.08	1.27	1.48	1.72	1.99	2.30	3.06
9	1.09	1.30	1.55	1.84	2.17	2.56	3.52
10	1.10	1.34	1.63	1.97	2.37	2.64	4.05
11	1.12	1.38	1.71	2.10	2.58	3.15	4.65
12	1.13	1.43	1.80	2.25	2.81	3.50	5.35
15	1.16	1.56	2.08	2.76	3.64	4.78	8.14
20	1.22	1.81	2.65	3.87	5.60	8.06	16.37
25	1.28	2.09	3.39	5.43	8.62	13.59	32.92
30	1.35	2.43	4.32	7.61	13.27	22.89	66.21
35	1.42	2.81	5.52	10.68	20.41	38.57	133.18
40	1.49	3.26	7.04	14.97	31.41	65.00	267.86
45	1.56	3.78	8.99	21.00	48.33	109.56	538.77
50	1.64	4.38	11.46	29.46	74.36	184.56	1,083.66

To see the cumulative impact of an 11% growth rate over a period of 30 years, look at the 11% column on the Growth Rate Table. You can see that at 11%, a $1000 investment will grow in value to $22,890 ($1000 × 22.89) at the end of 30 years. Admittedly this is not a net total return. It is what you have before you subtract (a) broker's fees, (b) taxes, and (c) the impact of inflation, but the result is still most impressive.

THE RULE OF 72

One of the easiest ways to calculate the effects of compounding, and one which brokers and advisors often refer to, is the Rule of 72. This rule says that, if an asset grows x% a year, its value will double in $72 \div x$ years. So in order to find how long it takes an investment to double, divide 72 by the annual rate of return.

Example How long will it take for an investment which is growing 10% a year to double in value?

Answer $72 \div 10$ or 7.2 years

FOUR BASIC RULES FOR INVESTORS

Based on many years of experience, the NAIC has developed *Four Basic Rules* for taking advantage of the long-term power of investing:

1. **Invest on a regular basis over a long period of time.**

   Dollar cost averaging is a process of investing roughly equal amounts of money at regular intervals. When you do that you get more shares when the price is down and fewer shares when the price is up, and the net effect is a favorable average price per share overall.

2. **Reinvest all earnings (dividends, interest, capital gains).**

   Reinvesting your earnings compounds the profitability of your investment. You put the money you invest to work for you, and the money you earn on that investment works for you as well.

3. **Invest in the common stock of good quality growth companies.**

   These are companies with established, consistent growth track records for at least 5 years and preferably 10 years. Rather than jumping in and out of stocks, look for companies that you can stay with for an extended period of time.

4. **Diversify your portfolio to reduce overall risk.**

   It is not advisable to tie your investment future to just one or two firms or industries. You want to buy stocks in a number of companies representing different industries.

You are just beginning to discover the wealth-building power of life-long investing. It is based on putting time and money to work for you. It is the art of using money to make money. By beginning young and investing modest sums of money on a regular basis over the years, you can produce very impressive long-term results.

78278 9031

2.1 The Power of Investing

UNDERSTAND TERMS AND IDEAS

1. What is the difference between merely saving money and investing it?

   That the interest in saving money is not compared to invest it this one makes much more

2. What are some of the rewards of investing?

   The rewards can last a lifetime, you beat inflation Is a way of owing a corporation

3. What is inflation and how does it affect saving and investing? How can someone earn 3% on a bank account and lose purchasing power?

   Inflation is when the value of money decreases. And earning 3% in a long period of time makes the money value go down

4. Why is knowledge of investing becoming more important?

   because its a good way of making your money grow / It's a better deal than savings

5. Describe compounding and how it works in your own words.

   (Earning interest over interest) Compounding is ed culotus in how long the investment will double your money. Is the rate of 72 (72% by the owed interest)

6. What are the two basic ways people make money from stocks?

   Through the dividends and by increases of the prices of the stock

7. What is the S&P 500, and what kind of returns have the S&P 500 stocks delivered over the past 70 years?

   These are the best 500 companies to invest in and it gives you a return of 10% - 12%

8. How long will it take for an investment that is growing 11% a year to double?

   72% 11% for 5 6,5 years

9. What are NAIC'S **Four Basic Rules** for investors?

   Invest on a regular basis over a long period of time Reinvest all earnings Invest in the common stock of good quality growth companies Diversify your portfolio to reduce overall risk

39

LESSON 2.2

The Corporation

I n this course, you are learning how to make your money grow by investing in the stock market. Each share of stock you buy is a piece of ownership of a very small part of a corporation. Whenever you buy anything, you should know where your money is going and what you are getting for it. This lesson will help you understand what a corporation is and how you can participate in corporate ownership as a stockholder .

GOALS

■ **Explain different forms of businesses.**

■ **Compare primary and secondary capital markets.**

ORGANIZING A BUSINESS

Whether it is General Motors or a plumber who works alone, all businesses offer products and services that satisfy consumer wants and needs in order to earn money. Businesses begin with an idea for a product or service and an interest in profiting from that idea, but before any business can begin to operate, it must meet two basic needs:

Labor refers to those people who will do the work.

Capital is money to buy real estate, equipment, raw materials and underwrite other start-up costs.

Generally, a new business needs more capital than a single owner or a small team of owners can provide, and it must look to two primary sources of business capital:

Lenders are people who lend money to the business in return for a contracted rate of interest or return for their investment.

Stockholders are those who buy shares of stock in the company and, in effect, become part owners. Instead of receiving a fixed rate of interest, stockholders profit from the success of a business.

This dynamic process of creating and sustaining businesses through private investments is called capitalism. Capitalism is very different from socialism where businesses are funded and owned by all taxpayers through their government.

SOLE PROPRIETORSHIPS, PARTNERSHIPS, AND CORPORATIONS

Many small businesses are owned by a single person or a small group of people, and they are legally organized as sole proprietorships or partnerships. The owners are personally liable for their company's losses and are subject to lawsuits by parties with a claim against their businesses.

In order to broaden company ownership and protect shareholders, many businesses are organized under state and federal laws as corporations. These laws stipulate that corporate shareholders have only a limited liability for the losses incurred by their company. The maximum amount they can lose is the money they have invested in the corporation. This means that some unhappy consumer who developed a hideous rash using a product manufactured by a pharmaceutical company in which you own two shares of stock cannot come after your computer, your snow board, and your baseball card collection. Limited liability is one of the chief advantages of the corporate form of business.

PRIVATE AND PUBLIC CORPORATIONS

The vast majority of corporations in the United States are private corporations. Shares in private corporations are not sold on the stock market, and can only be purchased from current stockholders - generally, a pretty small group of people. Private companies are a little like private parties. You have to be invited. Shares in a public corporation, however, can be purchased from dealers and other shareholders and traded openly.

HOW BUSINESSES RAISE MONEY

When a corporation is raising new money for some venture, it may sell stocks and bonds directly to investors. This process of raising new money and selling stock directly to the public is called a **primary capital market**.

As a rule, however, the stock you buy will be sold in a secondary market. A **secondary capital market** is created when stockholders buy and sell shares from one another on a stock market with the help of brokers. None of the proceeds of these sales go back to the corporation, which got its money when it first issued the stock.

The New York Stock Exchange, the American Stock Exchange, and the NASDAQ over-the-counter market are predominantly involved in this secondary market of stocks and bonds.

One form of primary capital market develops when a company "goes public" and offers its stocks and bonds to the general public for the first time. This is called an initial public offering (IPO). The IPO market consists of many new and relatively small companies with very limited track records. IPOs are risky and often quite volatile (subject to steep price changes), and are not appropriate investments for inexperienced investors.

THE STOCK MARKETS

There are two kinds of stock markets: exchanges and the over-the-counter (OTC) market. Exchanges such as the New York Stock Exchange (NYSE) and the American Stock Exchange (AMEX) are auction markets where buyers and sellers come together to do business. The over-the-counter (OTC) or NASDAQ (National Association of Securities Dealers Automated Quotes) market is a dealer marketplace where securities dealers buy or sell from their own accounts (for themselves). As a rule, smaller and newer firms are traded OTC, although some well established firms and a number of technology companies are traded on the NASDAQ as well.

STOCKBROKERS

A stockbroker is essentially a person who assists you in purchasing stocks and bonds. With few exceptions, most buy and sell orders on the stock market are handled through brokers, who either act as agents or as principals (buying or selling for their own account). There are different kinds of brokers and brokerage houses. A full-service broker provides more customer service and investment advice and research, but charges a high-end fee. A discount broker charges less but may do little more than assist you in purchasing securities you have selected.

A broker's advice can be very useful, but you have to be wary. Brokers are usually compensated in commission fees, and some brokers may try to pad their commissions by encouraging you to participate in more stock transactions (buying and selling) than are good for you.

THE SECURITIES AND EXCHANGE COMMISSION

The Securities and Exchange Commission (SEC) is a federal agency which is considered the "policeman" of the securities (stocks and bonds) industry. The SEC is responsible for establishing and enforcing regulations which protect the investing public from unfair practices in the securities market.

When a company issues new stocks and bonds to the public, it is required to file registration information with the SEC. This information includes data on the company, its industry, competitors, management, and other important facts. The company is required to provide full and accurate information. There are severe penalties for a company's officers who do not comply with the full disclosure rules.

PROSPECTUS

The document that discloses financial information about the company and is filed with the SEC is called a prospectus. Usually, there are at least two prospectuses: a preliminary ("red herring") prospectus and a final prospectus. The nickname "red herring" points to the fact that the front page of the prospectus has red lettering to warn investors that this is a preliminary document. The preliminary prospectus does not include the price of the securities to be offered for sale. This decision is made on the day of offering.

ACCOUNTING

Publicly traded corporations are required to have their annual financial statements prepared by an outside accounting firm in conformity with generally accepted accounting principles. The statements are prepared by Certified Public Accountants (CPAs), accountants with extensive training who are licensed by the states in which they are doing business.

When the economy is strong and public confidence is high, virtually any common stock can go public and trigger amazing price volatility. For example, suppose a new issue is offered by Presstek Corporation, a laser printing company. On May 24, 1996 Presstek common stock was selling for $175 a share. In a four week period from May to June, 1996, the stock price dropped from $175 to $69, based on disappointing earnings news. How do you calculate the percent decline of the drop in the stock's value?

Solution Calculate the percent decline using the rate of change formula where r = rate of increase or decrease, P_o = original price, and P_n = new price.

$$r = \frac{|P_n - P_o|}{P_o} \qquad \textit{Rate of Change formula}$$

$$r = \frac{|69 - 175|}{175} = \frac{106}{175} = 0.606 \approx 61\%$$

It was a decline of more than 60% in one month!

UNDERSTAND TERMS AND IDEAS

1. What is the primary advantage to organizing a business as a corporation?

   Seperating your personal finance from the company, people would invest in you (its easier to obtain financing)
   (liability)

2. What are the two major sources of capital for a business?

   Stock holders or lenders

3. Distinguish between the rights and expectations of a shareholder and a lender.

   A lender would only gain a percentage of the initial investment a share holder depend gets dividends plus a apreciation

4. When you buy corporate stock, where does the money go? Does it ever go to the company named on the stock?

   If it is an IPO it will go to the company for them to invest in their field/When you buy it for the first time from the company

5. What is the difference between buying stock in a private company and a public company?

   The private can only be buyed from some own that owes it directly and public from the stockmarket

6. Why is an IPO considered high risk?

   Because its newly comming out

7. What is the difference between stock exchanges and the OTC market?

   Exchange is an auction and OTC is dealers selling their stocks

8. What is a stockbroker? Why do you have to be careful in relying on brokers?

   he provides you all the information but they work on their own benefits

9. What have you learned about the accounting requirements for corporations?

   They are required by law to have their financial statements prepared by an outside accountant.

The Investment Supermarket

For anyone starting out, the world of investments can be very confusing. There are so many different kinds of investments to choose from. Where do you begin? How do you keep from getting lost? A modern supermarket contains an amazing profusion of products and brands, but a shopper soon learns not to search the pro-duce and pet food sections for a loaf of bread. By grouping investments in categories based on different levels of risk and potential return, this lesson will help you find your way. It will help you form a better picture of the investment supermarket.

GOALS

■ Describe the relationship between risk and return.

RISK AND POTENTIAL RETURN

As you learn about investing, one factor you will encounter over and over is the relationship between risk and potential return. What you would like, of course, is low risk and high return on your investments, but that is not something you are likely to find. Investments with very little risk can attract investors with a relatively low rate of return. Ventures with a considerable risk of losing money have the potential to pay a lot more, which persuades people to invest in them. For investors, this relationship between risk and return is a basic fact of life.

Seasoned investors agree that there are times for avoiding risk and times when a calculated degree of risk is in order. If you are saving money for a purchase or expenditure that will take place in a year or two, you should probably play safe and not take the risk of coming up short. But if you are trying to make your money grow over an extended period of time greater than three years, you should assume a greater level of risk. In general, buying stocks entails more risk than an investment that pays a guaranteed rate of interest. But over the long run, a stock market investor rides out downturns in the stock market (bear markets) in order to take advantage of the substantial returns generated by the market's overall upward trend.

This appraisal of risk and return reminds us that one kind of investment is not necessarily better than another. You have to choose investments that are suited to your particular needs and goals. Often, what you want is a mix of investments that helps you achieve a balance of risk and potential return. To assist you as an investment shopper, this lesson organizes investment opportunities by their risk and return potential.

LEVEL 1—LOWEST RISK/LOWEST RETURN

Loans to the Federal Government Savings instruments and securities issued by the U.S. Government are considered risk free. They are guaranteed by the federal government, which has the power to tax and create money.

Series EE Bonds These federal government savings bonds are issued in denominations as small as $50, but are discounted to be sold at $25. The interest on a Series EE bond is a variable rate based on 85% of the average rate on five-year Treasury notes. The major advantages of Series EE bonds are: (1) safety and (2) deferred taxes on the interest until the bonds are redeemed.

Series HH Bonds Series HH bonds are similar to EE bonds, except for the fact that they are sold in larger denominations and at face

HIGHEST RISK & RETURN

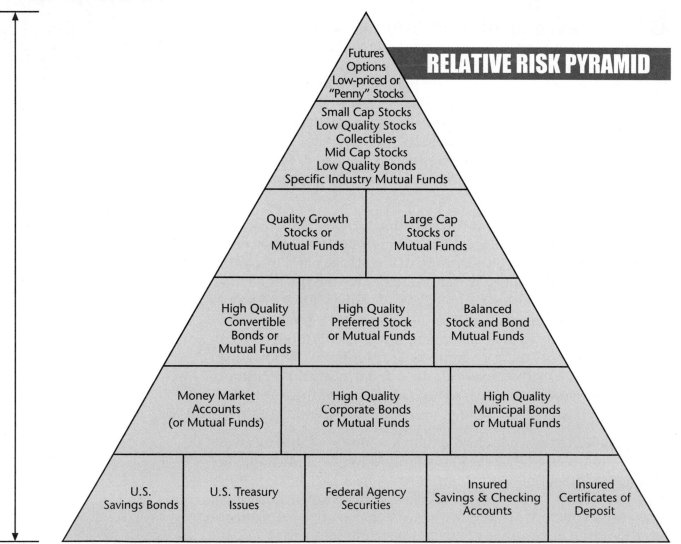

RELATIVE RISK PYRAMID

Futures
Options
Low-priced or
"Penny" Stocks

Small Cap Stocks
Low Quality Stocks
Collectibles
Mid Cap Stocks
Low Quality Bonds
Specific Industry Mutual Funds

Quality Growth Stocks or Mutual Funds

Large Cap Stocks or Mutual Funds

High Quality Convertible Bonds or Mutual Funds

High Quality Preferred Stock or Mutual Funds

Balanced Stock and Bond Mutual Funds

Money Market Accounts (or Mutual Funds)

High Quality Corporate Bonds or Mutual Funds

High Quality Municipal Bonds or Mutual Funds

U.S. Savings Bonds

U.S. Treasury Issues

Federal Agency Securities

Insured Savings & Checking Accounts

Insured Certificates of Deposit

LOWEST RISK & RETURN

value rather than being discounted. The interest on HH bonds is currently taxable. Both types of savings bonds are bought by conservative investors who want low risk and are prepared to accept a low interest rate. The bonds are non-marketable. They cannot be sold. An investor must redeem them, usually through a commercial bank.

Treasury Bills T-Bills are short-term government securities sold in $10,000 to $1,000,000 denominations. Like EE bonds, T-Bills are issued at a discount to their face (par) value. They mature in 3-12 months. As low-risk securities, the returns are very low and vary in response to the overall interest rate environment.

Treasury Notes and Treasury Bonds These securities have longer maturities than T-Bills. The notes mature in 1 to 10 years, the bonds in more than 10 years. Both are issued in minimum denominations of $1000. Because of their longer maturities, Treasury notes and bonds normally pay higher interest rates than T-bills.

Federal Agency Securities In addition to the federal government, many federal agencies issue debt securities:

- Government National Mortgage Association: (a Ginnie Mae)
- Federal Home Loan Mortgage Corporation (a Freddie Mac)
- Federal National Mortgage Association (a Fannie Mae)

These federal agency securities tend to offer higher interest rates than the treasury securities, but they are still considered low risk. Treasury bills, notes, and bonds and the various federal agency securities are negotiable. They can be bought and sold in secondary markets.

Insured Savings and Checking Accounts Most commercial banks and savings and loan banks offer checking and savings accounts which are insured by the federal government (the Federal Deposit Insurance Company, FDIC) for up to $100,000. Perhaps you already have a savings account in a local bank. If the bank or S&L where you have an account were to run into financial difficulties, your money would still be safe. The money in these accounts earns a low rate of interest which changes from time to time. Checking and savings accounts are low-risk, low-return investments, suitable for short-term money.

Insured Certificates of Deposit Certificates of Deposit (CDs) are slightly longer-term investments ranging from 3 months to several years. The bank or S&L offers you either a fixed or variable interest rate over a determined time period. The CDs are also insured for up to $100,000 per account. Because you are tying up your money for a longer time period, CDs pay more interest than savings accounts, but like other low-risk investments, offer relatively low returns.

LEVEL 2—LOW RISK/LOW RETURN

Money Market Accounts (or Money Market Mutual Funds)
These accounts consist of low-risk, relatively short-term securities such as T-bills, large CDs, and notes issued by large, stable corporations. Money market mutual funds are based on portfolios of these securities. Because these mutual funds are made up of low-risk securities and because the funds are diversified, they are considered safe places to park money for short periods of time.

High Quality Corporate Bonds (or Corporate Bond Mutual Funds) By buying corporate bonds or shares in a mutual fund that buys corporate bonds, investors are loaning money to corporations. These loans are riskier than loans to the federal government, but if they are investment-grade bonds (AAA/Aaa to BBB/Baa3 as rated by Standard & Poor or Moody's), the risk of default is still very low.

High Quality Municipal Bonds (or Municipal Bond Mutual Funds) These bonds are similar to high quality corporate bonds, but with an important difference. They are issued by federal, state, and city government entities, and the interest is tax free. A number of high quality municipal bonds are insured against default by municipal bond insurers, thus reducing the risk that investors will not get their money back. Municipal bonds only really make sense for investors in a high tax bracket, who have the most to gain from the tax exemption.

LEVEL 3—RELATIVELY LOW RISK

High Quality Convertible Bonds (or Mutual Funds) A convertible bond is a corporate bond which pays a fixed rate of interest, but can be exchanged for a specific number of shares of common stock in the same company. The flexibility has a price. The rate of return (coupon rate) is usually lower than the rate on a "straight" (non-convertible) bond.

High Quality Preferred Stock (or Mutual Funds) The name is deceptive. Although it is called preferred stock, it is really a fixed-income security more like a corporate bond. For most individual investors, it does not make sense to invest in preferred stock because the yields are very close to the yields on similarly rated bonds and because preferred stockholders lack legal power to force dividend payment.

Balanced Stock and Bond Mutual Funds A little higher on the risk ladder are mutual funds which offer an opportunity to invest in a mixed bag of stocks and bonds. You can even choose your level of risk. A fund with 75% of its money in common stock and 25% in bonds has a higher risk profile than a fund with 50% in each.

LEVEL 4—INTERMEDIATE RISK

Quality Growth Stocks (or Mutual Funds) Quality growth stocks are shares in companies which are leaders in their industry and have demonstrated consistent growth rates for both earnings and revenues in excess of 12%. These companies usually pay low dividends, but offer opportunities to profit from rising stock prices. Over the long run, quality growth stocks produce excellent returns, well above inflation. In Part Two, you will learn how to select quality growth stocks to invest in.

> **DOLLAR SENSE**
> *I have enough money to last me the rest of my life, unless I buy something.*
> —*Jackie Mason*

Large Capitalization (Large Cap) Stocks (or Mutual Funds) Large capitalization refers to companies in which a lot of money has already been invested and which have a high market value. Market value is calculated by multiplying the number of common stock shares owned by stockholders times the current price per share. For example, a company with 100,000,000 shares outstanding at $50 a share has a market value of $5 billion—considered by many to be the minimum for a large cap stock.

LEVEL 5—RELATIVELY HIGH RISK

Medium Capitalization (Mid Cap) Stocks or (Mutual Funds) Stocks with market capitalizations that range from $1 billion to $5 billion are considered mid cap stocks. These are smaller companies which may have demonstrated high growth rates in revenues and earnings.

Small Capitalization (Small Cap) Stocks or (Mutual Funds) These are stocks in companies with under $1 billion in market capitalization. Because many of these are small companies with short track records, they represent high risk and relatively high return potential.

Specific Industry Mutual Funds When you buy shares in a specific industry mutual fund, you are investing in a number of companies in the same industry. For example, you can buy funds specializing in health care, financial services, technology, or the Internet. If this kind of investment represents a major share of your investment portfolio, you are taking the risk of staking a great deal of your financial future on developments in one industry.

Low Quality Stocks (or Mutual Funds) The definition of "low quality" is subjective, but these are high-risk stocks for a variety of reasons: small revenue and earnings base, erratic past performance, not being leaders in their industry, concentration on one product or service, market price of stock under $5 a share, questionable management, the possibility that the stock is overpriced.

Low Quality Bonds (or Mutual Funds) Because these are non-investment grade bonds, there is a higher likelihood that they could default and not pay the interest due and/or the face value of the bond at maturity. At the bottom of this group are the so-called "junk bonds." But that term is deceptive. Some excellent companies are included in this group, and their bonds may very well be upgraded because of improvements in corporate operations. There is a high level of risk, but low quality bonds have produced excellent returns over the past 10 to 15 years.

Collectibles Collectibles include items such as rare coins, art work, baseball cards, and historical memorabilia. Collectibles are often used as investments by people who want to take advantage of their potential to increase in value over a period of time. Collectors need a knowledge of the market for the items they are collecting, and they must take appropriate storage and insurance precautions. Some would argue that collectibles are high risk because they are subject to changing public tastes and can be difficult to market.

LEVEL 6—HIGH RISK

Futures Commodity futures are contracts to buy and sell items that are mined and grown—soy beans, coffee, cattle, crude oil, etc.—at some time in the future. The investor is betting on the future movement of prices, a speculative activity even for those who know the markets well. This is treacherous territory for a beginner. Beware of radio advertisements and telephone solicitations offering you a once-in-a-lifetime chance to make a killing in commodities. Financial futures and currency futures are contracts involving future price directions of items such as Treasury bonds, bank CDs, the NYSE Index, the British pound, the Japanese yen, etc. This is a highly speculative area and is used by professionals for complicated hedging purposes.

Options An option is a contract to buy or sell a stock at a certain price during a specified period of time. The investor is betting on the future direction of the price of that stock. Small price swings in the underlying stock will have a multiplier effect on an option's price. Large percentage gains or losses are characteristic of options. An option is a short term vehicle used primarily by people who trade stocks. It is not for long-term investors, especially beginners.

Low-Priced and "Penny" Stocks A low-priced stock sells for under $5 a share, a penny stock for under $1 a share. In general, these are stocks from small companies with no track record. In the penny stock arena, you may even find companies with no revenues and no earnings, only a corporation set up to pursue a future dream. Low-priced stocks are high risk. Although the low price may look tempting, beginning investors should avoid them.

UNDERSTAND TERMS AND IDEAS

1. Describe the relationship between risk and potential return.

   _____

   _____

   _____

2. Which government securities are marketable and which non-marketable?

   _____

   _____

   _____

3. Characterize the risk/return profiles of the following investments.

   a. bank savings account _____

   b. Treasury notes _____

   c. quality growth stock _____

   d. commodity futures _____

   e. municipal bonds _____

   f. corporate bonds _____

   g. balanced stock _____

   h. bond mutual funds _____

   i. small cap stocks _____

   j. mutual funds _____

4. When should an investor play it safe, and when should an investor take on a calculated level of risk?

   _____

   _____

   _____

   _____

5. What is a Certificate of Deposit? Why is it regarded a safe investment?

   _____

   _____

   _____

   _____

LESSON 2.4

Buying and Selling Stock

You have probably seen stock tables in the business section of your newspaper. If you have never used them—and most young people have not—the tables can look pretty scary, like a sea of incomprehensible letters and numbers. But what the tables contain is a surprisingly simple, shorthand report on the status of the stocks traded on the different stock markets. You will use this information when you buy and sell stocks.

GOALS

■ **Determine how to buy and sell stocks.**

■ **Explain how to read a newspaper stock table.**

THE STOCKBROKER

Generally, you buy and sell stock by placing your order with a stockbroker. Brokers go through training and testing to qualify for various kinds of securities licenses. One organization that administers proficiency exams is the National Association of Securities Dealers (NASD). By passing the exam, the broker becomes a registered representative of the NASD.

You may choose a full-service broker or a discount broker. After you have mastered the NAIC method for evaluating stocks, you may feel more comfortable using a discount broker to place your securities orders.

A full-service brokerage firm usually has a staff of investment analysts who are assigned to follow various industries and companies in order to compile investment information on them. A full-service broker can provide advice based on these reports. In particular, the broker will tell you whether the firm's research indicates that a company's stock seems to be overvalued (overpriced), undervalued, or fairly-valued. There are two basic kinds of investment research:

Fundamental analysis is an analysis of the company itself, its operations, its position within its industry.

Technical analysis is an analysis of the company's stock, its price, price movement, trading volume, etc.

LET THE BUYER BEWARE

A full-service stockbroker is a salesperson first and an advisor second. A broker may sincerely want to help you achieve your goals, but in order to make money, the broker ultimately has to sell the product to you. As an advisor, the broker has a conflict of interest. In addition, because full-service brokers are usually paid entirely in commissions and make money only on stock transactions, they will often encour-

COMMISSION COMPARISONS

Compare Our Price	200 shares @ $25	300 shares @ $20	500 shares @ $18	1000 shares @ $14
Full Service	129.50	164.85	225.23	308.28
Discount 1	89.00	95.60	106.60	123.50
Discount 2	88.50	95.10	106.10	123.10
Discount 3	60.50	65.00	81.50	94.00
Discount 4	35.00	40.82	57.62	90.33

age you to buy and sell stocks when you really ought to hold on to the ones you have.

Even the advice of investment analysts has to be treated with skepticism. Analysts rely heavily on information they obtain by interviewing the managers of the companies they are following. Analysts do not want to lose these valuable contacts, and as a result, they are reluctant to criticize corporate management teams. It is no surprise that analysts' buy recommendations exceed their sell recommendations by a margin of 5 to 1. Because neither stockbrokers nor investment analysts are fully dedicated to the needs and goals of individual investors, it is absolutely imperative for each investor to develop the knowledge and skills to be self-reliant.

PLACING AN ORDER

Remember that you are looking only at procedures for placing orders. Later, you will learn how to choose the stocks you want to buy.

You can place your order (a) verbally over the telephone, (b) through a touch-tone automated system, or (c) by computer over the Internet. You will need to learn some of the buzzwords for the different kinds of orders:

Market Order You want to buy or sell a certain number of shares of stock at the best current available price and you assume your order will be executed as soon as possible.

Limit Order You want to buy or sell when the stock reaches a certain price. You will not buy or sell if the specified price is not reached.

Stop Order Your order to buy or sell at a specific price changes to a market order when the specific price is reached.

In addition to these three basic kinds of orders, you can attach a time limit to your order. A *day order*, for example, is good only on the day it is entered. When the market closes at the end of the day, the order expires.

Stocks are often ordered in even hundreds of shares (that is, 200, 500, 1000). When you order this way, it is called a *round lot*. An order that is not in even hundreds (for example, 60, 128) is called an *odd lot*. It usually costs more in commissions to buy and sell odd lots.

FILLING AN ORDER

Using computers, your order goes in a matter of minutes from your broker to the appropriate stock market. If the security you are interested in is listed on the New York Stock Exchange or the American Stock Exchange, a specialist there will handle your order. If it is stock in a company not listed on one of these exchanges, your order will go to a dealer in the over-the-counter market.

On a stock exchange (an auction market), a "specialist" acts as an agent, matching buy orders and sell orders. When you are buying, you pay the asking price (ask). When you are selling, you receive the bid price (bid). Sometimes the specialist will buy or sell from his or her own account to maintain an orderly market. In the NASDAQ and over-the-counter markets, a dealer handles the buying and selling. The dealer acts not as an agent, but as a principal, using his or her own funds.

INSTITUTIONAL INVESTORS

Institutional investors do approximately 75-80% of all stock market trading. These include banks, bank trust departments, mutual fund companies, pension funds, and insurance companies. Usually, they are large companies with professional staffs dedicated to investment decisions. Because of the size of their purchases, these institutions have a lot of influence on stock prices.

TYPES OF ACCOUNTS

There are two basic types of accounts with brokerage firms: cash accounts and margin accounts. As a beginning investor, you should have a cash account, which means that you will be required to pay for your security purchases within three business days of your order.

Margin accounts are for more sophisticated investors, who are actually borrowing money to purchase securities. Margin accounts are sometimes used to conduct a stock transaction known as selling short. In a short sale, an investor is selling borrowed stock, which he will pay for at a later date. He is betting that the price will drop between the time of sale and the time of purchase, and he hopes to pocket the difference. If the price rises in the interim, however, he loses money. Selling short is a high-risk, short-term transaction, and it is certainly not an appropriate investment activity for a beginner.

STOCK TRANSACTION DOCUMENTS

After the brokerage firm has executed your order, you will receive a confirmation statement. This written document summarizes the transaction - number of shares of a specific security bought or sold, price, date, transaction fees, and the amount due.

The securities you buy may be registered in your name or in street name, the name of your brokerage firm. If they are registered in your name, you will receive a stock certificate several weeks after the transaction date. If the stock remains with the brokerage firm in an account and the firm acts as custodian, you will receive a monthly account statement from the firm summarizing your security positions.

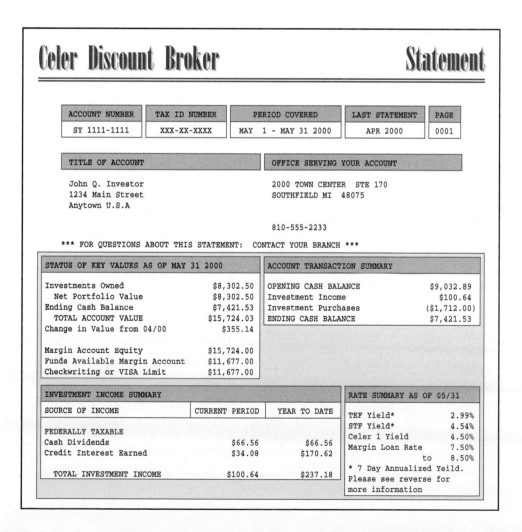

Celer Discount Broker · Statement

ACCOUNT NUMBER	TAX ID NUMBER	PERIOD COVERED	LAST STATEMENT	PAGE
SY 1111-1111	XXX-XX-XXXX	MAY 1 - MAY 31 2000	APR 2000	0001

TITLE OF ACCOUNT

John Q. Investor
1234 Main Street
Anytown U.S.A

OFFICE SERVING YOUR ACCOUNT

2000 TOWN CENTER STE 170
SOUTHFIELD MI 48075

810-555-2233

*** FOR QUESTIONS ABOUT THIS STATEMENT: CONTACT YOUR BRANCH ***

STATUS OF KEY VALUES AS OF MAY 31 2000

Investments Owned	$8,302.50
Net Portfolio Value	$8,302.50
Ending Cash Balance	$7,421.53
TOTAL ACCOUNT VALUE	$15,724.03
Change in Value from 04/00	$355.14
Margin Account Equity	$15,724.00
Funds Available Margin Account	$11,677.00
Checkwriting or VISA Limit	$11,677.00

ACCOUNT TRANSACTION SUMMARY

OPENING CASH BALANCE	$9,032.89
Investment Income	$100.64
Investment Purchases	($1,712.00)
ENDING CASH BALANCE	$7,421.53

INVESTMENT INCOME SUMMARY

SOURCE OF INCOME	CURRENT PERIOD	YEAR TO DATE
FEDERALLY TAXABLE		
Cash Dividends	$66.56	$66.56
Credit Interest Earned	$34.08	$170.62
TOTAL INVESTMENT INCOME	$100.64	$237.18

RATE SUMMARY AS OF 05/31

TEF Yield*	2.99%
STF Yield*	4.54%
Celer 1 Yield	4.50%
Margin Loan Rate	7.50%
to	8.50%

* 7 Day Annualized Yeild.
Please see reverse for
more information

READING STOCK TABLES

Part of the reason why the tables are difficult to read at first is the fact that company names are abbreviated, but the problem quickly fades away as you become familiar with the abbreviations for the companies whose stock you are interested in. Another source of difficulty is the tradition of quoting stock prices in dollars and fractions of a dollar (without the dollar sign). Fortunately, this custom is coming to an end. Stock prices will soon be listed like everything else you buy and sell in dollars and cents.

STOCK TABLE

Sym	Div	Yld %	PE	Vol 100s	Hi	Lo	Close	Net Chg
-A-A-A-								
AIR	.34	1.3	23	3104	$27\,^{11}/_{16}$	$26\,^{15}/_{16}$	27	$-\,^{3}/_{4}$
ABM	.48	1.5	25	248	$31\,^{1}/_{4}$	$30\,^{7}/_{16}$	31	$-\,^{3}/_{16}$
AAN	.25	...	...	553	24	$23\,^{9}/_{16}$	$23\,^{3}/_{4}$	$+\,^{1}/_{8}$
ACG	.90	7.9	...	792	$11\,^{7}/_{16}$	$11\,^{5}/_{16}$	$11\,^{3}/_{8}$	...
AOF	.63	7.9	...	1058	8	$7\,^{3}/_{4}$	$7\,^{15}/_{16}$	$-\,^{1}/_{16}$
ADF	1.35	9.4	...	228	$14\,^{5}/_{16}$	$14\,^{1}/_{4}$	$14\,^{5}/_{16}$	$+\,^{1}/_{16}$
AMF	.90	9.2	...	420	$9\,^{7}/_{8}$	$9\,^{3}/_{4}$	$9\,^{3}/_{4}$	$-\,^{1}/_{8}$
AMU	.90	6.2	...	109	$14\,^{5}/_{8}$	$14\,^{9}/_{16}$	$14\,^{9}/_{16}$	$-\,^{1}/_{16}$
ACX		...	25	825	$24\,^{5}/_{16}$	$23\,^{5}/_{8}$	$24\,^{5}/_{16}$	$+\,^{3}/_{16}$
AES		...	48	3089	$53\,^{5}/_{16}$	$52\,^{1}/_{8}$	$53\,^{1}/_{4}$	$+\,^{7}/_{8}$
AFL	.46	.7	16	1243	$65\,^{3}/_{4}$	$65\,^{3}/_{16}$	$65\,^{5}/_{16}$	$+\,^{9}/_{16}$
AG	.04	.1	11	3216	$29\,^{5}/_{8}$	$29\,^{3}/_{8}$	$29\,^{9}/_{16}$	$+\,^{1}/_{8}$
ATG	1.08	5.0	16	1643	$21\,^{7}/_{16}$	$21\,^{3}/_{16}$	$21\,^{7}/_{16}$	$+\,^{3}/_{16}$
ASV		...	18	30	$17\,^{1}/_{8}$	17	$17\,^{1}/_{16}$	$+\,^{1}/_{16}$
AJP	1.44	13.9	...	324	$10\,^{1}/_{2}$	$10\,^{1}/_{4}$	$10\,^{3}/_{8}$	$+\,^{1}/_{8}$
AMB	1.37	5.5	...	228	$24\,^{15}/_{16}$	$24\,^{1}/_{2}$	$24\,^{3}/_{4}$	$+\,^{7}/_{16}$
AML	1.76	7.7	16	332	23	$22\,^{13}/_{16}$	23	$+\,^{1}/_{16}$
AMP	1.08	2.5	20	3245	$43\,^{1}/_{8}$	$42\,^{1}/_{8}$	$42\,^{5}/_{8}$	$-\,^{1}/_{2}$
AMR		...	13	6676	$139\,^{1}/_{4}$	$136\,^{3}/_{4}$	$137\,^{7}/_{8}$	$-1\,^{1}/_{2}$
ASA	.80	3.6	...	1920	$22\,^{3}/_{16}$	$20\,^{7}/_{8}$	$22\,^{1}/_{16}$	$+1\,^{5}/_{16}$
AXA	.65	...	...	638	$51\,^{3}/_{4}$	$50\,^{7}/_{8}$	$51\,^{3}/_{8}$	$-1\,^{7}/_{8}$
AAM	.13	.9	15	1640	$14\,^{3}/_{4}$	$14\,^{5}/_{16}$	$14\,^{5}/_{8}$	$+\,^{1}/_{8}$
ABT	1.20	1.6	29	17530	$75\,^{3}/_{4}$	$74\,^{5}/_{8}$	$75\,^{3}/_{8}$	$+\,^{13}/_{16}$
ANF		...	...	1716	$43\,^{1}/_{16}$	$42\,^{9}/_{16}$	$42\,^{11}/_{16}$	$-\,^{5}/_{16}$
ABY	.40	...	...	9684	$15\,^{3}/_{4}$	$15\,^{3}/_{8}$	$15\,^{11}/_{16}$	$+\,^{3}/_{16}$
AIF		...	10	120	$22\,^{15}/_{16}$	$22\,^{11}/_{16}$	$22\,^{7}/_{8}$	$+\,^{3}/_{16}$
ASI		...	34	10096	$33\,^{13}/_{16}$	33	$33\,^{1}/_{16}$	$-\,^{7}/_{8}$
ACL	.32	.8	16	5445	$40\,^{15}/_{16}$	$39\,^{1}/_{8}$	$40\,^{15}/_{16}$	$+3\,^{11}/_{16}$
AK	.02	.1	21	355	$22\,^{13}/_{16}$	$21\,^{7}/_{16}$	$21\,^{15}/_{16}$	$-1\,^{3}/_{8}$

In addition to the alphabetical listing of stocks on the New York Stock Exchange (NYSE) and the American Stock Exchange (AMEX) and major issues on the NASDAQ, you may notice summary boxes with items such as: top gainers, top losers, and most active (in terms of trading volume).

When people ask, "How did the market do today?" they are asking about the average change in stock market prices. One of the oldest and most common ways of describing the overall performance of the stock market is to report on the Dow Jones Industrial Average and to note how these 30 representative "blue chip" American stocks did on a given day.

The Dow Jones is not the only representative stock market index, and it makes good sense to pay attention to some other more comprehensive averages or indexes: the NYSE Index, Standard & Poor's 500 Index, the NASDAQ Composite Index, and the AMEX Index.

The labels for the columns in the Newspaper Stock Table are explained below:

1. **Sym** ticker symbol for the company.
2. **Div** current dollar amount of the annual dividend per share. The dividend is income paid to stockholders.
3. **Yld%** dividend of the stock as a percentage of stock price (column 2 Div divided by column 8 Close). *Return on your investment*
4. **PE** price earnings ratio (price per share divided by earnings per share). In later chapters, you will learn about the significance of the P/E ratio in evaluating stock prices. *You looking for a low P/E ratio in order to buy*
5. **Vol 100s** trading volume, the number of shares traded that day in *the day that jus past* hundreds of shares (round lots). 1026 means 102,600 shares.
6. **Hi** the highest price the stock sold for that day. A footnote "u" means this was a 52-week high.
7. **Lo** the lowest price the stock sold for that day. A footnote "d" means this was a 52-week low.
8. **Close** (or Last) the price per share when the trading day ended.
9. **Net Chg** the amount the closing price moved up or down from the prior day's closing price.

Some newspapers include columns for the high price and the low price for the stock during the past 52 weeks, as well as a column called Stock which gives the abbreviated name of the company.

UNDERSTAND TERMS AND IDEAS

1. Why should you consider a stockbroker a salesperson first and an advisor second?

   _____

   _____

2. Why would someone go to a full-service broker? To a discount broker?

   _____

   _____

3. Why is it important for investors to become self-reliant?

   Stockbrokers don't control de Market

   _____

4. Explain the concepts of fundamental and technical analysis and why both of them are important.

   analizis of the company itself and technical

   the analysis of the stock

   _____

5. What are the differences among market, limit, and stop orders?

   _____

   _____

   _____

6. What is a confirmation statement and what does it contain?

   Price date fees of you stocks

   _____

7. What information is contained in a newspaper stock table?

   Price, symbol, high-low - PD/ratio, valuo,

   _____

   NASDAQ S&P 500

8. What is the Dow Jones Industrial Average, and why should we pay attention to other stock market indexes?

   D. J. has 30 diferent companies to do the average

   Index showing an averages of all the companyd that up and down

   _____

Stock Market Literacy

N ow comes the critical part of making an investment—finding the informa-tion you need and using it to choose securities. The investment process begins with acquiring information. The old adage "knowledge is power" is certainly true when it comes to choosing stocks. There are many sources of investment informa-tion. Some are free. Others cost hundreds, even thousands of dollars. Some are available free of charge at your local library.

GOALS

■ **Name the various categories of investment information sources.**

■ **Discuss why acting on inside information is illegal.**

THE NEED FOR INFORMATION

As a new long-term investor, you are interested in selecting and hold-ing onto a portfolio of good quality common stocks. That means you want to choose the companies you invest in very carefully based on a knowledge of their past performances, their present management, and their future objectives. You are not interested in a lot of short-term buying and selling, which would increase your transaction costs, but you do need to keep track of how your portfolio is doing in terms of achieving your investment expectations.

INFORMATION PROVIDED BY PUBLIC CORPORATIONS

The starting point is investment information provided by the compa-nies themselves. Public corporations (companies whose stock trades on a stock market) are required by law to disclose financial informa-tion in various reports to their shareholders. Here are the major re-ports provided by public companies.

Annual Report The annual report is a widely used source of investor information. Although publicly owned companies are required by law to send annual reports only to their stockholders, many of them will also send annual reports to non-stockholders on request. The annual report contains an explanation of the financial results of the past year. But many companies also use the annual report as a public rela-tions tool and a showcase for their products and services. An excellent booklet on reading annual reports, "Understanding the Annual Re-port," is available free of charge from the Chrysler Corporation.

The typical report starts with a letter to shareholders from the presi-dent or the chairman of the board of directors. It highlights the past year—management changes, organizational changes, dividend changes—and it may look ahead to the future and the company's fu-ture outlook.

The 10-K Report The 10-K is a report filed by a public company each year with the Securities and Exchange Commission (SEC). It is much longer and more detailed than the annual report to stockholders. Professional investment analysts use the 10-K report as the backbone of their research into company operations. The report is provided free to shareholders, if they formally request it, and may be provided free to non-shareholders.

Corporate Quarterly Reports Public companies usually provide quarterly reports to their shareholders. These reports summarize activities in that quarter including unaudited financial statements. The 10-Q, a quarterly report filed with the SEC, is more detailed than the quarterly report to stockholders.

OTHER CORPORATE SOURCES OF PUBLIC INFORMATION

Many companies publish news bulletins whenever a significant event occurs: an acquisition of another company, a merger, the sale of a division or subsidiary, introduction of a new major product.

Companies must file an 8-K report within 15 days of an event that could affect the value of the firm's securities. Changing accounting firms is usually considered serious enough to require filing an 8-K.

If an investor acquires 5% of a company's stock, that person or his/her firm must file a 13-D report with the SEC. This report also alerts management that someone may be trying to gain control of outstanding shares.

Quentin Sampson

When Quentin Sampson grew up in the Great Depression, neither he nor his parents could have imagined how much success he would have investing in the stock market. His parents taught him about the importance of saving, but like many who had seen banks fail, they mistrusted banks. Quentin's parents kept their savings in hiding places in their home. Now retired, he lives on the income from his investments, and he invests his Social Security checks. What's even more amazing is that he started investing in1986!

Quentin Sampson worked for People's Gas, a utility company in Chicago, his entire professional life. He tried investing on his own, but he was investing without a plan and without much of an understanding of how the stock market works. He ended up losing money. Once he joined an NAIC investment club in 1986, however, all that changed. Now he teaches investing basics and the wonders of dividend reinvestment plans to high school students.

He wishes that he had known earlier about investing. Even though Quentin hasn't invested for very long, he has been able to earn returns of 12 to 12.5% each year on his investments. It would be higher, he says, but he takes money out for his comfortable retirement.

INSIDE INFORMATION

Inside information refers to information that exists inside a corporation, but has not yet been released to the public. The securities laws of the United States forbid investors from acting on inside information.

Here's an example of an illegal use of inside information. Your brother works for a company that is in the process of being acquired by a much larger company. That information has not yet been released to the public. Over lunch, however, your brother tells you about it. As soon as you can, you contact your broker and buy 1000 shares in your brother's company. A week later, when the acquisition is announced, the price per share of your brother's company jumps 25%. It is the SEC's job to enforce securities laws. Using computers, the SEC discovers your well-timed purchase of 1000 shares. You face severe penalties including the possibility of becoming an insider in an institution that does not trade on the stock market.

NEWSSTAND AND SUBSCRIPTION PUBLICATIONS

There are many newsstand and subscription publications with timely news and analysis for investors. While these publications can range in price from $15 a year to several hundred dollars a year, many are available free of charge at your public library.

NEWSPAPERS AND MAGAZINES

Your local daily newspaper probably has a business section with stock tables and articles about corporate activities (especially those of local firms). This is an excellent place to find stories about corporations that are located right in your own back yard.

In the investment community, *The Wall Street Journal* is one of the most respected sources of financial information. Published Monday through Friday, the WSJ is packed with a wealth of data and in-depth analyses of companies and industries. You already may have seen the Journal's "Classroom Edition" in your school. Other excellent newspaper sources are *Investor's Business Daily*, *The New York Times*, *Barron's* (weekly), and *The Wall Street Transcript*.

There are dozens of financial magazines which offer analyses of corporations, management, and industries. The better general financial news magazines are *Business Week*, *Forbes*, and *Fortune*. These magazines offer excellent lists and studies. For example, *Business Week* and *Forbes* offer periodic industry studies, comparing companies within an industry. Another excellent source of information for the beginning investor is NAIC's *Better Investing* magazine. This monthly publication offers articles on stocks to study and undervalued stocks, along with many helpful ideas for beginners.

INVESTMENT ADVISORY SERVICE PUBLICATIONS

Hundreds of investment advisory information sources are available for purchase. Among the best known are *Value Line Investment Survey* and *Moody's*, as well as *Standard and Poor's Stock Guide*, *Bond Guide*, *Corporation Records*, and *The Outlook*. The *S&P Stock Guide* and *Value Line Investment Survey* will play an important role in the stock selection process you will learn later.

With all the investment advisory services out there, how do you know who is reliable and who isn't? There is a publication, *The Hulbert Financial Digest*, which provides monthly appraisals of the investment advice dispensed by many of the more popular advisors.

BROKERAGE FIRM RESEARCH REPORTS

If you use a full-service stockbroker, you will have access to the research reports written by the firm's analysts. These reports may be several pages long and conclude with a buy, hold, or sell recommendation. As a new investor using these brokerage firm services, you should be cautious about accepting their experts' opinions. The major advantage of the reports is the fact that they are free to the firm's customers. The costs are absorbed by the commissions you pay on stock transactions. You should also note whether the brokerage firm is a dealer (market maker) for a recommended stock or whether the firm was an underwriter of any recent stock offerings for that company. These facts could influence the investment opinion offered in the reports.

INVESTMENT INFO ON THE INTERNET

The Internet is a whole new frontier of investment information that can be obtained quickly and conveniently, usually for minimum cost. The easiest way to learn of the many web sites out there is to use browser software and possibly a search engine to search for specific topics. New web site information is being added to the Internet every day. Here are some of the more important web sites.

BROKERAGE FIRMS OR MUTUAL FUND COMPANIES

www.ml.com This is the Merrill Lynch web site, where you can get the firm's daily market analysis and read about different financial planning ideas.

www.schwab.com Trading on the Internet is available through discount broker Charles Schwab.

www.fid-inv.com Fidelity Investments is located at this site offering planning ideas, mutual fund information, and brokerage service information.

www.vanguard.com This very professional site from Vanguard Group includes helpful planning tools such as an assessment of your investment personality profile. Check out the Investor Education section which has a broad array of investment courses.

www.mfmag.com *Mutual Funds* magazine offers a searchable database on mutual fund performances and many interesting articles on the topic.

SITES FOR INDIVIDUAL INVESTORS

www.investorama.com This award-winning web site produced by Doug Gerlach is a directory with 28 categories and more than 2,155 links to leading investment sites. There is information on how to invest in individual stocks and mutual funds, plus many feature articles.

www.pathfinder.com/money This is *Money* magazine's Personal Finance Center, an excellent starting point to explore many sites.

INVESTMENT INFORMATION ON A SPECIFIC COMPANY

www.sec.gov/edgarhp.htm This is the SEC's Edgar (Electronic Data Gathering and Retrieval) database containing the electronic filings of public companies.

www.hoovers.com This is Hoover's Online Database, which provides information on more than 8,500 companies.

CYBER SLEUTH

Numerous web sites exist that can make all of your financial planning quicker and easier. There are sites which can help you develop your own financial plan and personal budget, or even help you pick the best stocks or mutual funds to invest in when you are ready. Enter keywords or phrases such as *investing* or *financial planning* into your search engine.

GENERAL INVESTMENT EDUCATION INFORMATION

www.better-investing.org This is the NAIC web site, which provides extensive services for Association members, both as individuals and investment clubs.

www.aaii.org This is the web site of the American Association of Individual Investors (AAII) and it contains many helpful articles on the basics of investing.

RADIO AND TELEVISION PROGRAMS

One of the best-known investment information television programs is Wall Street Week, which airs on Friday nights on PBS. Each week, host Louis Rukeyser and three panelists quiz a special guest on a specific investment topic. Every night on PBS the Nightly Business Report summarizes that day's stock market results and presents interviews with market experts. There are other daily and weekly television shows on CNBC and CNN.

For radio listeners there are The Dolans, a call-in show with Ken and Daria Dolan (M-F, WOR Radio Network), Marketplace (M-F, Public Radio International), and SOUND Money (weekly, Public Radio International).

Investment information is available in great supply. Much of it is free. In the future, more and more of this information will be accessible on-line. As a new investor, you need to know how to get this information. Analyzing a company is like putting together a jigsaw puzzle. After a period of time, when enough pieces are in place, you have a pretty good idea what the whole puzzle is about.

UNDERSTAND TERMS AND IDEAS

1. Go to your public library and see which of the newsstand and subscription publications they have. Skim through them to get a sense of their different formats. Report on your findings.

_____

_____

_____

2. See which investment advisory service publications the library has. Report your findings.

_____

_____

_____

3. Write a letter to request a corporate annual report.

_____

_____

_____

4. Contact a local full-service brokerage firm and request an analyst's research report. Check over it to see what approach it takes.

_____

_____

_____

5. Visit several of the web sites mentioned in this chapter. Describe the results.

_____

_____

_____

6. For several weeks, watch one of the weekly television programs mentioned in the chapter with a parent or another adult who has some investment knowledge. Describe the results.

_____

_____

_____

Chapter 2 REVIEW

SUMMARY

LESSON 2.1 **THE POWER OF INVESTING**

Investing puts your money to work earning more money. Invest regularly over a long period of time, reinvest all earnings, purchase common shares of a quality growth company, and diversify your portfolio.

LESSON 2.2 **THE CORPORATION**

Companies can be created under different organizational models. Stockbrokers are needed to trade shares of public companies on the stock markets.

LESSON 2.3 **THE INVESTMENT SUPERMARKET**

Investments that have a high rate of return often have more risk of losing money. A mix of investments will give you a balance of risk and possible return.

LESSON 2.4 **BUYING AND SELLING STOCK**

Stockbrokers earn a commission on each stock transaction. Wise investors buy quality stocks and hold them for a long period of time. After every transaction, your broker will send a confirmation statement that provides details about the transaction. Stock prices can be tracked in the newspaper.

LESSON 2.5 **STOCK MARKET LITERACY**

Public corporations must publish their financial information. You can find this information on the Internet, in various magazines and newspapers and in company publications. Company information that is not published is considered insider information. Trading based on unpublished information is illegal.

REVIEW INVESTING TERMS

Write the letter of the term that matches each definition. Some terms may not be used.

1. ____l____ those who buy shares of stock in the company and, in effect, become part owners

2. ____f____ people who lend money to the business in return for a contracted rate of interest or return for their investment

3. ____j____ putting money aside for a rainy day

4. ____i____ the process of raising new money and selling stock directly to the public

5. ____b____ earn interest on the initial deposit and earn interest on the interest

6. ____c____ an analysis of the company itself, its operations, its position within its industry

7. ____h____ buy or sell certain shares of stock at the best current available price as soon as possible

8. ____a____ money to buy real estate, equipment, raw materials and underwrite other start-up costs

9. ____n____ an analysis of the company's stock, its price, price movement, trading volume, etc.

10. ____d____ buying stocks or properties that will increase in value over a period of time

11. ____g____ buy or sell when a stock reaches a certain price

12. ____e____ the people who do the work

13. ____k____ stockholders buy and sell shares from one another on a stock exchange with the help of brokers

a. capital

b. compound interest

c. fundamental analysis

d. investing

e. labor

f. lenders

g. limit order

h. market order

i. primary capital market

j. saving

k. secondary capital market

l. stockholders

m. stop order

n. technical analysis

UNDERSTAND TERMS AND IDEAS

11. Today's career trends are increasing the importance of investing. Why?

_____

_____

_____

_____

12. Which government agency monitors the trading of stocks and bonds? How does the agency do this?

_____

_____

_____

_____

13. You want to make a major purchase in two years. What type of investments would you make?

_____

_____

_____

_____

14. What information can you find in the newspaper stock tables?

_____

_____

_____

_____

15. Describe two documents a company produces that provide information for investors or potential investors

_____

_____

_____

_____

SHARPEN YOUR RESEARCH SKILLS

16. A company can be created as a limited liability corporation (LLC). Look on the Internet or in your local library to identify two primary advantages of an LLC.

_____

_____

_____

_____

_____

_____

_____

17. Think of a collectible that interests you. Look on the Internet for information. What type of items can you collect? How much can you expect an item to increase in value? How long would this increase take?

_____

_____

_____

_____

_____

_____

_____

THINK CRITICALLY

18. You and a friend decide to start a business. What type of product or service would you sell? Why would your company succeed? Who would be your competition? How would you get investors interested in your company?

_____

_____

_____

_____

_____

_____

_____

19. Describe the types of investments you would make to create a good investment portfolio.

_____

_____

_____

_____

_____

_____

_____

_____

PROSPECTIVE PORTFOLIO PROJECT

In the first chapter, you looked up the companies that make products you see every day. As you progress through this class, you will return to your portfolio at the end of every chapter. As you apply the skills you learn, some companies may move up in your portfolio. Others may be eliminated.

In this chapter, you learned about reading stock charts. Locate your companies from Chapter 1 in the newspaper or on the Internet to fill in the following table.

Company	Sym	Yld %	PE	Vol 100s	Hi	Lo	Close	Net Chg

Continue to track the prices for your stocks. If the price increases or dips, check for news about the company, its industry or the economy.

MUTUAL INTERESTS

INDUSTRY INDICATORS
DEPARTMENT STORES

Wal-Mart Stores
Founded in 1962

Sam Walton opened the first Wal-Mart store in 1962. He was a small-town merchant who believed that a discount store with friendly service and a variety of product offerings would attract many customers. Since 1962, Wal-Mart has expanded nationwide and globally to become the world's largest retailer. Diversification into membership warehouse clubs (SAM's Clubs), grocery stores (Wal-Mart Supercenters), discount warehouse outlets, and international operations has fueled the company's growth.

Wal-Mart is known for its "hometown" image. The company facilitates this image by allowing each store to customize the merchandise it carries to match the needs of its community. Each store has the technology to track customer purchases. Since 1990, Wal-Mart stores have been compiling databases of purchasing information. By knowing what customers are buying, Wal-Mart stores can keep their shelves stocked with the most frequently sought items while reducing their inventory and expenses. Because Wal-Mart carefully controls its expenses, it can maintain lower prices. Database information also helps stores to place products in locations that are more convenient for customers.

The "hometown" image of Wal-Mart goes beyond meeting consumer demands. Wal-Mart Stores sponsors many college scholarships for high school seniors, provides money and manpower for local fundraisers, and presents awards to top teachers and public officials. Wal-Mart is the largest sponsor of the Children's Miracle Network and, in 1998, made charitable donations of over $127 million. Each Wal-Mart store has a commitment both to providing quality products and friendly service to their customers, and to helping their local community. The success of Wal-Mart means that it will continue to open new stores and, in so doing, help more communities.

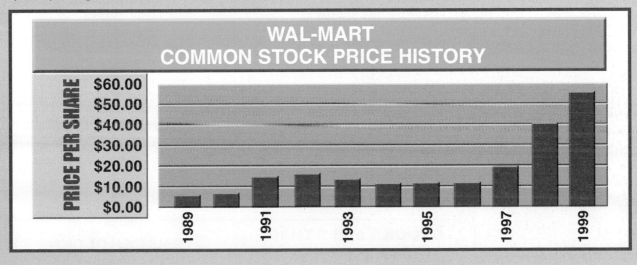

WAL-MART COMMON STOCK PRICE HISTORY

Mutual Funds

Why are so many investors using mutual funds? In this lesson, you will learn about mutual funds. Different kinds of mutual funds are suited to different investment objectives. As with stocks, you need to determine your goals and your tolerance for risk.

GOALS

■ **Describe mutual funds and explain the advantages of mutual fund investing.**

■ **Discuss the different types of mutual funds.**

WHAT ARE MUTUAL FUNDS?

Mutual funds offer an alternative way of investing. Instead of buying stocks in individual corporations, you buy shares in a fund, and professional fund managers take the money you and other shareholders have contributed and invest it in an assortment of stocks, bonds, and other investments. In other words, each shareholder owns a small piece of the fund's entire investment portfolio.

As a shareholder, you are counting on the fund's managers to invest wisely. It is up to them to make money on the mutual fund's investments through dividend income, interest income, increases in stock prices, and capital gains when they sell stocks. After the fund's operating costs are deducted, a portion of these profits belongs to you. And as the fund's investments increase in value, so does the value (net asset value) of your mutual fund shares. The opposite is also true.

SHAREHOLDER $ buys shares ⬇	**STOCKS and OTHER INVESTMENTS** $ pay dividends pay interest increase in price produce capital gains ⬇
MUTUAL FUND makes investments ⬇	**MUTUAL FUND** passes on dividend and interest value of shares increases ⬇
STOCKS and OTHER INVESTMENTS	**SHAREHOLDER**

MUTUAL FUND PRICES AND NET ASSET VALUE (NAV)

Unlike stocks, most mutual fund prices are not determined by what people are willing to pay for them at a given time. They are determined by the net asset value (NAV). The **NAV** is the total value of a fund's investment portfolio minus liabilities divided by the number of shares outstanding. Because the value of the portfolio changes as the stocks and other items are traded throughout the day, the NAV is calculated at the end of each business day.

$$\text{NAV (net asset value)} = \frac{\text{Value of Portfolio} - \text{Liabilities}}{\text{Number of Shares}}$$

WHY ARE SO MANY PEOPLE BUYING THEM?

There are several important advantages to investing in mutual funds.

Diversification The first is diversification. It is not a good idea to own stocks in only a handful of companies. If one of them were to fall on hard times, you would lose a lot of your money. What you want is a diversified portfolio with stocks in a dozen or more companies including companies in separate industries. A severe decline in one stock would be balanced by the performance of others. It is not unusual for a mutual fund to hold stocks in over a hundred different companies.

Suppose of the total assets of a mutual fund are listed as $97,594,050,000 and the liabilities are listed as 0.60% of the assets. There are 769,481,127 shares. Find the net asset value.

Solution Calculate the value of the liabilities by multiplying the total assets by 0.60%.

$97,594,050,000 \times 0.006 = \$585,564,300$

Next, calculate the new net asset value using the net asset value formula.

$$\text{NAV} = \frac{\text{Value of Portfolio} - \text{Liabilities}}{\text{Number of Shares}}$$

$$\text{NAV} = \frac{97,594,050,000 - 585,564,300}{769,481,127}$$

$$= \frac{97,008,485,700}{769,481,127}$$

$$= 126.07$$

The net asset value is $126.07 per share.

Professional Fund Management The second advantage of mutual funds is professional fund management. Many ordinary investors do not feel secure about investing directly in the stock market. They do not have the knowledge or dedication it takes to choose and track individual stocks. In a mutual fund, experienced full-time managers and analysts handle your investments. These investment professionals are compensated through the management fees that are part of the fund's operating expenses.

Convenience The third advantage is convenience. Mutual funds are easy to buy and sell. You can conduct mutual fund transactions through a brokerage firm, or you can deal directly with the mutual fund company. You can obtain a prospectus and an application from the fund by calling or by visiting the fund's web site and downloading the materials. You then mail the completed application and enclose a check to cover your purchase.

FAMILY OF FUNDS

If you own shares in a fund that belongs to a family of funds (funds managed by the same company), you can transfer from one fund to another whenever your investment needs or goals change. Mutual funds also offer the option of automatic reinvestment of dividends and capital gains, and they allow you to arrange for monthly payment deductions from a bank account.

THE MUTUAL FUND UNIVERSE

Mutual funds have become very popular, and they account for much of the stock market's phenomenal growth in the past decade. But people who think that mutual funds are an easy ride had better be careful. Mutual funds have their winners and losers just like stocks, and as you shall observe later, professional fund management is no guarantee of success.

GOALS AND RISK

There are now thousands of mutual funds representing a variety of investments and objectives. That means you have to be clear about your investment goals and the level of risk you are willing to accept if you want to choose a fund that is right for you. You may choose Fund A because you are interested in secure short-term income or Fund B because you are prepared to take some risks in order to achieve more dramatic long-term growth.

After you have chosen the type of fund you want, examine specific funds in that category very carefully before you buy. Compare their performance records, their management, and the growth and income potential of their investment portfolios. Buying a mutual fund is not all that different from buying stock. You have to do your homework.

CATEGORIES OF MUTUAL FUNDS

You begin to get some idea of the complexity of mutual fund investing when you look at how the funds are grouped into categories based on the investments they make and their overall objectives. For example, here is one way of grouping them.

- Common stock funds
- Balanced funds (stocks and bonds)
- Municipal (tax exempt) bond funds
- Corporate bond funds
- Government bond funds
- Money market funds

IMPORTANCE OF COMMON STOCK FUNDS

The stock market funds provide the greatest growth potential and carry the greatest risk. Within the stock funds, however, there are some important subdivisions.

- Aggressive growth (small companies with high growth potential)
- Long-term growth (better known steady-growth companies)
- Growth and income (a mixed portfolio of stocks and bonds)
- Sector funds (stocks from one industrial sector)
- International funds (stocks from other parts of the world)

Sometimes the names of mutual funds let you know what kinds of funds they are: T. Rowe Price Equity Income Fund (mix of stocks and bonds), Montgomery Small Cap Fund (aggressive growth), Fidelity Utilities Fund (sector). But often (The New America Fund, The New Era Fund), you need to examine a prospectus or a profile to find out.

INDEX FUNDS

Recently a special type of common stock fund has jumped into the spotlight: the index fund. An **index fund** buys a little of everything. It invests in a representative sample of the entire stock market, or in the case of a sector index fund, in a cross-section of some industrial sector.

When you buy a total market index fund, you are trying to profit from the general upward movement of the entire stock market over a period of time without making any judgments about the special potential of individual stocks. You are also casting a vote of no confidence in fund managers, who, in spite of their credentials and reputations, have not distinguished themselves. Recently 90% of professionally managed mutual funds have not outperformed the S&P 500 index!

UNDERSTAND TERMS AND IDEAS

1. What are mutual funds and why are they so popular?

   Investment option where you can put your money in one fund

2. How are mutual fund prices determined? What does NAV stand for, and how is it calculated?

   Net Asset Value It's in my note book

3. The value of the total assets of a mutual fund is listed as $64,985,458,000 and the liabilities are listed as 0.53% of the assets. Find the net asset value if there are 625,545,892 shares. _344423.40_

   $$\frac{64,985,458,000 - 344,422,927.4}{625,545,892}$$

4. What are some advantages to investing in mutual funds?

   Low risk, diversification, Professional fund mang. convience to buy or sell

5. What are the main categories of mutual funds? Which involve the highest risk and offer the highest growth potential?

   highest risk

6. What is an index fund? Why are many people choosing index funds today?

   They copy how the market is doing

Investigate Mutual Funds

L*earn where to look for mutual fund information and some of the factors you need to consider when you are trying to choose a mutual fund. For example, when you are considering buying mutual funds, be sure to look for sales charges and any other fees.*

LIGHTEN THE LOAD

All funds incur administrative and managerial costs, and investors must be prepared to pay certain charges to cover them. Still, the object should be to keep these charges as low as possible. **Load funds** charge an up-front sales commission or a "load" on your investment of an average of 3.5%. There are also plenty of **no-load funds** that charge no sales fee. Up-front charges are costly since they decrease the amount you are investing.

Example What is a 5% load on a $10,000 investment?

Solution To calculate 5% of $10,000, multiply $10,000 by 0.05.

$10,000 × 0.05 = $500

Since the load, or sales fee, is $500, you are only investing $9500.

There may also be *back-end loads* (also called contingent deferred sales charges). This charge is deducted at the time of sale of fund shares and commonly decreases from 5% within the first year to zero over a period of time.

ADVICE FROM A FINANCIAL ADVISOR

Some people buy load funds in order to obtain the assistance of a financial advisor. If you learn to make your own mutual fund decisions and buy primarily no-load funds, you will have more money to invest.

GOALS

■ Describe an expense ratio and why it is important.

■ Explain where to go for information on mutual funds.

EXPENSE RATIO

In addition to loads or commissions, a number of other fees are commonly associated with mutual funds. These fees are a part of the fund's **expense ratio** and are expressed as a percentage of assets deducted each fiscal year for fund expenses. Management fees, 12b-1 fees, administrative fees, operating cost and all other asset-based costs incurred by the fund are included in the expense ratio. Expense ratios range from 0.3% to 5%. You should probably avoid funds with expense ratios higher than 1.5%. Operating expenses have a dramatic impact on the long-term performance of a fund.

	Fund A	Fund B
Expense ratio	0.45%	2.1%
Value of $10,000 in 20 years	$61,979	$45,754

Assumes 10% annualized total return before operating expenses.

GETTING THE LOWDOWN

You can follow the progress of mutual funds, just like stocks, in many local newspapers or in *The Wall Street Journal*. Newspaper tables are good for a quick overview of mutual funds.

NEWSPAPER TABLE

NAME Name of mutual fund. Fund families are in bold face.

NAV (Net Asset Value) Per-share value calculated by the fund.

NET CHG Gain or loss in NAV, based on prior day's NAV.

YTD % RET The percent return for the year to date.

NAME	NAV	NET CHG	YTD %RET
Artisan Funds:			
Intl	19.60	+ 0.23	+ 21.6
MidCap	16.47	+ 0.09	+ 14.7
ScapVal	10.15	+ 0.10	+ 11.1
SmCap	10.99	+ 0.15	− 1.5
Buffalo Funds:			
Balanced	8.71	...	− 0.3
Equity	17.38	+ 0.17	+ 3.0
HiYld	10.58	− 0.02	+ 1.3
SmCap	10.91	+ 0.05	+ 13.3
USA Gbl	18.48	− 0.07	+ 13.3
DLB Fund Group:			
Disc Gr	16.78	+ 0.11	+ 5.6
FixInc	10.16	+ 0.03	− 1.2
Growth	12.31	+ 0.04	− 4.0
MicroCap	9.20	+ 0.07	+ 6.9
MidCap	11.32	+ 0.10	− 4.8
Value	14.49	+ 0.09	+ 0.1

IN-DEPTH INFORMATION

If you want to invest in mutual funds, you will also need to use an in-depth information source such as one of the following.

MORNINGSTAR MUTUAL FUNDS

Morningstar is available on a subscription basis. It is also found in the reference section of many public libraries and on the web at *www.morningstar.com*. The next lesson shows how to use *Morningstar* reports to compare various funds.

STANDARD & POOR'S/LIPPER MUTUAL FUND PROFILES

This mutual fund source is also available by subscription, at many public libraries, and on the web at *www.lipperweb.com* or at *www.personalwealth.com*.

MAGAZINES

Forbes magazine publishes a mutual fund issue in August each year. The larger, more popular funds are grouped by investment objectives. Performance data are available, with the added feature of ratings of fund performances in up and down markets. The *Forbes* mutual fund issue also contains sales charge and operating expense information. *Forbes* is probably available in your local library.

Another survey of 2500 mutual funds is found in *Money* magazine. The information includes type of fund, style of investing, risk level, annualized total returns for up to 10 years, sales loads, annual fees, size of portfolio, and the fund's telephone number.

Business Week magazine publishes a quarterly "Mutual Fund Scorecard," which has performance data on more than 700 funds. The Scorecard contains investment objectives, turnover, sales charges, operating fees, percent in cash, and largest stock holdings.

Other publications with mutual fund performance information are *Barron's, Fortune, Kiplinger's Personal Finance,* and *Consumer Reports.*

INTERNET INFORMATION SOURCES

Invest-o-rama is found at *www.investorama.com*. Clicking on Mutual Funds takes you to a list of major mutual fund families such as Vanguard, Fidelity, Federated, T. Rowe Price, Dreyfus, Value Line, and INVESCO. Clicking on any of these names takes you to that fund's web site. At each site, prospectus information is available for downloading.

Use the Internet to investigate different companies and the methods they use to evaluate mutual funds. Enter keywords or phrases such as mutual fund or net asset value. Most web sites will provide definitions of the terms used in the evaluation reports. Some sites will also rate different mutual funds against others that invest in similar stocks and products.

At **_www.quicken.com_**, you can search for information on the better performing funds by investment objective for different time periods. You can also check a list of the top 25 performing funds by investment objectives. Also available are net asset values (NAVs) for funds by their ticker symbols, abbreviated Morningstar fund profiles, and a feature that allows you to set up your own portfolio of mutual funds.

Another excellent site with good educational information on mutual funds is the Mutual Fund Investors Center at **_www.mfea.com_**.

Forbes magazine is available at **_www.forbes.com_**. *Forbes* has a mutual fund section where you can search for a particular fund and receive a summary report.

Mutual Funds magazine has a web site at **_www.mfmag.com_**. Current articles are available for screening and there is a search function that allows you to search prior issues. The screening functions are not free, but require you to register and subscribe.

Mutual funds provide a practical way for ordinary investors to participate in the stock market. Mutual funds may be used as an alternative to investing in individual stocks or they may be used to complement and diversify a stock portfolio. There are many different kinds of mutual funds with a wide range of stock, bond, and money market portfolios and a variety of investment goals. Intelligent mutual fund investors select fund categories that match their investment objectives. Then, they carefully evaluate the performance records, the management, the expense ratios, and the growth and income potential of individual funds before they invest.

Susan Curtis

Susan Curtis always knew her parents had invested so they could pay for her college tuition. After graduating from Cornell University, she realized how much financial freedom that gave her. When she asked her parents how she could repay them, they told her to do the same for her future children.

Susan is now a project engineer for an aluminum and zinc die casting manufacturer. She has been investing for more than seven years. Her long-term goals are to put her children through college and to have a comfortable retirement. Her short-term goal is to become a homeowner. With these goals in mind, she has disciplined herself to invest at least 10% of her income every month. Her employer did not offer a 401(k), so she researched and chose an IRA that was just right for her.

She invests using the NAIC principles. She enjoys researching new companies when the inspiration strikes. Some of her investments have been good, some not so good. Her annual return on her portfolio is 9%. Susan is on track to achieve her goals. She credits her parents with making sure she was not intimidated by investing, and for teaching her that it is not important how much you invest, just that you invest regularly.

UNDERSTAND TERMS AND IDEAS

1. Describe a load fund.   7 3 (5

Is a up "front sells comission or a load on your investment
Is an up front sell comission on your investment on
on overage of 3.5%.

2. Calculate a 7% load on a $5,000 investment.

5.000 × 0.0071 = 350

3. What is a fund's expense ratio, and why is it important?

Is a percentage of assets deducted each fiscal year
for fund expenses. Could be between 1 to five % of
the investment

4. What are some mistakes mutual fund investors must avoid?

5. Describe the information you should find in a mutual fund newspaper table.

Name of mutual fund, Net Asset Value, Net Change
(gain or los in NAV based on Prior's day, Ytd Return
The percent returned for the year to date

6. Name some sources of information about mutual funds.

Morning star mutual funds, standard and poor's/lipper
mutual fund profiles, magozine, internet

7. Surf the Net! Find a site that tells you about the top 25 aggressive growth stock funds.
Visit a mutual fund family web site and examine prospectus and application materials.

Oak association mutual funds

LESSON 3.3

Choose Mutual Funds

You now know what a mutual fund is, and you have a good picture of the different kinds of mutual funds. You know where to look when you need information on mutual fund objectives, portfolios, and performances. In this lesson, you will learn to use the NAIC Equity Mutual Fund Check List to identify the attributes of a given fund that will reveal whether it merits your consideration for investment.

GOALS

■ **Find information in the Morningstar Mutual Fund Reports.**

■ **Analyze a mutual fund's portfolio and asset allocation.**

■ **Evaluate statistical information related to performance, fees and costs, and risk.**

USE THE EQUITY MUTUAL FUND CHECK LIST

You can use the NAIC Equity Mutual Fund Check List to take a closer look at a fund and examine some of the key elements that define it. The Check List will make you aware of these key elements:

- How the fund invests
- What the fund invests in
- The tenure and effectiveness of current management
- Tax considerations
- What percentage of your investment is used to pay the fund's expenses

WHERE TO FIND INFORMATION

Where do you locate the information to fill in the Check List? Although mutual fund reports are provided by several sources, a widely available source is Morningstar's Mutual Funds publication. Morningstar tracks every established mutual fund company currently on the market and publishes detailed, full-page reports on a select group of 1,700 funds. The Morningstar Mutual Funds publication can be found at your local library. On the Morningstar Internet site (**www.morningstar.com**), you'll find a Quicktake Report that contains *most but not all* of the data required for the Check List.

Each Morningstar Mutual Funds Issue provides a cover page (shown on the next page) that lists all of the Morningstar fund categories under two main classifications, Equity Funds and Fixed-Income Funds. A dot located next to a category indicates that the category is covered in that issue. All individual funds contained within the category are listed under each category heading.

MORNINGSTAR

Mutual Funds

• June 6, 1999

Fund Highlights

390   At **Berger 100**, a change at the top gives long-suffering shareholders a reason to hope.

402   **Fidelity Advisor Equity Growth** has hit a few air pockets, but it's still flying high.

421   **Kemper Growth** is getting another facelift.

423   **Marsico Focus'** red-hot performance owes to more than just a favorable market.

480   A huge bet on Australia continues to hamper **AIM New Pacific Growth**.

516   Standing apart from the crowd is finally paying off for **FPA New Income**.

Individual Funds

Domestic-Equity Funds

Large Blend (continued)

355   Stein Roe Growth & Income ★★★★
356   Strong Equity Income ★★★★★
357   Strong Growth & Income ★★★★★
358   Strong Value
359   TIAA-CREF Growth & Income ★★★★
360   United Accumulative A
361   United Income A ★★★★
362   USAA Growth
363   Van Kampen Growth & income A
364   Van Kampen Pace A
365   Vanguard 500 Index ★★★★★
366   Vanguard LifeStrat Growth ★★★★
367   Vanguard Morgan Growth ★★★★
368   Vanguard Primecap ★★★★★
369   Vanguard Tax-Mgd Grth & Inc ★★★★★
370   Vanguard Tot Stk Mkt Idx ★★★★
371   Victory Diversified Stock A ★★★★★
372   Vintage Equity S ★★★★★
373   Warburg Pincus Cap Appr Comm ★★★★★
374   WM Growth & income A
375   Adams Express (CE) ★★★★
376   General American Investors (CE) ★★★★
377   Liberty All-Star Equity (CE) ★★★★
378   Tri-Continental (CE) ★★★★

379 ◎ Large Growth Overview
380   AIM Weingarten A ★★★★
381   Alger Capital Appreciation B ★★★★

Fund Category ③

382   Alger Growth B ★★★★★
383   Alleghany/Chicago Tr Gr & In ★★★★★
384   Alleghany/Montag Growth N ★★★★★
385   Amcap
386   American Cent Growth inv
387   American Cent Select Inv ★★★★
388   American Cent Ultra Inv ★★★★
389   Babson Growth ★★★★
390   Berger 100
391   Berger Growth & Income ★★★★
392   Bramwell Growth ★★★★
393   CitiFunds Large Cap Growth A
394   Citizens Index ★★★★★
395   Columbia Growth ★★★★
396   *Dreyfus Premier WldwideGrA* ★★★★
397   Dreyfus Third Century ★★★★
398   Eaton Vance Tax-Mgd Growth A ★★★★
399   Enterprise Growth A ★★★★★
400   Evergreen Omega A ★★★★
401   Evergreen Strategic Growth B
402   Fidelity Adv Eqty Grth T ★★★★
403   Fidelity Growth Company ★★★★
404   Fidelity Large Cap Stock ★★★★★
405   Founders Growth ★★★★
406   Franklin DynaTech A ★★★★
407   Gabelli Growth ★★★★★
408   Hancock Growth A
409   Harbor Capital Appreciation ★★★★★
410   Idex JCC Growth A ★★★★★
411   IDS Growth A ★★★★
412   IDS New Dimensions A ★★★★★
413   Invesco Blue Chip Growth ★★★★
414   ISG Large Cap Equity A ★★★★★
415   Janus ★★★★★
416   Janus Equity-Income
417   Janus Growth & Income ★★★★★
418   Janus Mercury ★★★★★
419   Janus Olympus ★★★★★
420   Janus Twenty ★★★★★
421   Kemper Growth A
422   MainStay Capital Apprec B ★★★★★
423   Marsico Focus
424   Marsico Growth & income
425   MFS Growth Opportunities A
426   MFS Managed Sectors B
427   MFS Massachusetts Inv Grth A ★★★★★
428   MFS Strategic Growth A ★★★★★
429   MSDW American Opp B ★★★★★
430   MSDW Capital Growth Secs B
431   Oppenheimer Capital Ap A ★★★★
432   Papp America-Abroad ★★★★★

Continued on next page

Analysis Section
Volume 35, Issue 3

Equity Funds

Domestic Equity
Large Value
• Large Blend
• Large Growth
Mid-cap Value
Mid-cap Blend
Mid-cap Growth
Small Value
Small Blend
Small Growth
Specialty
Convertible
Domestic Hybrid

International Equity
Europe
Latin America
Diversified Emerging Markets
• Pacific
• Pacific ex-Japan
Japan
Foreign Stock
World Stock
International Hybrid

Fixed-Income Funds

Taxable Bond
Long-Term Government
Intermediate-Term Government
Short-Term Government
Long-Term Bond
• Intermediate-Term Bond
Short-Term Bond
Ultrashort Bond
High-Yield Bond
Multisector Bond
International Bond
Emerging Markets Bond

Municipal Bond
Muni National-long-Term
Muni National-Intermediate
Muni NY Long-Term
Muni NY Intermediate
Muni CA Long-Term
Muni CA Intermediate
Muni Single State-long-Term
Muni Single State-Intermediate
Muni Bond-Short-Term

The next publishing date for Analysis Section Issue 3 is October 6, 1999.

MFBIO990606
2nd Section of 2 Sections

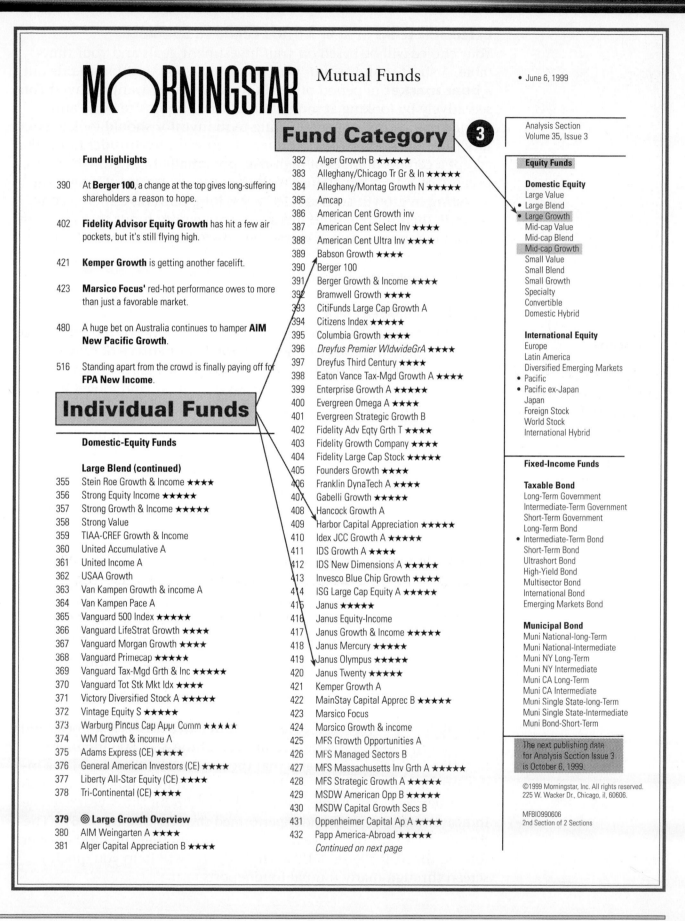

DETERMINE WHAT KIND OF MUTUAL FUNDS TO CONSIDER

Your choice will be based on your investment goals and your time-table. A short-term investor who is not in a good position to ride out a **bear market** (a period of declining prices) may want to invest conservatively by looking at mutual funds that emphasize bond and money market investments. A long-term investor should look at equity (common stock) funds and may even want to consider funds that accept a certain number of high-risk, potentially high-growth stocks. Because of NAIC's experience with the superior results of long-term investing in growth stocks, NAIC urges long-term investors to concentrate their mutual fund investments in equity funds that invest in growth companies. Funds with this investment style can be found under Equity Funds in the Large Growth, Mid-cap Growth, and Small Growth categories.

CHOOSE A GROWTH FUND

One of the first challenges you face is narrowing down the number of growth funds to study. Limiting your choice of growth funds to those that have strong performance comparable to the S&P 500 index in the 3-year, 5-year, and longer periods will give you a good starting point.

S&P 500 INDEX

PERIOD	TOTAL RETURN Annualized
3 years	29.17%
5 years	27.94%
10 years	18.81%
15 years	19.25%
20 years	17.89%

The comparison of the fund's performance to the S&P 500 index is the most widely accepted and used benchmark in the industry. The historical total return figures for the S&P 500 index are shown at the left. Investing in a fund that performs closely to the returns of the S&P 500 index would do any investor's portfolio proud.

SAMPLE MORNINGSTAR REPORT

Suppose you are a long-term investor and decide to evaluate Vanguard U.S. Growth Fund, an equity fund that invests in large firms with strong continuing growth prospects. This fund represents a large growth fund that has performed comparably to the S&P 500 index in the 3-, 5-, 10-, and 15-year total return periods. This information is highlighted on the middle left side of the sample Morningstar report on page 90.

The +/– S&P 500 figures measure the difference between a stock fund's total return (%) and the total return (%) of the S&P 500 index. A negative number (–) indicates that the fund under-performed the index by the given amount, while a positive number indicates a positive performance. For example, the listing of –0.96 for the 3-year average indicates that the fund under-performed the S&P 500 by 0.96%. The listing of 1.12 for the 10-year average indicates that the fund out-performed the S&P 500 by 1.12%. These figures will help you quickly screen through many mutual fund reports.

SAMPLE OVERVIEW SHEET

An Overview sheet is provided for each fund category in the Morningstar Mutual Funds publication. The Overview sheet for the Large Growth category that Vanguard U.S. Growth Fund is listed under is shown on page 89. The Overview sheet summarizes the performance of all the funds in that category. It will enable you to compare information about a fund with averages from its category.

SAMPLE EQUITY MUTUAL FUND CHECK LIST

A completely filled-in Sample Equity Mutual Fund Check List is shown on pages 91 and 92. It is color-keyed with the Vanguard U.S. Growth Fund on pages 90 and 93 and the Morningstar Overview sheet on page 89. A blank Check List is provided in Appendix B.

The Check List has four sections. In addition to the spaces used to fill in the raw data, there are some informative bullet points to help you interpret the data (for example: "A cash holding of 20% or more may indicate the fund manager is trying to time the market...very risky!"). Occasionally a bullet point will pose a question (for example: "Are the assets spread out evenly across the various categories?").

Section 4 is a review section that asks questions about the key elements that impact a fund's performance. You are prompted to reread the Check List Summary. This will help you give informed answers as you determine whether the fund, even if a fine performer, is suitable for you. Definitions for the Check List Summary are found in Appendix A.

CHECK LIST SUMMARY

COMPLETE THE TITLE BLOCK

(A-L) Complete the data in the upper right-hand corner of the Check List. Check for accuracy. Do the minimum and additional purchase amounts meet your needs? Can the fund be used in a tax-deferred account?

Section 1

(1 A) The **Prospectus Objective** shown on the Morningstar Report classifies funds based on stated goals from the fund's prospectus. Read this section and the analysis section carefully.

(1 B) Is the fund investing the way it says it will? For example, suppose the stated objective is growth and at least 85% of assets will be invested in common stocks. A look at the fund's composition reveals only 35% of assets are currently invested in stocks, 60% are in bonds and 5% is cash. Instead of a growth fund, you are, in reality, looking at a *bond* fund. If breaking down a fund's composition reveals a cash holding of 20% or more, the fund's manager may be trying to

time the market. That is, waiting for the market to reach a low point just before a hoped-for up swing. However, predicting the rise and fall of the overall stock market is not an exact science and is more like gambling than investing. Long-term investors buy and hold growth stocks for a period of years, thus defusing the effects of market/price fluctuations. The composition of a growth fund whose objective is to buy and hold stocks in growth companies ideally should be almost fully invested in stocks (90% or more of assets) and should have a small cash holding (less than 10%).

There will be times, as seen on the Sample Check List, when the percentage totals for each category exceed 100%. According to Morningstar, this happens because the libilities are taken out of the total net assets. Therefore, investments, repurchase agreements, and cash can add up to more than the total net assets. Also, this can happen when the fund borrows.

1 C Are the holdings representative of the stated objective and spread out across a sufficient number of different sectors and categories of market capitalization? Concentration in company size or sector tends to increase volatility. Diversification, while spreading risk, does not increase the earnings potential of the portfolio.

1 D A fund is only as good as the sum of the individual stocks in its portfolio. The experienced investor will recognize whether these stocks comprise a group of good quality, growing companies. You can check out each company individually in Value Line reports. When looking at the Total at the bottom of the assets column ask yourself, "Do the top ten holdings together make up a majority of the funds assets?" If not, then you may want to pay additional attention to the other companies in the funds portfolio listed on the fund report. Morningstar provides up to twenty-five of the top holdings in the fund.

1 E The more stocks in different industries a fund holds in its portfolio, the more likely the portfolio represents the broader market. It becomes increasingly more difficult to out-perform the market in this case. When a fund concentrates on relatively few stocks (less than 50) the manager's chance of doing significantly better increases. But note the opposite holds true as well.

Section 2

2 A Who's going to be investing your money, and how's the manager been doing? Be sure to distinguish which data refers to the period that the current manager has been in control of the fund. In the bar graph near the top of the Morningstar report, triangular symbols are placed to indicate any changes in manager. If you see a lot of triangular symbols, the fund may be having a hard time retaining managers. Because the fund manager determines which securities are bought and sold, you need assurance that the current manager is the same manager that has produced the current total returns.

Volume 35, Issue 3, June 6, 1999.

◎ Overview: Large Growth

Large-growth funds invest in big companies that are projected to grow faster than the overall stock market. Most of these funds focus on companies in rapidly expanding industries, such as technology or health care, or multinational companies with a high percentage of earnings coming from sales in foreign markets. A typical holding for one of these funds would be Microsoft or Johnson & Johnson.

Highlights 06-06-99

Good Timing: Marsico Focus fortuitously moved into consumer-cyclical stocks, adding automakers and airline companies, just prior to that sector's April rally.

Big Bet: Janus Mercury isn't shying away from new technology plays: It currently invests 16% of its assets in Internet names.

Group Inflows: Though the large-growth category isn't the most popular place for new investments in 1999, the average fund in the group has seen cash inflows of more than 8%.

Update Amy Granzin 06-06-99

If you think this is the long-heralded large-cap growth correction, think again.

The stock market, which has shown a strong bias for large-growth companies in recent years, has definitely broadened its embrace in 1999. The implementation of oil-production controls by OPEC sent the sluggish energy sector soaring in April. Cyclical stocks also bounced back this spring, buoyed by optimistic global economic news and stronger-than-expected earnings. Over the same period, many technology stocks have stumbled, and giant pharmaceuticals, some of the surest things in 1998's market, have also foundered.

Investors who own the funds that buy and love these aggressive companies may be tempted to believe that the recent storm hitting these growth stocks, while distressing, is now blowing its way out of town. But while the price tags on drug stocks and tech leaders such as Microsoft have seen a few markdowns this year, providing managers in the group with decent buying opportunities, this event hardly qualifies as a large-growth correction.

In fact, while several categories now boast better year-to-date returns, the average large-growth vehicle still posts a pretty gratifying 8% through mid-May. What's more, the most successful offerings in the group in 1999 have been the most aggressive ones. In 1999, a handful of tech-laden, high-P/E Janus funds, including Olympus and Mercury, along with several entrants from the hyperaggressive Alger shop boast returns around 20%.

Like many of their higher-returning peers these Janus and Alger funds have taken advantage of the big boom in Internet stocks, participating in the almost overnight ascent from IPO to behemoth of companies like Amazon.com and Ebay. And while not every fund in the category owns these rather risky names, the more established America Online is one of the most-widely held, not to mention highest-returning, stocks in the group this year.

Those still thinking that the large-growth sector has seen a reasonable price adjustment and experienced the worst for awhile might want to take a gander at the group's average P/E. At the end of April 1999, it came in at 41, a number that doesn't even reflect the Internet stocks that have yet to post earnings. While there's no telling when this group will take a reality check, it's pretty clear that it hasn't happened yet.

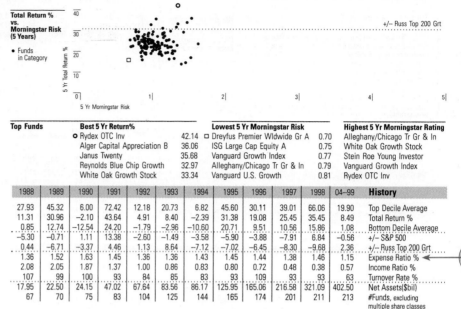

Total Return % vs. Morningstar Risk (5 Years)					+/– Russ Top 200 Grt
● Funds in Category					

Top Funds

	Best 5 Yr Return%		Lowest 5 Yr Morningstar Risk		Highest 5 Yr Morningstar Rating
○	Rydex OTC Inv	42.14	□ Dreyfus Premier Wldwide Gr A	0.70	Alleghany/Chicago Tr Gr & In
	Alger Capital Appreciation B	36.06	ISG Large Cap Equity A	0.75	White Oak Growth Stock
	Janus Twenty	35.68	Vanguard Growth Index	0.77	Stein Roe Young Investor
	Reynolds Blue Chip Growth	32.97	Alleghany/Chicago Tr Gr & In	0.79	Vanguard Growth Index
	White Oak Growth Stock	33.34	Vanguard U.S. Growth	0.81	Rydex OTC Inv

1988	1989	1990	1991	1992	1993	1994	1995	1996	1997	1998	04–99	History
27.93	45.32	6.00	72.42	12.18	20.73	6.82	45.60	30.11	39.01	66.06	19.90	Top Decile Average
11.31	30.96	−2.10	43.64	4.91	8.40	−2.39	31.38	19.08	25.45	35.45	8.49	Total Return %
0.85	12.74	−12.54	24.20	−1.79	−2.96	−10.60	20.71	9.51	10.56	15.86	1.08	Bottom Decile Average
−5.30	−0.71	1.11	13.38	−2.60	−1.49	−3.58	−5.90	−3.88	−7.91	6.84	−0.56	+/– S&P 500
0.44	−6.71	−3.37	4.46	1.13	8.64	−7.12	−7.02	−6.45	−8.30	−9.68	2.36	+/– Russ Top 200 Grt
1.36	1.52	1.63	1.45	1.36	1.36	1.43	1.45	1.44	1.38	1.46	1.15	Expense Ratio %
2.08	2.05	1.87	1.37	1.00	0.86	0.83	0.80	0.72	0.48	0.38	0.57	Income Ratio %
107	99	100	93	84	85	83	93	109	93	93	63	Turnover Rate %
17.95	22.50	24.15	47.02	67.64	83.56	86.17	125.95	165.06	216.58	321.09	402.50	Net Assets($bil)
67	70	75	83	104	125	144	165	174	201	211	213	#Funds, excluding multiple share classes

Performance 04-30-99

	1st Qtr	2nd Qtr	3rd Qtr	4th Qtr	Total
1996	5.17	4.92	3.70	4.19	19.08
1997	−1.66	16.93	9.98	−0.80	25.45
1998	14.62	5.01	−10.80	25.94	35.45
1999	7.86	—	—	—	—

Trailing

	Total Return %	+/– S&P 500	+/– Russ Top 200 Grth	% Rank All Funds
3 Mo	1.96	−2.71	2.34	52
6 Mo	28.66	6.35	4.28	14
1 Yr	26.11	4.28	−4.56	11
3 Yr Avg	25.22	−3.84	−9.13	9
5 Yr Avg	23.32	−3.55	−8.12	10
10 Yr Avg	17.54	−1.27	−3.36	14
15 Yr Avg	16.33	−2.37	—	23

Tax Analysis

	Tax-Adj Ret%	% Rank All	%Pretax Ret	% Rank All
3 Yr Avg	22.31	4	88.5	34
5 Yr Avg	20.50	6	87.9	38
10 Yr Avg	14.87	8	84.8	34

Risk Analysis

	Morningstar Score		Morningstar
	Return	Risk	Risk-Adj Rating
3 Yr	1.81	1.03	★★★★
5 Yr	1.54	1.05	★★★★
10 Yr	1.48	1.11	★★★★
Wtd Avg	1.57	1.07	★★★★

Other Measures

			Standard Index S&P 500
Standard Deviation	24.67	Alpha	−4.50
Mean	24.59	Beta	1.10
Sharpe Ratio	0.92	R-Squared	85

Morningstar Category Correlation

Style	Value	Blend	Growth	
	0.91	0.97	1.00	Large
	0.89	0.93	0.90	Med
	0.76	0.76	0.76	Small

Average Expense Ratios

Front-End Load	1.29	Level Load	2.16
Deferred Load	4.32	No-Load	1.11

Portfolio Analysis 04-30-99

Avg number of equity holdings: 82	% Portfolios in Category	% Net Assets
Microsoft	91	3.97
Cisco Sys	87	2.51
Pfizer	84	2.37
Intel	80	1.90
MCI WorldCom	78	2.58
Home Depot	76	1.46
EMC/Mass	71	1.59
General Elec	70	2.25
American Intl Grp	68	1.69
Schering–Plough	64	1.11
Lucent Tech	63	0.99
America Online	61	2.66
Wal-Mart Stores	60	1.53
Merck	58	1.38
Warner–Lambert	57	1.06

Most Common Purchases	Value $mil
Qwest Comms Intl	14,209.5
Microsoft	10,067.7
America Online	3,956.5
AT & T	3,235.4
Time Warner	2,949.9

Most Common Sales	Value $mil
Johnson & Johnson	−712.5
Bell Atlantic	−707.4
Media One Grp	−655.6
Tribune	−618.9
Washington Mutual	−579.3

Sector Weightings	% of Stocks	Rel S&P 500
Utilities	0.4	0.16
Energy	2.0	0.34
Financials	12.2	0.75
Industrials	7.3	0.65
Durables	1.4	0.59
Staples	6.0	0.73
Services	16.7	1.10
Retail	10.5	1.58
Health	15.7	1.28
Technology	27.9	1.40

Investment Style	Stock Port Avg	Rel S&P 500
Price/Earnings Ratio	40.7	1.15
Price/Book Ratio	10.6	1.19
3 Yr Earnings Gr%	22.3	1.26
Price/Cash Flow	28.4	1.20
Debt % Total Cap	26.4	0.84
Med Mkt Cap $mil	57,292.6	0.83
Yield	0.1%	

Market Cap	
● Giant	50.3
◐ Large	34.1
◔ Medium	13.8
○ Small	1.6
○ Micro	0.2

Composition % of assets 03–31–99	
Cash	3.5
Stocks*	95.0
Bonds	0.6
Other	0.9
*Foreign (% of stocks)	3.2

Cash Inflows	Cash Flow %	% Total Assets	
		Equity	All
1995	10.9	11.67	6.77
1996	11.9	11.50	7.13
1997	4.5	11.04	7.32
1998	12.7	13.04	8.91
1999	8.6	15.33	10.58

M◯RNINGSTAR **Mutual Funds** 379

Volume 35, Issue 3, June 6, 1999.

Vanguard U.S. Growth

	Ticker	Load	NAV	Yield	SEC Yield	Total Assets	Mstar Category
	VWUSX	None	$38.61	0.5%	—	$15,647.9 mil	Large Growth

Prospectus Objective: Growth

Vanguard U.S. Growth Fund seeks long-term growth of capital.

The fund invests primarily in common stocks and convertible securities issued by established U.S. companies. In selecting investments, the advisor emphasizes companies that it believes to have exceptional growth records, strong market positions, reasonable financial strength, and relatively low sensitivity to changing economic conditions.

On Sept. 30, 1985, the Ivest Fund divided into this fund and Vanguard World International Growth Fund. From that date until May 3, 1993, the fund was named Vanguard World Fund U.S. Growth Portfolio.

Portfolio Manager(s)

David Fowler. Since 1-87. MBA'73 Northwestern U. Fowler is a portfolio manager and an equity strategist for Lincoln Capital Management. He joined the company in 1984 as a security analyst, focusing on the technology sector. Previously, Fowler worked for 12 years as an analyst and portfolio manager with Stein Roe & Farnham.

J. Parker Hall III. Since 8-87. BS'55 Swarthmore C.; MBA'57 Harvard U. Hall is president of Lincoln Capital Management, his employer since 1971.

Performance 04-30-99

	1st Qtr	2nd Qtr	3rd Qtr	4th Qtr	Total
1995	9.26	10.51	7.46	6.70	38.44
1996	6.88	7.13	4.08	5.78	26.05
1997	0.59	16.71	3.12	4.02	25.93
1998	15.51	7.27	−9.42	24.73	39.98
1999	3.81				

Trailing	Total Return%	+/− S&P 500	+/− Russ Top 200 Grth	% Rank All Cat	Growth of $10,000
3 Mo	−2.30	−6.97	−1.92	93 94	9,770
6 Mo	20.03	−2.28	−4.35	24 88	12,003
1 Yr	21.91	0.08	−8.76	7 56	12,191
3 Yr Avg	28.11	−0.96	−6.25	4 31	21,024
5 Yr Avg	27.24	0.38	−4.20	2 15	33,357
10 Yr Avg	19.94	1.12	−0.96	4 19	61,592
15 Yr Avg	17.52	−1.17	—	11 34	112,666

Tax Analysis	Tax-Adj Ret%	%Rank Cat	%Pretax Ret	%Rank Cat
3 Yr Avg	25.96	27	92.4	34
5 Yr Avg	25.50	11	93.6	19
10 Yr Avg	18.82	10	94.4	9

Potential Capital Gain Exposure: 40% of assets

Analysis by Christopher Traulsen 05-17-99

Read This

Vanguard U.S. Growth Fund isn't above trying to plug a gap.

This fund, long a stellar performer in the large-growth category, is struggling mightily in 1999. Through mid-May, it had eked out a 2.7% return, leaving it with just a bottom-decile showing relative to its category peers.

So have manager David Fowler and the team at advisor Lincoln Capital suddenly lost their touch? Well, stock-picking is partly to blame. Names such as Compaq (which Fowler sold, but not before it did some damage), 3Com, and Philip Morris have plummeted in 1999. The fund's style, though, is probably the bigger reason for its lethargy. Fowler favors companies with consistent, long-term earnings growth over flashier plays, so the portfolio sports big weightings in the giant consumer-staples firms and drugmakers that have been relatively sluggish this year.

Fowler isn't about to change course, but he is thinking about tweaking the fund's mix in

at least one respect. Specifically, he now wants to give it some exposure to pure Internet stocks (an area that he has thus far avoided). The team is still trying to figure out a suitable means of valuing them and hasn't yet made any purchases, but a Net name or two could well be in the fund's future. Fowler also added MCI WorldCom to the portfolio earlier in 1999 as a play on the growing demand for bandwidth.

Despite its woes in 1999, the fund has generally flourished under Fowler's guidance. Its trailing returns for periods longer than a year all rank in or close to the large-growth category's top third, and it hasn't been nearly as volatile as some of its peers. Investors considering it should take heed of its 1999 performance, though. The fund does well when its giants soar, but many of those stocks have already enjoyed extremely strong runs. If the market should rotate in earnest away from them, it could suffer more than most.

Address:	Vanguard Financial Ctr. P.O. Box 2600 Valley Forge, PA 19482 800−662−7447 / 610−669−1000
Inception:	01-06-59
Advisor:	Lincoln Capital Management
Subadvisor:	None
Distributor:	Vanguard Group
NTF Plans:	N/A

Minimum Purchase:	$3000	Add: $100	IRA: $1000
Min Auto Inv Plan:	$3000	Add: $100	
Sales Fees:	No-load		
Management Fee:	0.40% max./0.10% min.		
Actual Fees:	Mgt: 0.38%	Dist: —	
Expense Projections:	3Yr: $32*	5Yr: $230*	10Yr: $518*
Avg Brok Commission:	—	Income Distrib: Annually	

Total Cost (relative to category)

Historical Profile

Return	High
Risk	Average
Rating	★★★★★ Highest

Investment Style: 90% 87% 91% 95% 96% 96% 97% 95%

	1988	1989	1990	1991	1992	1993	1994	1995	1996	1997	1998	04–99	History
	7.51	10.21	10.49	15.20	15.36	14.93	15.33	20.35	23.74	28.70	37.49	38.61	NAV
	8.76	37.70	4.60	46.76	2.76	−1.45	3.88	38.44	26.05	25.93	39.98	2.99	Total Return %
	−7.85	6.01	7.72	16.27	−4.86	−11.50	2.57	0.91	3.10	−7.42	11.41	−6.06	+/− S&P 500
	−2.12	0.01	3.24	7.35	−1.14	−1.37	−0.97	−0.21	0.53	−7.81	−5.12	−3.14	+/− Russ Top 200 Grt
	0.86	1.73	1.86	1.81	1.18	1.37	1.21	1.89	1.28	1.14	0.66	0.00	Income Return %
	7.90	35.97	2.74	44.94	1.57	−2.81	2.68	36.55	24.77	24.79	39.32	2.99	Capital Return %
	56	23	9	36	72	94	8	12	9	49	26	90	Total Rtn % Rank Cat
	0.06	0.13	0.19	0.19	0.18	0.21	0.18	0.29	0.26	0.27	0.19	0.00	Income $
	0.00	0.00	0.00	0.00	0.08	0.00	0.00	0.57	1.62	0.89	2.31	0.00	Capital Gains $
	0.88	0.95	0.74	0.56	0.49	0.49	0.52	0.44	0.43	0.42	0.41	—	Expense Ratio %
	1.23	1.44	1.77	1.82	1.52	1.50	1.30	1.59	1.32	1.13	0.69	—	Income Ratio %
	38	48	49	30	24	37	47	32	44	35	48	—	Turnover Rate %
	132.2	198.2	355.9	978.1	1,813.9	1,847.2	2,109.3	3,624.1	5,532.0	8,054.6	13,023.6	15,647.9	Net Assets $mil

Risk Analysis

Time Period	Load-Adj Return %	Risk %Rank[1] All Cat	Morningstar Return Risk	Morningstar Risk-Adj Rating
1 Yr	21.91			
3 Yr	28.11	68 18	2.17 0.85	★★★★★
5 Yr	27.24	66 11	2.03 0.81	★★★★★
10 Yr	19.94	68 8	1.92 0.89	★★★★★

Average Historical Rating (161 months): 3.3★s

[1]=low, 100=high

Category Rating (3 Yr)

Worst 1 2 3 4 5 Best

Return: Above Avg
Risk: Below Avg

Other Measures	Standard Index S&P 500	Best Fit Index S&P 500
Alpha	−0.7	−0.7
Beta	1.00	1.00
R−Squared	92	92
Standard Deviation	21.96	
Mean	28.11	
Sharpe Ratio	1.18	

Portfolio Analysis 03-31-99

Share change since 12−98 Total Stocks: 79

	Sector	PE	YTD Ret%	% Assets
⊕ Microsoft	Technology	64.3	17.26	6.02
⊕ General Elec	Industrials	36.6	3.67	5.51
⊕ Cisco Sys	Technology	NMF	22.90	4.96
⊕ Merck	Health	31.7	−4.25	4.56
⊕ Intel	Technology	31.5	3.24	4.46
⊕ Procter & Gamble	Staples	33.9	3.38	3.92
⊕ Pfizer	Health	43.6	−7.79	3.50
⊕ Lucent Tech	Technology	49.8	9.23	2.93
⊕ Dell Comp	Technology	77.7	12.55	2.69
⊕ Bristol−Myers Squibb	Health	39.2	−4.37	2.54
⊖ Coca−Cola	Staples	49.3	1.83	1.98
⊕ American Home Products	Health	38.1	8.63	1.98
⊖ American Intl Grp	Financials	32.8	21.15	1.95
⊕ Wal−Mart Stores	Retail	46.5	13.09	1.91
⊕ CVS	Retail	45.4	−13.10	1.78
⊖ Chase Manhattan	Financials	17.3	17.38	1.73
⊕ Gillette	Staples	54.4	9.71	1.61
⊕ Nokia Cl A ADR	Technology	22.4	24.11	1.61
⊕ Amgen	Health	35.2	17.51	1.55
⊕ Schering−Plough	Health	39.0	−12.30	1.54
⊕ IBM	Technology	29.6	13.61	1.49
⊕ Johnson & Johnson	Health	42.0	16.59	1.45
⊕ Automatic Data Processing	Services	41.6	11.21	1.42
⊕ Monsanto	Industrials	—	−4.68	1.37
⊕ Philip Morris	Staples	14.9	−33.70	1.36

Current Investment Style

Style: Value Blnd Growth
Size: Large Med Small

	Stock Port Avg	Relative S&P 500 Current	Hist	Rel Cat
Price/Earnings Ratio	40.9	1.20	1.31	1.00
Price/Book Ratio	12.4	1.43	1.61	1.16
Price/Cash Flow	29.6	1.24	1.29	1.04
3 Yr Earnings Growth	23.0	1.37	1.31	1.03
1 Yr Earnings Est%	20.9	1.24	—	0.92
Debt % Total Cap	26.3	0.84	0.86	1.00
Med Mkt Cap $mil	104,105	1.6	2.0	1.82

Special Securities % of assets 03-31-99

○ Restricted/Illiquid Secs	0
○ Emerging−Markets Secs	0
○ Options/Futures/Warrants	No

Composition % of assets 03-31-99

Cash	1.9
Stocks*	97.7
Bonds	0.0
Other	0.5
*Foreign (% of stocks)	2.8

Market Cap

Giant	67.8
Large	26.5
Medium	5.7
Small	0.0
Micro	0.0

Sector Weightings

	% of Stocks	Rel S&P	5-Year High	Low
Utilities	0.0	0.0	5	0
Energy	0.0	0.0	3	0
Financials	9.1	0.6	24	5
Industrials	9.7	0.8	19	9
Durables	0.0	0.0	3	0
Staples	13.8	1.7	27	13
Services	5.0	0.3	20	4
Retail	9.4	1.5	20	3
Health	23.6	2.1	24	8
Technology	29.5	1.5	29	0

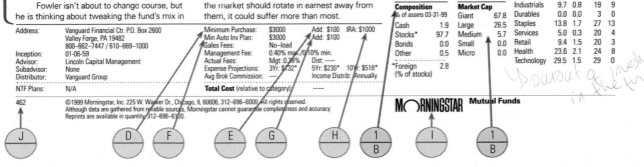

M✩RNINGSTAR Mutual Funds

NATIONAL ASSOCIATION OF INVESTORS CORPORATION

NAIC

INVESTMENT EDUCATION
FOR INDIVIDUALS AND CLUBS
SINCE 1951

EQUITY MUTUAL FUND
Check List®

(A) Fund Name _Vanguard U.S. Growth_
(B) Fund Ticker Symbol _VWUSX_
(C) Fund Category _Large Growth_
(D) Minimum Purchase($) _3,000_   (E) Add ($) _100_
(F) Min Auto Inv Plan($) _3,000_   (G) Add ($) _100_
(H) IRA($) _1,000_
(I) Data Reference _Morningstar_   (J) Page No. _462_
(K) Portfolio Analysis Date _03-31-99_
(L) Current NAV($) _$38.61_
Prepared by _My Name_   Date _11-04-99_
Taxable Account _____   Tax-Deferred Account _✔_ 401(k)
                                                    (IRA)
                                                    Other

1. FUND INVESTMENT CHARACTERISTICS

(A) Stated Investment Objective _Long-term growth of capital_

- What are the fund's investment criteria & investment policies?

(B) Portfolio Composition

Cash	Stocks	Bonds	Other	Foreign
1.9 %	97.7 %	0 %	0.5 %	2.8 %

- Does this composition reflect the fund's stated investment policies? _yes_
- A cash holding of 20% or more may indicate the manager is trying to time the market...very risky!

(C) Market Capitalization

Giant	Large	Medium	Small	Micro
67.8 %	26.5 %	5.7 %	0 %	0 %

- Are the assets concentrated accorcing to the stated objective? _yes_
- Does this provide you with the diversification you are looking for? _yes_

(D) Top 10 Company Holdings

No.	Company Name	Sector	Assets
1	Microsoft	Technology	6.02 %
2	General Electric	Industrials	5.51 %
3	Cisco Sys	Technology	4.96 %
4	Merck	Health	4.56 %
5	Intel	Technology	4.46 %
6	Proctor & Gamble	Staples	3.92 %
7	Pfizer	Health	3.50 %
8	Lucent Technology	Technology	2.93 %
9	Dell Computers	Technology	2.69 %
10	Bristol-Myers Squibb	Health	2.54 %
			41.09 % Total

- Does any one holding make up a far greater % of assets than the other holdings? _no_
- How many differeny sectors do the top ten holdings cover? _4_
- The fewer number of holdings and sectors that the fund's assets are spread over the greater likelihood for volatility within the portfolio.

(E) Total Number of Stocks in Portfolio _79_

- It becomes more difficult to perform better than the market as a whole, the more stocks held by the fund.
- A fund is likely to become more volatile over the short term, the fewer (less than 50) stocks it holds.

2. FUND MANAGEMENT CHARACTERISTICS

(A) (1) Fund Manager David Fowler   **Years** 12   **(2) Date Fund Started** 01-06-59

Fund Manager #2 J. Parker Hall, III   **Years** 12

If manager has been with fund five years or less, give name of previous fund managed, length of service, and investment style.

_____

- Fund reports do not always include previous employment information, to get this you may have to call the fund directly.

(B) Management Record   Initial Year   (shade in blocks above years pertaining to current manager)

enter all years ⇒	1989	1990	1991	1992	1993	1994	1995	1996	1997	1998
(1) Current Management Period	1989	1990	1991	1992	1993	1994	1995	1996	1997	1998
(2) Net Asset Value (NAV)	10.21	10.49	15.20	15.36	14.93	15.33	20.35	23.74	28.70	37.49
(3) Annual Total Return %—Subject Fund	37.70	4.60	46.76	2.76	−1.45	3.88	38.44	26.05	25.93	39.98
(4) +/− Total Return %—S&P 500 Index	6.01	7.72	16.27	−4.86	−11.50	2.57	0.91	3.10	−7.42	11.41

- Has the current manager consistently out-performed the index? yes
- Has the NAV increased in value over the years? yes

(C) Turnover Rate (%)
(Most recent five years)

Initial Year

Years	1994	1995	1996	1997	1998	Total	Average	Average = total of all turnover rates / # of years entered
Turnover Rate	48	35	44	32	47	206	41.2	

- Turnover rated in excess of 20% indicate that a buy and hold investment style is not being implemented.
- Higher turnover rates can cause high capital gains and brokerage fees.

(D) Tax Analysis

	3 Yr.	5 Yr.	10 Yr.	
Fund Total Return %	28.11	27.24	19.94	(line 1)
Fund Tax-Adjusted Return %	− 25.96	− 25.50	− 18.82	(line 2)
Taxes (%) (subtract line 2 from line 1)	2.15	1.74	1.12	(line 3)

how much toto pay

- The lower the number on line 3 the more tax-efficient the fund is.
- The higher the number the more tax liability you will incur.

(E) (3-Year) Average Portfolio Earnings Growth Rate _____ 23.0 %

return of your money

- Earnings Growth leads to Higher Stock Prices which leads to increase in Fund Value.

(F) Average Price-to-Earnings (P/E) Ratio of Stocks in Portfolio 40.9

Price of mutual fund compare to the earning it give

- High P/E ratios may indicate that stocks are being bought at high prices or that the current holdings may not produce gains in the near future

3. COST CONSIDERATIONS

(A) Management Fee .... _____ 0.40 %   Fund Expense Ratio   Peer Group Avg. Expense Ratio (listed on overview sheet)

it low

(B) Expense Ratios .... _____ 0.41 %   **(C)** _____ 1.15 %

(D) Avg. Broker Commission (if applicable).. _____ %

(E) 12b-1 Charges (if any) .... _____ %

(F) Load / No Load .... _____ %   **(G) Deferred Sales Charge or Redemption Fee** (if any) _____ %

- High costs will greatly impact your return on investment.

4. REVIEW (Read Check List Summary prior to answering questions)

(a) Is it clear to you how the fund invests?   Yes ✔   No _____
(b) Are you familiar with the types of companies the fund manager invests in?   Yes ✔   No _____
(c) Are these growth companies? (What does Value Line say?)   Yes ✔   No _____
(d) Does the average earnings growth rate indicate growth companies?   Yes ✔   No _____
(e) Does the fund manager appear to follow a buy and hold method for investing in stocks?   Yes ✔   No _____
(f) Has the fund manager been with the fund for at least five years?   Yes ✔   No _____
(g) Has the manager's record shown consistency in outperforming the S&P 500 index?   Yes ✔   No _____
(h) Are the taxes being generated so high that the fund belongs in a tax-deferred account?   Yes ✔   No _____
(i) Are the costs of the fund reasonable to you?   Yes ✔   No _____

Completing this checklist will provide you with a better understanding of how this mutual fund invests, what it invests in, how long and how effective the current management tenure has been, and what percentage of your investment dollars will be used to pay the fund's expenses.

Volume 35, Issue 3, June 6, 1999.

Vanguard U.S. Growth

Ticker	Load	NAV	Yield	SEC Yield	Total Assets	Mstar Category
VWUSX	None	$38.61	0.5%	—	$15,647.9 mil	Large Growth

Prospectus Objective: Growth

Vanguard U.S. Growth Fund seeks long-term growth of capital. The fund invests primarily in common stocks and convert-ible securities issued by established U.S. companies. In selecting investments, the advisor emphasizes companies that it believes to have exceptional growth records, strong market positions, reason-able financial strength, and relatively low sensitivity to changing economic conditions.

On Sept. 30, 1985, the Ivest Fund divided into this fund and Vanguard World International Growth Fund. From that date until May 3, 1993, the fund was named Vanguard World Fund U.S. Growth Portfolio.

Historical Profile

Return	High
Risk	Average
Rating	★★★★ Highest

Investment Style: 90% 87% 91% 95% 96% 96% 97% 95%

Investment Style
Equity
Average Stock %

▼ Manager Change
▽ Partial Manager Change
◢ Mgr Unknown After
◣ Mgr Unknown Before

Fund Performance vs. Category Average
Quarterly Fund Return
+/– Category Average
Category Baseline

Performance Quartile (within Category)

	1988	1989	1990	1991	1992	1993	1994	1995	1996	1997	1998	04–99	History
NAV	7.51	10.21	10.49	15.20	15.36	14.93	15.33	20.35	23.74	28.70	37.49	38.61	NAV
Total Return %	8.76	37.70	4.60	46.76	2.76	−1.45	3.88	38.44	26.05	25.93	39.98	2.99	Total Return %
	−7.85	6.01	7.72	16.27	−4.86	−11.50	2.57	0.91	3.10	−7.42	11.41	−6.06	+/– S&P 500
	−2.12	0.01	3.24	7.35	−1.14	−1.37	−0.97	−0.21	0.53	−7.81	−5.12	−3.14	+/– Russ Top 200 Grt
	0.86	1.73	1.86	1.81	1.18	1.37	1.21	1.89	1.28	1.14	0.66	0.00	Income Return %
	7.90	35.97	2.74	44.94	1.57	−2.81	2.68	36.55	24.77	24.79	39.32	2.99	Capital Return %
	56	23	9	36	72	94	8	12	9	49	26	90	Total Rtn % Rank Cat
	0.06	0.13	0.19	0.19	0.18	0.21	0.18	0.29	0.26	0.27	0.19	0.00	Income $
	0.00	0.00	0.00	0.00	0.08	0.00	0.00	0.57	1.62	0.89	2.31	0.00	Capital Gains $
	0.88	0.95	0.74	0.56	0.49	0.49	0.52	0.44	0.43	0.42	0.41	—	Expense Ratio %
	1.23	1.44	1.77	1.82	1.52	1.50	1.30	1.59	1.32	1.13	0.69	—	Income Ratio %
	38	48	49	30	24	37	47	32	44	35	48	—	Turnover Rate %
	132.2	198.2	355.9	978.1	1,813.9	1,847.2	2,109.3	3,624.1	5,532.0	8,054.6	13,623.6	15,647.9	Net Assets $mil

Portfolio Manager(s)

David Fowler. Since 1-87. MBA'73 Northwestern U. Fowl-er is a portfolio manager and an equity strategist for Lincoln Capi-tal Management. He joined the company in 1984 as a security ana-lyst, focusing on the technology sector. Previously, Fowler worked for 12 years as an analyst and portfolio manager with Stein Roe & Farnham.

J. Parker Hall III. Since 8-87. BS'55 Swarthmore C.; MBA'57 Harvard U. Hall is president of Lincoln Capital Manage-ment, his employer since 1971.

Performance 04-30-99

	1st Qtr	2nd Qtr	3rd Qtr	4th Qtr	Total
1995	9.26	10.51	7.46	6.70	38.44
1996	6.88	7.13	4.08	5.78	26.05
1997	0.59	16.71	3.12	4.02	25.93
1998	15.51	7.27	−9.42	24.73	39.98
1999	3.81	—	—	—	—

Trailing	Total Return%	+/– S&P 500	+/– Russ Top 200 Grth	% Rank All	% Rank Cat	Growth of $10,000
3 Mo	−2.30	−6.97	−1.92	93	94	9,770
6 Mo	20.03	−2.28	−4.35	24	88	12,003
1 Yr	21.91	0.08	−8.76	7	56	12,191
3 Yr Avg	28.11	−0.96	−6.25	4	31	21,024
5 Yr Avg	27.24	0.38	−4.20	2	15	33,357
10 Yr Avg	19.94	1.12	−0.96	4	19	61,592
15 Yr Avg	17.52	−1.17	—	11	34	112,666

Tax Analysis	Tax-Adj Ret%	%Rank Cat	%Pretax Ret	%Rank Cat
3 Yr Avg	25.96	27	92.4	34
5 Yr Avg	25.50	11	93.6	19
10 Yr Avg	18.82	10	94.4	9

Potential Capital Gain Exposure: 40% of assets

Risk Analysis

Time Period	Load-Adj Return %	Risk %Rank¹ All	Risk %Rank¹ Cat	Morningstar Return	Morningstar Risk	Morningstar Risk-Adj Rating
1 Yr	21.91					
3 Yr	28.11	68	18	2.17	0.85	★★★★★
5 Yr	27.24	66	11	2.03	0.81	★★★★★
10 Yr	19.94	68	8	1.92	0.89	★★★★★

Average Historical Rating (161 months): 3.3★s

¹1=low, 100=high

Category Rating (3 Yr)	Other Measures	Standard Index S&P 500	Best Fit Index S&P 500
①②③④⑤	Alpha	−0.7	−0.7
Worst ← → Best	Beta	1.00	1.00
	R-Squared	92	92

Return	Above Avg	Standard Deviation 21.96
Risk	Below Avg	Mean 28.11
		Sharpe Ratio 1.18

Portfolio Analysis 03-31-99

Share change since 12–98 Total Stocks: 79	Sector	PE	YTD Ret%	% Assets
⊕ Microsoft	Technology	64.3	17.26	6.02
⊕ General Elec	Industrials	36.6	3.67	5.51
⊕ Cisco Sys	Technology	NMF	22.90	4.96
⊕ Merck	Health	31.7	−4.25	4.56
⊕ Intel	Technology	31.5	3.24	4.46
⊕ Procter & Gamble	Staples	33.9	3.38	3.92
⊕ Pfizer	Health	43.6	−7.79	3.50
⊕ Lucent Tech	Technology	49.8	9.23	2.93
⊕ Dell Comp	Technology	77.7	12.55	2.69
⊕ Bristol–Myers Squibb	Health	39.2	−4.37	2.54
⊖ Coca–Cola	Staples	49.3	1.83	1.98
⊖ American Home Products	Health	38.1	8.63	1.98
⊖ American Intl Grp	Financials	32.8	21.15	1.95
⊖ Wal–Mart Stores	Retail	46.5	13.09	1.91
⊖ CVS	Retail	45.4	−13.10	1.78
⊖ Chase Manhattan	Financials	17.3	17.38	1.73
⊕ Gillette	Staples	54.4	9.71	1.61
⊕ Nokia Cl A ADR	Technology	22.4	24.11	1.61
⊕ Amgen	Health	35.2	17.51	1.55
⊕ Schering–Plough	Health	39.0	−12.30	1.54
⊕ IBM	Technology	29.6	13.61	1.49
⊕ Johnson & Johnson	Health	42.0	16.59	1.45
⊕ Automatic Data Processing	Services	41.6	11.21	1.42
⊕ Monsanto	Industrials	—	−4.68	1.37
⊕ Philip Morris	Staples	14.9	−33.70	1.36

Current Investment Style		Stock Port Avg	Relative S&P 500 Current	Relative S&P 500 Hist	Rel Cat
Style: Value Blnd Growth	Price/Earnings Ratio	40.9	1.20	1.31	1.00
Size: Large Med Small	Price/Book Ratio	12.4	1.43	1.61	1.04
	Price/Cash Flow	29.6	1.24	1.29	1.04
	3 Yr Earnings Growth	23.0	1.37	1.31	1.03
	1 Yr Earnings Est%	20.9	1.24	—	0.92
	Debt % Total Cap	26.3	0.84	0.86	1.00
	Med Mkt Cap $mil	104,105	1.6	2.0	1.82

Special Securities	% of assets 03-31-99
○ Restricted/Illiquid Secs	0
○ Emerging–Markets Secs	0
○ Options/Futures/Warrants	No

Composition	% of assets 03-31-99		Market Cap	
Cash	1.9		Giant	67.8
Stocks*	97.7		Large	26.5
Bonds	0.0		Medium	5.7
Other	0.5		Small	0.0
			Micro	0.0

*Foreign 2.8 (% of stocks)

Sector Weightings	% of Stocks	Rel S&P	5-Year High	5-Year Low
Utilities	0.0	0.0	5	0
Energy	0.0	0.0	3	0
Financials	9.1	0.6	24	5
Industrials	9.7	0.8	19	9
Durables	0.0	0.0	3	0
Staples	13.8	1.7	27	13
Services	5.0	0.3	20	4
Retail	9.4	1.5	20	3
Health	23.6	2.1	24	8
Technology	29.5	1.5	29	0

Analysis by Christopher Traulsen 05-17-99

Vanguard U.S. Growth Fund isn't above trying to plug a gap.

This fund, long a stellar performer in the large-growth category, is struggling mightily in 1999. Through mid-May, it had eked out a 2.7% return, leaving it with just a bottom-decile showing relative to its category peers.

So have manager David Fowler and the team at advisor Lincoln Capital suddenly lost their touch? Well, stock-picking is partly to blame. Names such as Compaq (which Fowler sold, but not before it did some damage), 3Com, and Philip Morris have plummeted in 1999. The fund's style, though, is probably the bigger reason for its lethargy. Fowler favors companies with consistent, long-term earnings growth over flashier plays, so the portfolio sports big weightings in the giant consumer-staples firms and drugmakers that have been relatively sluggish this year.

Fowler isn't about to change course, but he is thinking about tweaking the fund's mix in at least one respect. Specifically, he now wants to give it some exposure to pure Internet stocks (an area that he has thus far avoided). The team is still trying to figure out a suitable means of valuing them and hasn't yet made any purchases, but a Net name or two could well be in the fund's future. Fowler also added MCI WorldCom to the portfolio earlier in 1999 as a play on the growing demand for bandwidth.

Despite its woes in 1999, the fund has generally flourished under Fowler's guidance. Its trailing returns for periods longer than a year all rank in or close to the large-growth category's top third, and it hasn't been nearly as volatile as some of its peers. Investors considering it should take heed of its 1999 performance, though. The fund does well when its giants soar, but many of those stocks have already enjoyed extremely strong runs. If the market should rotate in earnest away from them, it could suffer more than most.

Address:	Vanguard Financial Ctr. P.O. Box 2600 Valley Forge, PA 19482 800–662–7447 / 610–669–1000	Minimum Purchase:	$3000 Add: $100 IRA: $1000
		Min Auto Inv Plan:	$3000 Add: $100
		Sales Fees:	No-load
Inception:	01-06-59	Management Fee:	0.40% max./0.10% min.
Advisor:	Lincoln Capital Management	Actual Fees:	Mgt: 0.38% Dist: —
Subadvisor:	None	Expense Projections:	3Yr: $132* 5Yr: $230* 10Yr: $518*
Distributor:	Vanguard Group	Avg Brok Commission:	— Income Distrib: Annually
NTF Plans:	N/A	Total Cost (relative to category):	—

M⊕RNINGSTAR Mutual Funds

The fund manager makes this type of investing completely different from investing on your own. You have no control over the fund manager or the decisions the manager makes. You may contact a fund—even before you invest in it—and request a resume or biography of the fund manager or management team. A fund manager who has been in control for less than five years probably has little responsibility for the fund's performance record. It does little good to look at the performance record of any previous manager since that person is not making the current investment decisions. If the manager is new and had a good record running another fund, it will be helpful for you to review the record of the fund previously managed. Be sure the type of fund is the same as the one you are studying (objective, size, etc.).

2 B The total return figures used here *do* take into account any management, administrative, 12b-1 fees, and other costs that are *automatically* deducted from the fund's assets. Morningstar *does not* adjust these figures for sales charges (loads) or for redemption fees.

Looking at the record for each individual year reminds you that there can be some years when the fund under-performs the S&P 500 index. While stock market gains are good over time, there will be many times when movement in the market is down rather than up. These fluctuations are common and should not alter your goal as a long-term investor. You make your purchase into the fund at the net asset value (NAV) per share, which is based on the value of securities and any cash held. You share in the fund's gains and losses according to your portion of the fund's total value.

2 C The **Turnover Rate** of a fund shows how often the manager buys and sells stocks in the portfolio. Some managers believe that the more often stocks are sold the more money the fund is likely to make. It happens, but rarely. Statistics show that frequent turnover does not necessarily produce favorable returns. What frequent turnover does do—100% of the time—is increase brokerage costs, which are passed along to the investor.

2 D If stock sales are profitable, the fund will generate taxable income in the form of capital gains. While gain is certainly better than loss, you are liable for taxes on these gains, even if you haven't sold any shares of your fund. If you hold the fund in a tax-deferred account, taxes will come due when you make withdrawals from the fund. A buy and hold investment style designation is not justified when the turnover rate starts to exceed 20%.

The difference between total return percentage and tax adjusted return percentage represents the percentage of the total return that is paid in taxes. If the taxes the manager generates are more than you can afford, consider placing the fund in a tax-deferred account or find a more tax-efficient fund to invest in.

The Acorn fund is a no-load mutual fund that invests in small and mid-sized companies. On September 30, 1999 its top ten holdings included Softbank (Internet services company based in Japan), AES Corporation (global power plant company), Carnival Corp. (cruise lines), and Harley Davidson (motorcycles). An investment of $10,000 on June 10, 1970 would have grown to $883,409 by September 30, 1999, representing an average annual total return of 16.5%.

(2 E) Whether investing in a mutual fund or in an individual stock, you become a proportionate owner in a company or companies and your profits are determined by the earnings of those companies. The Earnings Growth Rate represents an average for the fund's current holdings. You can check the earnings per share growth rate for each separate holding by reviewing the company's Value Line report. NAIC looks for growth of about 7% per year for a giant company to 12% or more for a small company, with average of 15% on the total portfolio.

(2 F) The P/E Ratio represents a weighted average of the price-to-earnings ratio for all the fund's holdings. The average P/E of stocks held by the fund is an indication of the risk in the portfolio. Morningstar publishes the P/E of the 500 stocks comprising the S&P 500 index. Compare your fund's figure with that of this market barometer.

If a company is just starting out or has recently gone public, a rising P/E ratio may mean that investors have high expectations for the company. The rate at which a company increases its sales and earnings per share, and how consistently it maintains such an increase, and the judgment of how long such an increase can continue, can combine to have a dramatic effect on a company's P/E.

Higher growth rates generally suggest higher P/E ratios. Well-managed growth companies generally have higher P/E ratios. Here's a little history for you. The average P/E of the S&P 500 index over the 30 year period October 1969 through October 1999 was 14.7. It has been as high as 35.4 and as low as 6.6 during the same period. Currently the P/E is 33.2. A high P/E usually indicates that the market is willing to pay a higher price to own a stake in the business. A low P/E usually indicates that the market has less confidence that the company's earnings will increase.

Section 3

(3 A)
(3 B) There are costs associated with all types of investing. The mutual fund investor must therefore carefully examine all expenses that will be incurred in such an investment, and note the differences from fund to fund. Some funds have costs that, on balance, may be higher than those you'd pay to retain a private money manager.

There has never been a proven relationship between high expenses and high returns. In fact, a fund with high costs *must* perform better than a similar fund with lower expenses just to stay even! Paying a front-end load means the fund has to perform that same amount better than the S&P 500 index just to match the Index total return performance.

(3 C) The Overview sheet on page 89 shows peer group performance listings. If the average expense ratio for the peer group is lower than the fund you are studying, you may want to consider a fund with lower expenses. These listings are helpful, but how the fund performs relative to the S&P 500 index is more important.

Section 4

The questions in this section put the basics of the Check List into personal perspective. You should have a clear understanding of these issues before making an investment decision.

SUMMARY

Past performance is never a guarantee of future results. You will see a notice like this in almost every publication or advertisement you see or read about a particular fund. If the fund manager responsible for the past performance (3 to 5 years minimum) remains the fund's manager and maintains the investment style and fundamental characteristics that were responsible for the past performance, then the investor can expect similar results under similar market conditions. But there are no guarantees in investing.

NOT A RECOMMENDATION

For illustration purposes, we used information on a real mutual fund, Vanguard U.S. Growth Fund. This company was used to illustrate how to complete the Equity Mutual Fund Check List and we are not making a recommendation to purchase shares in this fund.

REVIEW YOUR PORTFOLIO

Morningstar's reports are updated every five months. Look at the cover page on page 85. The highlighted area near the bottom shows the next publication date for that issue. When new figures become available, update your Check List. Look for announcements from the fund, or from an outside source that could affect future performance, such as manager change, change in recent data figures, fund closings, fee changes, and overall market changes.

As with all types of investing, it is important that you educate yourself as much as possible and continuously in order to become a well-informed investor. Be sure to read as many sources on mutual funds as you have time for prior to investing.

Be skeptical of what you hear and read in the financial media. Their agenda is different than yours. You'll find that most publications list the current top performing or "hot" funds. These funds should be examined closely. The caution here is you may find that they are the top performing funds at that moment in time, but it is not unusual to find that the high rated fund of the moment is not in that position at the next rating period.

You may want to invest a portion of your portfolio in mutual funds. This lesson has shown you one approach that uses Morningstar Mutual Fund Reports and the NAIC Equity Mutual Fund Check List to compare, evaluate, and select funds which are appropriate for your investment objectives and risk profile. As with selecting common stocks and all investments, knowledge is power.

DOLLAR SENSE

There are no secrets to success. It is the result of preparation, hard work, learning from failure.

—*Colin Powell*

UNDERSTAND TERMS AND IDEAS

1. When you are comparing mutual funds, how do you make sure you are comparing apples with apples?

   Compare cotogories - high growth fund - or investing in bonds

2. Why is it important to determine whether a fund is investing the way it says it will?

   Look at the compostion to see it they are really doing what they se

3. Why is fund manager tenure important when looking at a fund's performance?

   Cause the results changes when manger changes

4. Why is portfolio turnover an important factor to consider when comparing funds?

5. Fund A has a cash position of 22%. Fund B's cash position is 4%. What is the significance of this difference for an investor?

   A wout give as much return as B

6. Complete the NAIC Equity Mutual Fund Check List in Appendix B for Harbor Capital Appreciation fund in Appendix C. What do you conclude about this fund?

Chapter 3 REVIEW

SUMMARY

LESSON 3.1 MUTUAL FUNDS

Mutual funds offer an alternative way of investing. Instead of buying stocks in individual corporations, you buy shares in a fund. The fund is made up of an assortment of stocks, bonds, and other investments. Professional fund managers select investments for the fund.

LESSON 3.2 INVESTIGATE MUTUAL FUNDS

A number of charges and other fees are commonly associated with mutual funds. Several sources, such as reports, magazines, and web sites, provide in-depth information about mutual funds.

LESSON 3.3 CHOOSE MUTUAL FUNDS

The NAIC Equity Mutual Fund Check List helps you take a closer look at a fund and examine some of the key elements. Review your portfolio periodically. Morningstar publishes new reports every five months.

REVIEW INVESTING TERMS

Write the letter of the term that matches each definition. Some terms may not be used.

1. __h__ how often the manager buys and sells stocks in the mutual fund's portfolio

2. __e__ the total value of a fund's investment portfolio minus liabilities divided by the number of shares outstanding

3. __b__ operating expenses, expressed as a percentage of your total investment, for a mutual fund

4. __g__ classifies funds based on stated goals from the fund's prospectus

5. __a__ a period of declining prices in stock market trades

6. __f__ mutual fund that does not charge a sales fee

7. __d__ mutual fund that charges an up-front sales commission on your investment

a. bear market
b. expense ratio
c. index fund
d. load funds
e. NAV
f. no-load fund
g. prospectus objective
h. turnover rate

UNDERSTAND TERMS AND IDEAS

8. How is the price of a mutual fund determined? When is it calculated?

   By the NAV at the end of each buss, day

   NAV = Assets - Libilities
   _____
        N° of share

9. Explain the three advantages of buying mutual funds instead of individual stocks.

   - Diversify the portoplio
   - Profesionel Mangment
   - Easy to by or sell

10. Explain the difference between a load fund and a no-load fund.

    load fund - It charges fee on investment

11. How would you select the type of mutual fund that is right for you? Explain your options.

    look prospectus
    Composition

Chapter 3 REVIEW

SHARPEN YOUR RESEARCH SKILLS

12. The fund manager is critical to the success of a mutual fund. Use the library or Internet. Identify one fund manager. Evaluate the manager's performance.

_____

_____

_____

13. Identify three load funds. List the name of the fund and the amount of the load. Use the Internet or library.

_____

_____

_____

THINK CRITICALLY

14. What type of mutual funds fit the ideal NAIC investor?

_____

_____

_____

15. You have been in a mutual fund for seven years. You have been very pleased with its performance. You receive a letter informing you that the fund has a new manager. What would you do?

_____

_____

_____

16. Your friend doesn't think her growth mutual fund is investing correctly. What information would you tell her to check?

_____

_____

_____

PROSPECTIVE PORTFOLIO PROJECT

In this chapter, you learned about mutual funds. A mutual fund may be a good addition to your portfolio. Remember that the NAIC urges long-term investors to concentrate their mutual fund investments in equity funds that invest in growth companies. Funds with this investment style can be found under Equity Funds in the Large Growth, Mid-cap Growth, and Small Growth categories. Use the NAIC Equity Mutual Fund Check List to fill in the table.

Mutual Fund	Invests How	Invests In	Management Tenure and Record	Tax	Expense Percentage

Will you add any of these funds to your portfolio?

Chapter 4

THE BIG PICTURE

LESSON 4.1   PLUG THE LEAKS

LESSON 4.2   PROTECT YOURSELF

LESSON 4.3   A CAR AND A HOUSE

INDUSTRY INDICATORS
ENTERTAINMENT

Walt Disney Company
Founded in 1929

Walt Disney and his brother Roy began the Walt Disney Company in 1923. In a small Los Angeles office, the two brothers produced a series of live-action/animated comedies called the *Alice Comedies.* The success of these short films allowed Disney to purchase a large studio lot two years later and, in 1928, Mickey Mouse was born. Walt Disney had dreams of making more animated and family movies, and he also dreamed of creating a theme park to celebrate his animated characters. The world-wide popularity of Disney's 1937 full-length animated movie, *Snow White and the Seven Dwarves,* proved that there was a market for animation and family entertainment.

Today, the Walt Disney Company is one of the largest diversified entertainment companies in the world. It operates in three business segments: Creative Content, Broadcasting, and Theme Parks and Resorts. The Creative Content division produces live-action and animated motion pictures, television programs, and music. This division also includes

The Disney Store, Walt Disney Pictures, Touchstone Pictures, Miramax, and programs such as *The Wonderful World of Disney* and Disney's *One Saturday Morning*. The Broadcasting segment of the company operates the ABC Television Network, Radio Disney, and The Disney Channel. Walt Disney World Resort in Florida (which is made up of Disney-MGM Studios, Epcot, and the Magic Kingdom) is part of the Theme Parks and Resort division. This division also includes the Disneyland theme parks in California, Tokyo, and Paris; Disney Cruise Lines; the Anaheim Mighty Ducks hockey team; and the Anaheim Angels Major League Baseball team.

The Walt Disney Company is one of the best known companies in the world. As an entertainment company, its success is based on public appeal, which is unpredictable and subject to change. The net income of Disney in 1999 was approximately $1.4 billion. Drawing customers of all ages, the Walt Disney Company plans to continue offering new and exciting alternatives in the world of entertainment.

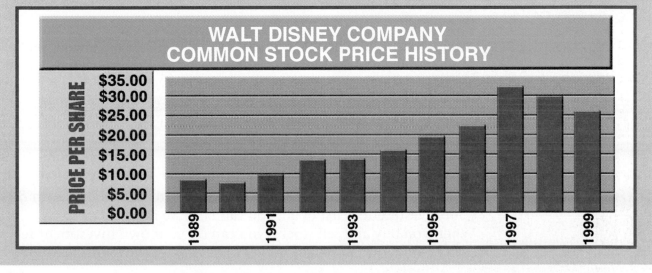

WALT DISNEY COMPANY COMMON STOCK PRICE HISTORY

PRICE PER SHARE: $35.00, $30.00, $25.00, $20.00, $15.00, $10.00, $5.00, $0.00

1989, 1991, 1993, 1995, 1997, 1999

LESSON 4.1

Plug the Leaks

W̶hen you are working hard to make your money grow through carefully chosen investments, you want to retain as much of your returns as you can. This lesson discusses the three main factors that tend to erode your returns, and it describes measures you can take to protect your investments.

GOALS

- **Describe how inflation, transaction costs, and taxes can reduce the returns on investments.**

- **Describe how retirement plans can benefit you.**

- **Calculate nominal and real total returns.**

THE BIG THREE

When you say that your salary is $25,000 a year, you mean total or **gross salary**. The amount you receive after taxes are deducted, **take-home pay**, is considerably less than that. If your work involves certain expenses—commuting, parking, lunches, wardrobe, tools, and supplies—your **net income**, what you actually have to live on, is reduced even further. From an economic perspective, the best job is not always the one with the biggest salary. It may be a job that actually pays less, but reduces your travel costs and allows you to live where housing and other expenses are lower.

A similar logic holds for investing. The actual return on your investments is what you get back after all your costs, losses, and taxes have been deducted. There are three primary factors that tend to drain off investment income, and investors have to do whatever they can to minimize them. These three investment leaks are

   a. inflation

   b. fees and transaction costs

   c. taxes

INFLATION

Although inflation has been unusually low for the past several years in the United States, it remains a simple fact of life. You are as powerless to stop inflation as you are to keep the wind from blowing. What you must do instead is allow for inflation and choose investments with a good prospect of delivering returns that are considerably higher than historical inflation rates.

FEES AND TRANSACTION COSTS

There are a number of measures you can take to reduce this drain on your investments. First of all, you can become more self-reliant. When you buy and sell stocks, you can do your own investment research, and you can reduce brokerage fees by dealing with discount brokers. You can make stock transactions over the Internet, which is very inexpensive compared to dealing with a full-service broker.

Long-term Investing If you are truly a long-term investor, you should not constantly buy and sell stocks in response to changing stock prices. You should buy high-quality growth stocks in the first place and, with few exceptions, hang on to them for a long period of time. Every time you buy or sell a stock you incur transaction costs, and these costs have a negative effect on real total returns.

Zero Transaction Costs Transaction costs can be zero with certain types of direct purchase plans and dividend reinvestment plans (DRIPs). Several hundred corporations, mostly large ones, provide opportunities to purchase their common stock directly from the corporation. Low cost plans are very similar, except for the fact that there is a nominal fee to purchase the first share, but no commission on subsequent shares. NAIC offers a low cost plan with a very low one-time set-up fee.

Low Turnover Rates The obvious way to reduce your fees and transaction costs when investing in mutual funds is to do your own research and buy low-cost, no-load mutual funds. Mutual fund expense ratio information is readily available. But there is also a second way for mutual fund investors to lower these costs. Select funds with relatively low turnover rates in their stock portfolios. Overactive fund managers, who buy and sell stocks too frequently, can really reduce the profitability of mutual fund investments.

TAXES

Investment income is subject to federal, state, and local income taxes at the same rates as other income. Interest and dividends are taxable income, and when you sell an investment for a higher price than you originally paid for it, you are subject to taxes on the capital gain.

As a young investor, still in school and not working on a full-time basis, taxes may not have much effect on your investments, at least at the present time. However, you need to be aware of the fact that taxes will have a significant impact on your ability to accumulate larger sums of money in the long run. It is not too early to build tax-deferred retirement plans into your investment strategy. When you are investing over the course of a lifetime, these plans can make a huge difference in the amount of money you will be able to accumulate.

RETIREMENT PLANS AND TAXES

The U.S. Congress has established several kinds of tax-deferred retirement plans in order to encourage you to save money for your retirement. These laws defer taxes on accounts that have been established for retirement purposes until you begin to withdraw the money and use it. Although ultimately the capital gains will be taxed, tax deferral allows you to accumulate a much larger amount of money over the years.

There is a second major tax benefit to these retirement plans. The money you contribute to them is deducted from your income before your income taxes are assessed, thus lowering the amount of your salary that is subject to taxes. Because of these tax benefits and because of a sharp decline in traditional company pension plans, tax-deferred retirement accounts should play a central role in life-long investment strategies. Federal laws provide for a number of different plans.

401(K) AND 403(B) PLANS

These plans are tax-deferred retirement savings plans offered to you by your employer. A 403(b) plan is similar to a 401(k) plan except that 403(b) plans are for the employees of non-profit organizations such as schools, hospitals, religious organizations, and foundations. You can contribute a percentage of earned income, up to a maximum limit. Some employers match employees' savings as much as 50 cents per

dollar invested. For example, your employer might add $50 for each $100 that you contribute. The employer automatically withholds from your paycheck the amount you designate and deposits the money in a professionally managed investment account.

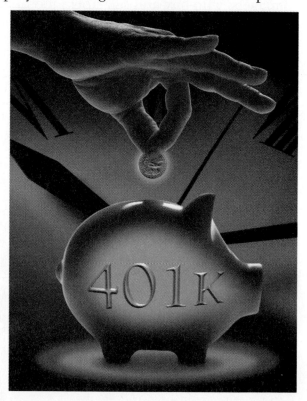

Typically, the employee has a choice of funds to invest in such as a growth stock fund, a balanced fund, a bond fund, or a money market fund. A 401(k) or 403(b) plan provides a significant tax advantage since dividends, interest, and capital gains are not taxed until you make withdrawals (after age $59\frac{1}{2}$). When you retire, you may have a lower income so your tax rate may be lower when you withdraw money. Note that there are expensive penalties for early withdrawal. However, you may be allowed to make a withdrawal from some plans for college tuition or medical emergencies before age $59\frac{1}{2}$.

INDIVIDUAL RETIREMENT ACCOUNTS (IRAS)

These are for workers who are not covered by an employer-sponsored retirement plan. There are two basic types—the traditional IRA and the Roth IRA.

Traditional IRA The IRA is set up by an individual and currently allows that person to contribute up to $2,000 a year (plus $2,000 a year for a non-employed spouse) to a tax-deferred account. You can choose to invest in any approved IRA investment.

Roth IRA Savings in a Roth IRA are not tax-deferred. Instead you pay taxes on your income before investing in a Roth IRA. The advantage is that you will not pay income tax on the money you earn on your investment in the Roth IRA even when you withdraw it. This can be a significant tax advantage for you.

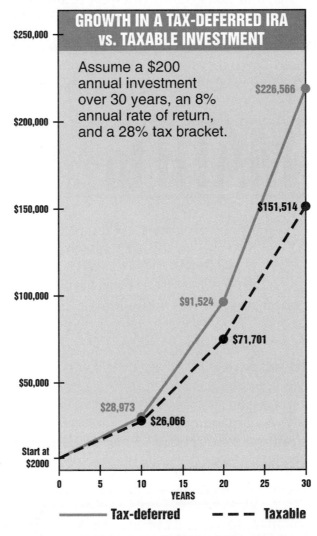

OTHER TAX SAVING OPTIONS

SEP IRAs and Keogh Plans These are tax-deferred retirement plans for self-employed persons. They permit a larger maximum annual contribution than an IRA.

Life Insurance Contracts: Tax Deferred In addition to tax-deferred retirement plans, people may purchase annuity contracts and certain types of life insurance contracts with tax deferral features.

NOMINAL AND REAL TOTAL RETURNS

You don't always make as much money as you think. Inflation, expenses and taxes impact the income you earn on investments as well as the salary you earn from working. The example in from Math to Riches shows how to measure the impact of inflation, transaction costs, and taxes on the one-year returns of a stock investment by calculating and comparing nominal and real total returns.

Smart life-long investors always try to (a) outperform inflation, (b) hold down investment costs and fees, and (c) pay as little of their growing wealth as possible in taxes, without breaking any laws.

from MATH to RICHE$

Mr. Johnson purchased 100 shares of stock for $2,000 on March 1, 1999. The broker's fee (transaction cost) was $35. He held the stock for 12 months and a day and then sold it for $2,400 (less another transaction cost of $35). He received $40 in cash dividends. His income taxes on this transaction were $55 (15% tax bracket). The inflation rate was 3%. What were Mr. Johnson's nominal and real total returns?

Solution:

Nominal	$2400	selling price	
Total	– 2000	buying price	
Returns	400	capital gain	
	+ 40	dividend income	
	$440	**nominal total return**	22% (440 ÷ 2000)
Real	$2365	selling price ($2400 – $35 fee)	
Total	– 2035	buying price ($2000 + $35 fee)	
Returns	330	capital gain	
	+ 40	dividend income	
	– 55	income tax	
	$315	**net return**	16% (315 ÷ 2000)
	– 60	inflation ($2000 × 0.03%)	– 3% inflation rate
	$255	**real total return**	13% (255 ÷ 2000)

The real total return ($255) is 9 percentage points less than the nominal total return.

UNDERSTANDING TERMS AND IDEAS

1. Why does it sometimes make economic sense not to take the job with the biggest salary?

   Because the cost of going to that job could be very high and that would reduce your net take home pay

2. As an investor, what can you do about inflation?

   Choose investments with higher returns than historical inflation rates.

3. Name two things you can do to save on transaction costs.

   Become self reliant or dealing with discount brokers

4. What do the different kinds of tax-deferred retirement plans have in common? How is each designed for a different group of workers?

   That the both plans allow you to contribute a percentage of your income upto a maximum limit. The 403b plan ar for non profit organizations schools hospitals, religion org. and foundations

5. How does a tax-deferred retirement plan save you money each time you contribute and over the entire life of the plan?

6. What is the difference between a Roth IRA and a traditional IRA?

   Roth IRA Is a non deffered tax, you won't pay tax on the money you earn from your investment

7. Look at the Real Total Returns calculations on the previous page.

   a. Why is $35 added to the buying price and subtracted from the selling price?

   b. Where do the $315 and $2,000 come from that are used to determine the net return percentage?

Protect Yourself

At this stage of your life, you probably do not know a lot about insurance. Usually, insurance is something your parents buy, and you are covered by their policies. If you get sick and go to the hospital, their insurance covers the bill. If you have a driver's license, they pay more to insure the family car so that you are covered on the policy, too. As you become involved in investing, insurance will become more important to you. It is a key element in life-long financial planning.

GOALS

■ **Explain what insurance is and how it works.**

■ **Describe the major kinds of insurance people need.**

WHAT IS INSURANCE?

The basic idea behind insurance is simple. Insurance provides protection against financial losses. Often it helps you survive an event such as one of the following that could have resulted in financial disaster.

Loss of income As a result of illness, disability, death.

Medical expenses Due to an accident or a health problem.

Damaged property From an accident, theft, natural disaster.

Lawsuit Because you and/or your property were involved in an injury or loss to another person.

HOW DOES INSURANCE WORK?

Insurance works by pooling the money of policyholders. Theoretically, any group of people with enough money could insure the group members. Each person would contribute a sum of money to the insurance pool, which would compensate a group member who suffers an accident or a loss. Insurance companies take on the work of forming pools, collecting payments from members, and distributing funds when losses occur. Insurance companies also increase the pool of money by investing it. They add charges to pay themselves for providing these services.

The policyholder's contribution for insurance coverage (monthly, annual, single payment, etc.) is called a **premium**. The size of the premium is determined by

(a) the potential size of the loss you are trying to cover

(b) the level of risk that this loss may occur

AUTOMOBILE INSURANCE

Automobile insurance protects you against losses of various kinds. You can buy various kinds of coverage, and most states require you to have certain kinds of automobile insurance.

Bodily Injury Liability Coverage Pays for injuries you may cause to other people in an accident.

Property Damage Liability Coverage Pays for damage you may cause to another person's property, but does not cover damages to your car.

Medical Payments Coverage Pays medical and funeral expenses for you and other passengers in your car, no matter who caused the accident.

Uninsured/Underinsured Motorist Coverage Pays medical and damage expenses for you and your passengers caused by a driver without insurance or with too little insurance to cover the loss. Does not cover that driver.

Comprehensive Coverage Pays for damage to your car caused by something other than a collision, such as earthquakes, fire, or theft.

Collision Coverage Pays for damage to your car.

As you may already know, auto insurance for teen drivers is very expensive. Together with the other costs involved in owning and operating an automobile, it may use most of a teenager's money so that there is little or nothing left over for short-term or long-term investing.

You may not like all the options, but the best ways of saving money on auto insurance include the following.

1. You decide not to own a car. Instead you rely on public transportation, a bicycle, or occasional use of a family car.

2. You buy a car that is more than five years old and carry no collision or comprehensive coverage. In other words, you carry insurance for bodily injury and liability, but do not insure your own car.

3. You avoid high-powered sports cars, which cost more to insure.

4. You insure your car, but with a $500 deductible. Your insurance reimburses you for damage to your car only after you have paid the first $500.

5. You do your best to maintain a flawless driving record. If you have an accident or a traffic violation, your insurance premiums will probably go up.

HEALTH INSURANCE

Although most people have medical insurance through their employers, more and more people need to buy their own insurance. Medical insurance varies greatly from plan to plan. Some company plans require you to pay a portion of the premium (say, 20%) while the company absorbs the rest (80%). In other plans, the employer may pick up 100% of the premium. Other common variables among medical insurance plans include:

Annual Deductible The amount you must pay on your medical bills each year before your insurance goes into effect.

Co-Insurance (Co-Pay) The percentage of medical costs the insured person must pay (after paying the deductible). The share ratio is typically 20% by the insured person and 80% by the insurance company. At a specified total out-of-pocket, $1,000 or $2,000 for example, the insurance company begins to pay 100% of the additional medical costs.

Maximum Coverage The lifetime limit on the total amount your insurance company will pay. Some HMOs (health maintenance organizations) have unlimited coverage because they can exercise greater control over costs than traditional policies.

DENTAL AND VISION CARE INSURANCE

Many employers also provide insurance to cover a wide range of dental services such as routine checkups, cleaning, X-rays, fillings and crowns. Vision care may also be provided which covers eye exams and a portion of the expense of eye glasses and contact lenses.

DISABILITY INSURANCE

Another type of health insurance is disability insurance. Many large employers provide disability insurance for their employees. Self-employed persons should consider purchasing their own. This type of insurance enables you to receive a certain portion of your salary when you are unable to work because of an accident or injury. Usually disability coverage is limited to one-half or two-thirds of gross salary. The limit is designed to give a worker an incentive to return to work as soon as possible.

LONG-TERM CARE INSURANCE

A chronic illness or disability could leave you unable to care for yourself for an extended period of time. Long-term care insurance covers nursing home care and care at home. This is an increasingly important type of insurance.

Protect your potential earnings with disability insurance. You are more likely to become disabled during your prime working years than you are to die. One in seven people becomes disabled for at least five years before reaching age 65.

LIFE INSURANCE

When you are older, hold a full-time job, and begin to take on family responsibilities, you will need life insurance. The main object of life insurance is to provide financial protection to people who depend on you. The insurance will replace income that is lost as a result of your death. Generally speaking, you do not need life insurance before you have a family. Before you buy life insurance, you should educate yourself about the different kinds of policies that are available.

TERM INSURANCE

The simplest and least expensive form of insurance, which allows you to buy coverage for a year or a specific period of time, and if you die during that time, pays your beneficiary a sum of money.

You may want to buy term insurance when you are in your 20s and 30s and coverage is very inexpensive and then stop buying life insurance when the value of your investments is large enough to protect your survivors. This is a cost effective way of using insurance in conjunction with a life-long investment program.

CASH VALUE INSURANCE

Like term insurance, cash value insurance pays a death benefit, but also builds up a cash value, which can be borrowed against or withdrawn when the policy is terminated.

Whole Life Premiums never change, offers death benefit, but also builds up a cash value over a period of time.

Variable Whole Life Allows you to choose how your insurance money is invested and decide how much risk you want to take in trying to achieve a higher level of return.

Universal Life Allows you to vary your annual contributions.

Some people consider cash value insurance a form of savings. However, funds invested in cash value insurance generally do not earn high returns over time. You will probably be better off buying term insurance and investing your remaining funds yourself.

Learn more about specific types of insurance on the Internet. Enter keywords or phrases such as deductible, life insurance or auto insurance into a search engine. You can find information such as insurance rates, types of coverage, and local agents.

PROPERTY INSURANCE

Property insurance includes real property insurance (a house or condominium) and personal property insurance (such as furniture, electronic equipment, or jewelry). Property insurance will compensate you for a loss of property due to fire, theft, natural disaster, and other hazards spelled out in your contract.

Two basic ways property insurance pays are:

Market Value The amount an item is worth now.

Replacement Value The cost of replacing the item, regardless of its market value at the time of the loss.

Your first living quarters outside your parents' house will probably be an apartment. You will not need real property insurance, but you may want renter insurance to cover personal property. You should have a list of all your property in case you need to file a claim. It may also be useful to keep receipts for the more expensive items in a safe deposit box and to videotape these items on a periodic basis.

LIABILITY INSURANCE

Liability insurance protects you from potential losses due to legal actions taken against you because of some alleged negligence. Liability coverage is included in auto and homeowner insurance. In a homeowner policy it covers lawsuits which may result from a person falling on your sidewalk or being bitten by your dog.

BUYING INSURANCE

Before you buy insurance you need to compare policies to see how they stack up against one another. You should do business with an experienced agent who is certified as a chartered life underwriter. Before you buy, go to the *Best's Insurance Reports* in your public library and make sure the company you are doing business with has an A rating or better from A.M. Best, an independent insurance rating company. The Internet also contains a number of web sites with insurance information.

Insuring your property, life, and health will be critical to your financial well being. You are learning how to build wealth over an extended period of time through investing. Appropriate insurance will protect you from losses that could wipe out your assets and undermine your investment program.

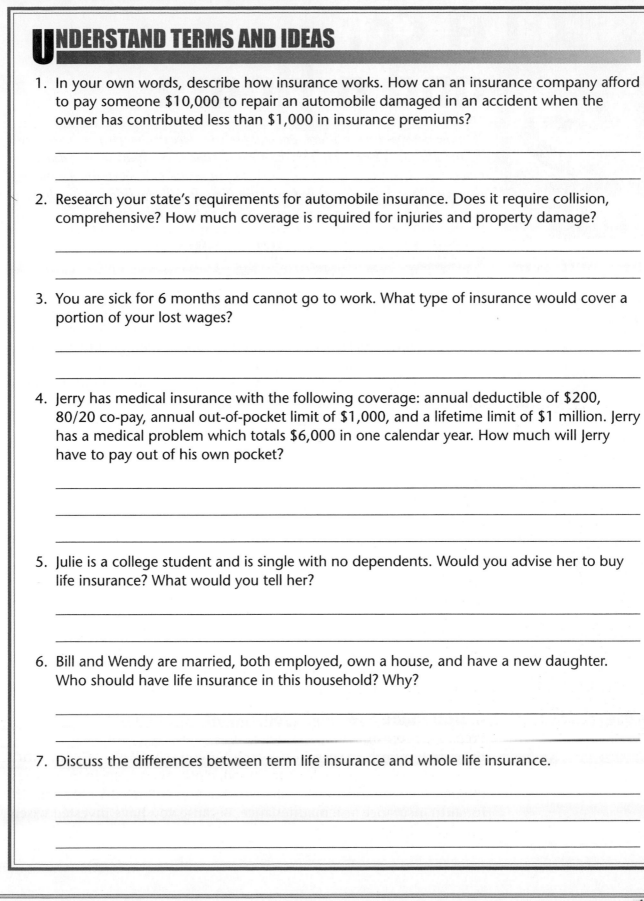

UNDERSTAND TERMS AND IDEAS

1. In your own words, describe how insurance works. How can an insurance company afford to pay someone $10,000 to repair an automobile damaged in an accident when the owner has contributed less than $1,000 in insurance premiums?

_____

_____

2. Research your state's requirements for automobile insurance. Does it require collision, comprehensive? How much coverage is required for injuries and property damage?

_____

_____

3. You are sick for 6 months and cannot go to work. What type of insurance would cover a portion of your lost wages?

_____

_____

4. Jerry has medical insurance with the following coverage: annual deductible of $200, 80/20 co-pay, annual out-of-pocket limit of $1,000, and a lifetime limit of $1 million. Jerry has a medical problem which totals $6,000 in one calendar year. How much will Jerry have to pay out of his own pocket?

_____

_____

_____

5. Julie is a college student and is single with no dependents. Would you advise her to buy life insurance? What would you tell her?

_____

_____

6. Bill and Wendy are married, both employed, own a house, and have a new daughter. Who should have life insurance in this household? Why?

_____

_____

7. Discuss the differences between term life insurance and whole life insurance.

_____

_____

_____

A Car and a House

*I*n the not-too-distant future, you will probably face two major purchases: a car and a house. These are important decisions, and they require a great deal of knowledge. This lesson will discuss the steps you should take when you are making these purchases and where to go for information. It will also help you weigh the impact of these "big ticket" items on your overall financial strategy.

GOALS

■ **Describe steps to take when you are ready to buy a car.**

■ **Distinguish among the three basic types of home mortgages.**

■ **Identify the advantages of home ownership.**

CONTRASTING THE TWO PURCHASES

Buying a car and buying a house have very different effects on your long-term finances. A car is a depreciating asset. It declines in value as it ages, and most of the money you put into a car you will never get back. This suggests that you should put off buying a car until you absolutely need one, and that you should not spend more on it than it takes to get a good, safe vehicle. A house, on the other hand, usually appreciates or increases in value through the years, and home ownership can make an important positive contribution to your long-term planning and investment strategy.

BUYING A CAR

Let's assume you have completed your education and are entering your chosen field of work. Your new employer pays a competitive salary and provides medical insurance, a 401(k) plan, and life insurance. You need a car for commuting, and you go through a step-by-step process like the one described in Lesson 1.1.

1. SET A GOAL
Buy a car that meets your needs.

2. ACQUIRE KNOWLEDGE

A. Determine how much you can afford to spend.
Prepare a monthly budget to determine how much money you will have each month to spend on a car after you have covered your other regular expenses (rent, telephone, food, clothing, college loan, savings, incidentals, recreation). You calculate that you will need $200 a month for auto insurance and maintenance. Because you have invested wisely

over the past 7 years, you can withdraw $3,000 from your stock portfolio for a down payment. You shop around for the best auto loan rate you can find. You determine that you can comfortably handle monthly car payments of $190.80 a month, which would be the payment on a car loan of $6,000 at a 9% interest rate for 36 months. You set a $9,000 limit on the car you will buy.

B. Research used cars.

Written Publications There are thousands of books, articles, and booklets on buying a car (new or used). Some contain checklists and pointers on how to make an intelligent car-buying decision. Start with back issues of car and consumer magazines in the public library. *Consumer Reports* and *Changing Times* rate different models and rank them on safety, economy, performance, and handling when new. These ratings will help you choose makes and models to look for. The *NADA Official Used Car Guide* has information on used car prices.

Internet Resources There are many excellent web sites for obtaining automobile information.

www.autos.yahoo.com At Yahoo! you can access many useful topics: used car checklists, used car databases, even a web site on cars and trucks for tall people. Particularly valuable are checklists of the items you should inspect (or have your mechanic inspect) before you buy.

www.edmunds.com This site includes Edmund's ratings (by safety, reliability, performance, comfort, driving fun, value, and overall), used car wholesale prices (what the dealer pays), and retail prices (what the dealer would charge you).

www.kbb.com Kelley Blue Book is another excellent site that has new car summaries with dealer invoice prices and suggested retail prices as well as trade-in prices for used cars.

carpoint.msn.com CarPoint is an information gold mine that includes interactive videos of new cars, road test results, help on selecting a car based on your requirements, and buying a car online.

3. COMPARE ALTERNATIVES

Visit used car lots and dealerships, and check dealer advertisements and classified ads in your local newspaper. Talk to knowledgeable friends and relatives. Look at a number of cars in your price range and narrow the field down to a manageable number of cars.

4. CHOOSE A STRATEGY

Using one of the checklists you have found, you should analyze the "pluses" and "minuses" for each of your finalists.

5. MAKE A COMMITMENT

You choose the car you think makes the most sense for you and make an offer. You do a little "haggling" and settle on a price.

6. KEEP FLEXIBLE

From time to time, you review your experience and consider what you will do differently the next time you have to purchase a car.

PURCHASING A HOUSE

If you are a teenager, buying a house is probably 10 to 15 years away, and you may wonder, "why worry about it now?" But buying a house is one of the most important purchases and investments you will ever make. It involves some real-life skills you will need to learn.

It is also important to realize that the investment skills you are learning can help you acquire money for the down payment. For example, if you save $10 a week and invest it in common stock or stock mutual funds on a monthly basis, at an annual return rate of 12%, your investment will be worth $21,648 at the end of 15 years. A total investment of $7,800 (780 weeks × $10) will grow to $21,648! If you invest $15 a week under the same conditions, in 15 years your investment will be worth $32,473! Over a period of time, small amounts of money invested regularly in common stocks or stock funds can grow into a "healthy" sum.

THE INVESTMENT ADVANTAGE OF BUYING A HOUSE

When you rent a house or an apartment, each monthly payment is money "out the door." On the other hand, a mortgage payment on a house you are buying increases your **equity**, which is the amount you actually own.

A mortgage is a loan, from a bank or mortgage company, to someone buying real estate. A mortgage is "secured" by the property. If the borrower doesn't pay the mortgage payments in a timely manner, the lender can take the real estate to pay off the loan. At first, most of each month's mortgage payment is interest on the loan and only a little is applied to the debt (the principal). But over a period of time, as the debt goes down, more and more of the payment goes to reduce the principal.

inve$tor profile

Jason Ramage

Jason started investing while still in high school. As with most investors, he was motivated by the prospect of making money. He didn't start out using the NAIC principles, so he has chalked up those early investments to a "learning experience." Jason made money on some investments, such as McDonald's, which is still in his portfolio. Other investments he made were in newer companies he thought would be performing better in the marketplace.

Jason is now a student at the University of Louisville, majoring in accounting and minoring in finance and international business. He and his dad joined the West Kentucky Stockpilers, an NAIC investment club. As he learned more about the NAIC way of investing, he began to sell off stocks that weren't performing well, and to spend more time researching stocks. Even though he has been investing for less than five years, and even with his "learning experience," Jason has been able to achieve an average annual return of 14.9%.

After he graduates, Jason would like to work for an accounting firm. Later, he will look into starting his own business, perhaps as a franchiser, or as a company executive.

Increasing Equity As you pay off your mortgage, your equity in the property increases. But your equity can also increase in another way. As the value of your property goes up, which property values normally do, your equity is growing. The house where you and your family are living is also an investment that is returning capital gains and increasing wealth.

THE TAX ADVANTAGES OF BUYING A HOUSE

The U.S. Tax Codes are designed to promote home ownership. These tax benefits are another important advantage of owning a house instead of renting.

The interest you pay on your mortgage may be deducted from your gross income in determining your income tax. The property taxes on your home are also deductible and reduce your federal taxes. Because of these tax savings, people can afford to pay larger monthly mortgage payments than they can afford in rent. Home ownership has another tax advantage, too:

■ When you sell a house and buy another, you generally do not have to pay a capital gains tax on the appreciated value of your house if it has been your main home for the previous two years.

AFFORDING A HOUSE

How much house can you afford? A bank or mortgage company will look at the following factors:

- Current monthly income of the applicant
- Expected future monthly income
- The down payment
- Current mortgage interest rates
- The price of the house
- Other debt obligations you may have
- The number of years for the mortgage

Generally, mortgage lenders look at gross monthly income in relation to the monthly housing payment, which includes the mortgage payment, property taxes, and homeowner's insurance. The general rule of thumb states that the monthly housing payment should not exceed 30% of gross monthly income. Thus, a person earning $30,000 per year or $2,500 per month could afford a monthly housing payment of $750 ($2,500 × 0.30). Lenders also examine your other debts including auto loans and credit card debt. It is not unusual to hear of upper limits for all debt payments at 35% or 36% of gross income.

THE DOWN PAYMENT

The **down payment** is the amount of money you pay at the closing (the time of sale) from your own funds. The rest of the money for the house is loaned to you (the mortgage). If the down payment is less than 20% of the purchase price, the mortgage lender will normally require you to buy private mortgage insurance (PMI). This insurance protects the lender in case you default on the loan. Depending on the size of the mortgage, this additional insurance could cost several hundred dollars a year.

Knowing how much a lender will lend you and how much money you have for a down payment, you can figure out what you can afford to pay for a house. This amount is not hard to calculate, and there are computer programs, especially on the Internet, which will walk you through the calculation. A real estate representative can also help. You can find web sites by searching on keywords such as *home buying* or *mortgages*.

TYPES OF MORTGAGES

When you shop for a mortgage, you will find three basic types: fixed rate mortgages, adjustable rate mortgages (ARMs), and balloon mortgages.

FIXED RATE MORTGAGES

A fixed rate mortgage is just that, a mortgage with an interest rate which is fixed for the life of the mortgage and is not affected by changes in overall interest rates. The monthly payments never change, and you always know how much to budget. When interest rates are low, it can be a great advantage to obtain a fixed rate mortgage where the interest rate will not go up even if the interest rates in the economy go up.

ADJUSTABLE RATE MORTGAGES

In contrast to a fixed rate mortgage, an adjustable rate mortgage, or ARM, has an interest rate that adjusts periodically (usually every 12 months) according to rising or falling interest rates in the overall economy. As a result, monthly housing payments may change on an annual basis, going up or down with overall interest rates. Usually, the initial rate on an ARM is lower than the rate on a fixed rate mortgage. ARMs may have a "cap limit" on the interest and a maximum change per year. Some ARMs allow you to convert to a fixed rate mortgage after a certain period of time.

BALLOON MORTGAGES

The name comes from the fact that the borrower must pay off the mortgage in full at the end of the loan term. In other words, the payment at the end "balloons" to a sizable amount. Balloon mortgages are typically 5 or 7 years in length. The interest rates on balloon mortgages are normally 3/8 to 3/4 of a percentage point below traditional fixed rate mortgages. Balloon mortgages are popular with home buyers who expect to move before the end of the 5- or 7-year mortgage period. If you decide to stay in the house, you will have to pay the balance on the mortgage, or more likely, get another mortgage to pay off (refinance) the first mortgage.

ADDITIONAL INFORMATION SOURCES FOR HOME BUYERS

Again, spending the time on research can save you big bucks. There are dozens of recent books for first-time homebuyers at your library or bookstore such as the following:

- *Kiplinger's Buying & Selling A Home*
- *J.K. Lasser's Guide to Buying Your First Home*
- *How to Buy Your Own Home in 90 Days*
- *Century 21 Guide to Buying Your Home*
- *100 Questions Every First-Time Home Buyer Should Ask*
- *The 106 Common Mistakes Homebuyers Make (And How to Avoid Them)*
- *Buy Your First Home Now*

Buying a car and buying a house are two of the largest purchases you will ever make. They require special preparation and study, and you have to consider them in your overall financial plan. This lesson has provided an introduction to the basic concepts and concerns involved in these "big ticket" purchases.

UNDERSTAND TERMS AND IDEAS

1. How should the fact that a car is a depreciating asset affect your thinking about buying a car?

2. You are now 19 or 20 years of age and about to purchase your first car. Make a list of steps you will have to take to find out how much you can afford to spend.

3. With information available on the Internet, select one lower priced (economy) new car, one medium priced new car, and one high priced (luxury) new car. Compare the three alternatives. Explain which one you think is the best value.

4. A potential home buyer with an annual gross income of $24,000 has approached a mortgage lender about receiving a mortgage on a house. How large a monthly housing payment would the typical lender say he could afford?

_____

_____

_____

_____

_____

5. What is included in a "monthly housing payment?"

_____

_____

_____

_____

6. In addition to monthly car payments, what other car costs does a car owner face?

_____

_____

_____

_____

7. What are the major advantages of home ownership over renting?

_____

_____

_____

_____

_____

8. Compare the three major types of home mortgages.

_____

_____

_____

_____

_____

SUMMARY

LESSON 4.1 **PLUG THE LEAKS**

Three main factors that drain your investment income are inflation, fees and transaction costs, and taxes. Tax-deferred retirement funds will protect your investments from taxes while you save for your retirement.

LESSON 4.2 **PROTECT YOURSELF**

Insurance provides protection against financial loss. Protect yourself with automobile, health, life, and property insurance.

LESSON 4.3 **A CAR AND A HOUSE**

A car loses value as it gets older. Always research before you select a car to purchase. In contrast, a house will usually increase in value over time. It also provides tax advantages. Therefore, a house should be considered an investment.

REVIEW INVESTING TERMS

Write the letter of the term that matches each definition. Some terms may not be used.

1. _c_ the total amount you receive as salary

2. _g_ the cost of replacing the item, regardless of its market value at the time of the loss

3. _d_ the amount of money you pay at the closing (the time of sale) from your own funds

4. _h_ the amount you receive as salary after taxes are deducted

5. _a_ the amount you actually own of a house you are buying

6. _e_ the amount you have to live on after job-related expenses are deducted from your take-home pay

7. _f_ the policyholder's contribution for insurance coverage (monthly, annual, single payment, etc.)

a. down payment

b. equity

c. gross salary

d. market value

e. net income

f. premium

g. replacement value

h. take-home pay

UNDERSTAND TERMS AND IDEAS

8. Explain the relationship between gross income, take-home pay and net income.

   Gross income is the amount you earn before any deductions, take home pay is the amount you take home after tax deduction, net income is what you get after paying the expenses you have

9. What type of taxes may be paid on investment income?

   Federal, state, capital gain taxes

10. What factors determine the size of the premium you must pay?

    lawsuit trying to cover, level of risk amount of lost that could take place

11. Name three types of automobile insurance that could provide money to fix your car if it is damaged.

    Comprehensive coverage, Underinsure motorist, Collision.

12. List three resources you could use to research new or used cars.

    Internet

13. What is private mortgage insurance?

    Insurance pay when your down payment is less than 20%.

SHARPEN YOUR RESEARCH SKILLS

14. What is the average cost of a house in your city? What is the size of the average house in your city? How did you locate this information?

_____

_____

_____

_____

15. Identify several factors that can raise or lower the cost of house insurance. How did you locate this information?

_____

_____

_____

_____

THINK CRITICALLY

16. Today, HMOs and insurance providers cannot be sued for rejecting a participant's claim. How does this impact specific patients and the health care industry in general?

_____

_____

_____

_____

17. When you work full-time for a company, it may offer insurance as one of your employee benefits. Describe the benefits the company may provide. Name additional insurance you may have to provide for yourself.

_____

_____

_____

_____

PROSPECTIVE PORTFOLIO PROJECT

Let's look at your portfolio again. Do you currently have any companies in the health care or insurance industry? If you do, take this opportunity to examine them closely. If you don't have a suitable company in your portfolio already, pick one or two that you might want to add.

Locate news items that might affect the price of these stocks such as health care legislation or natural catastrophes.

Company	Symbol	High	Low	Current	Recent News

Based on what you have seen so far, would you add any of these stocks to your portfolio? If so, add them to your list and continue to track them with the rest of the stocks in your portfolio.

Chapter 5

INVESTOR BLUEPRINT

Microsoft
Founded in 1975

Bill Gates was a sophomore in college when he and Paul Allen established Microsoft in 1975. They formed this partnership in response to the development of the first personal computer—the MITS Altair. Though MITS had created the Altair, it had not developed a language for the computer or programs to run it. Gates and Allen adapted a computer language known as BASIC to fit the needs of the Altair. The success of Microsoft BASIC for the Altair led to contracts with other emerging computer companies, such as Commodore and Apple. Years before the personal computer became popular, Microsoft had emerged as a leader in the software industry.

Since 1975, the mission of Microsoft has been to develop a wide range of products for both business and personal use. Microsoft Disk Operating System (MS-DOS) debuted in 1981 with the first IBM personal computer.

Microsoft Word and Microsoft Windows were released in 1983, and Microsoft Works was introduced in 1985. As the personal computer market expanded, Microsoft not only continued to update these early programs, but also introduced new software types. Educational and reference programs were developed to benefit software users of all ages. The introduction of programs such as the Microsoft Network (MSN) allowed more people to access and explore the growing world of the Internet.

In 1988, Microsoft surpassed its biggest competitor, Lotus Development Corporation, to become the leading software vendor in the world. Microsoft began with 3 employees and revenues of $16,005 in 1975. By 1999, the number of Microsoft employees reached 31,575 and revenues were estimated to be nearly $19.75 billion.

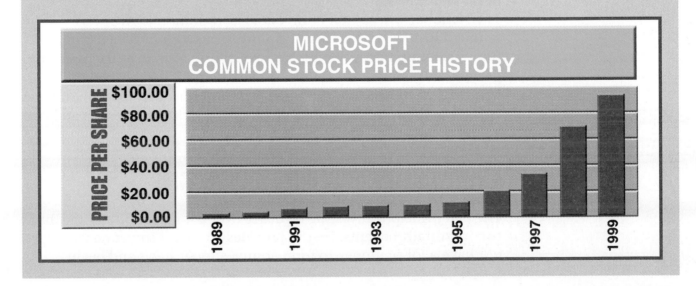

MICROSOFT COMMON STOCK PRICE HISTORY

PRICE PER SHARE: $100.00, $80.00, $60.00, $40.00, $20.00, $0.00

Years: 1989, 1991, 1993, 1995, 1997, 1999

LESSON 5.1

Investment Principles

Your best financial advisor should be the person you see when you look into a mirror. Your goal should be to double the value of your investments every five years. To do so will require an average 15% compounded annual gain in every five-year period. You do not have to make 15% every year. Some years will probably return more than that, other years less. But following NAIC's basic investment principles, you should be able to achieve this goal.

GOALS

■ **Summarize NAIC's four basic investment principles.**

■ **Identify four low-cost methods of investing.**

■ **Explain the concept of diversification.**

■ **Compare the investment characteristics of large and small sales volume companies.**

THE NAIC WAY OF INVESTING

The National Association of Investors Corporation (NAIC) has developed a long-term approach to investing, which has proven very successful. This approach is founded on a fundamental analysis of companies, rather than just a technical analysis of stock performances. It revolves around NAIC's four basic investment principles.

NAIC'S FOUR BASIC INVESTMENT PRINCIPLES

1. Invest on a regular basis over a long period of time.
2. Reinvest all earnings (dividends, interest, capital gains).
3. Invest only in good quality companies with proven track records of growth.
4. Diversify your portfolio to reduce overall risk.

WHAT IS THE NAIC?

The National Association of Investors Corporation (NAIC) was founded in 1951 by four Michigan investment clubs. The organization was set up to develop tools to assist long-term investors and to promote investment education. While originally established for investment clubs, the non-profit organization now provides investment education for both investment clubs and individual investors and has a total membership in excess of 500,000.

INVEST REGULARLY OVER A LONG TIME

The first principle, investing regularly over a long period of time, has two important benefits. First, it provides a way for someone who does not have a lot of money to form an investment habit and begin building a portfolio. People who wait to begin investing until after they have made major purchases—car, house, furniture—will probably find themselves always trying to catch up with their debts and will lose valuable time for their investments to grow and compound.

DOLLAR COST AVERAGING

Regular investing also allows you to "dollar cost average." **Dollar cost averaging** means investing roughly equal amounts of money at regular intervals. Stock prices may move up or down, but when you spread your purchases out like this, you get more shares when the price is down. As a result, you will buy most of your shares at a price lower than the average price. Sound tricky? Here's an example of how it works.

DOLLAR COST AVERAGING EXAMPLE

You invest $25 a month for a year in stock A.

Month	Amount Invested in Stock A	Stock Price	Shares Bought
1	$25.00	$15.00	1.666
2	$25.00	$15.50	1.612
3	$25.00	$16.00	1.562
4	$25.00	$16.50	1.515
5	$25.00	$17.00	1.470
6	$25.00	$17.50	1.428
7	$25.00	$18.00	1.388
8	$25.00	$18.50	1.351
9	$25.00	$19.00	1.315
10	$25.00	$19.50	1.282
11	$25.00	$20.00	1.250
12	$25.00	$20.50	1.219
Total	$300.00	$213.00	17.058
Average	$25.00	$17.75	$17.59

$213 ÷ 12 months = $17.75 average price per share

$300 ÷ 17.058 shares = $17.59 average cost per share

Note that the average cost per share was less than the average price per share. The value of those 17.058 shares at the year-end price of $20.50 is $349.69. Since you paid $300 for them, you made $49.69, or a 16.56% gain in one year.

Cisco Systems, Inc. first sold shares to the public on February 16, 1990 at $18 a share. Since then, Cisco has split its stock eight times: six 2-for-1 splits and two 3-for-2 splits. If you had bought $2,000 worth of Cisco stock at the end of its first day of trading, in October 1999 you would have had more than 16,000 shares worth $1.33 million.

LOW-COST WAYS OF INVESTING REGULARLY

There are many ways to invest regularly at low cost:

- NAIC's Low Cost Plan or NAIC's Stock Service
- Buying direct from companies which provide that opportunity
- Buying first shares from a broker and investing regularly in the dividend reinvestment plan (known as a DRIP plan)
- Joining or starting an investment club

REINVEST ALL EARNINGS

The second principle, reinvesting all earnings, compounds your investment. It makes your earnings work for you in the same way as the money you originally invested. Reinvesting means:

- Reinvesting capital gains from the sale of stock
- Reinvesting dividends
- Reinvesting any interest earned

Earnings should be reinvested in the stocks that produced the earnings (direct purchase or DRIP's) or in other common stocks. Remember, it is the power of compounding over a long period of time that produces superior performance.

RULE OF 72

Recall the Rule of 72: if an asset grows $x\%$ a year, its value will double in $72 \div x\% = y$ years. You can use also this formula to calculate the number of years it takes an investment to double since $72 \div y$ years $= x\%$.

So, an investment that will double in value every 7 years must grow $72 \div 7 = 10.29\%$ per year. If you look for companies that grow about 15% per year, by the Rule of 72 they should double in $72 \div 15\% = 4.8$ or approximately 5 years.

INVEST IN QUALITY GROWTH COMPANIES

What is a growth stock or growth company? It is a company that is perceived to have excellent prospects for above-average future growth in revenues and earnings—and thus, in the price of its common stock. Growth companies are usually defined as companies that are growing faster than the rate of growth of the overall U.S. economy.

Quality growth companies should have established, continuous growth records for sales and earnings per share for at least 5 years, and preferably 10 years. Remember that continuous growth reflects strong management. You are interested in growth records because you are looking for companies which can provide consistent 15% annual growth in net earnings over the next 5 years.

DIVERSIFY YOUR INVESTMENTS

By investing in different companies representing different industries, you reduce the risk of your overall portfolio. Investors call this **diversification**. An example of a poorly diversified portfolio: 15 companies, all in Internet-related businesses. A more diversified portfolio would contain stocks in several different industries.

In addition to diversifying by industry grouping, you can diversify by company size, based on sales volume.

Small Companies: sales under $500 million

Medium Companies: sales between $500 million and $5 billion

Large Companies: sales over $5 billion

ADVANTAGES OF A LARGE SALES VOLUME COMPANY

1. Business is more stable.
2. The stock price tends to be more stable.
3. The stock price should hold up better in a weak market.
4. Management should be able to control growth more efficiently through types of products sold.
5. The company may have a worldwide market.
6. Such companies should be purchased on dips in price.
7. Dividends may be larger as a percentage of earnings.

DISADVANTAGES OF A LARGE SALES VOLUME COMPANY

1. The growth rate in sales and earnings per share is normally less than 10%.

2. Sales have to increase by a much larger dollar amount to achieve the same percent of increase as a smaller company.

3. Dividends will be small if there is real potential for growth.

ADVANTAGES OF A SMALL SALES VOLUME COMPANY

1. Sales and earnings growth rates can be higher than those of larger companies—we hope between 15-25%.

2. Yearly high and low prices will be farther apart due to greater price fluctuations.

DISADVANTAGES OF A SMALL SALES VOLUME COMPANY

1. Smaller companies are more likely than larger companies to experience falling stock prices in a weak market, especially when the country's economy is slow.

2. A smaller company may have more problems obtaining experienced and effective management.

3. Many smaller companies are family controlled and lack management depth.

4. Smaller companies are frequently younger, and their survival rate is lower.

SUCCESS STORIES

NAIC has been helping investors for almost fifty years. Many years ago, Tom O'Hara, NAIC Chairman, told a young man that, if he saved $25 a month and invested it in good stocks, he could become a millionaire. The young man took the advice and invested $25 every month. Forty years later, at a NAIC conference, he showed Mr. O'Hara his stock portfolio. It had a total value of $1,300,000. "You were right," the man told Mr. O'Hara. Imagine what he will have if he continues to take advantage of the compounding effect of his investments and earnings and his portfolio doubles in value in the next five years!

> ### DOLLAR SENSE
> *If you don't want to work, you have to work to earn enough money so that you won't have to work.*
>
> Ogden Nash (1902 – 1971) humorist and poet

Many of you will have great stories to tell, too. Stories of starting young, doing your homework, and following NAIC's four basic principles. The NAIC life-long investment philosophy can pay off for you. It will take patience and diligent work, but your motivation will come from keeping your sights on the goal of doubling the value of your portfolio every five years and remembering how many five-year spans you have ahead of you to double and redouble your money.

Mone

UNDERSTAND TERMS AND IDEAS

1. If you start now with $1,000 and double that amount through investing and compounding every five years, how many spans of five years will it take for you to become a millionaire? How old would you be?

2. Suppose you buy 100 shares of a growth stock at $31.25 per share. If the value grows at 15% annually, how many years will it take to reach two hundred thousand dollars?

3. Many NAIC members have average returns of more than 15%. How many years will the growth stock investment in exercise 2 take to reach two hundred thousand dollars with a 18% annual growth rate?

4. Use the results in exercises 2 and 3 to find how many years it will take to reach two hundred thousand dollars if the growth rate is 24%.

5. Explain how dollar cost averaging enables you to buy stock at a below-average price.

6. Does diversification increase or decrease the risk in a portfolio? Explain.

7. Summarize the advantages and disadvantages of large sales volume as compared with small sales volume.

LESSON 5.2

Search for Companies to Study

GOALS

- Identify some methods for finding companies to study.

- Describe the information in *Value Line* and *Standard & Poor's* stock reports.

*I*n order to choose stocks and manage your investments wisely, you need good information about companies. There are many investment information resources, everything from corporate publications to newsstand magazines and from radio and television programs to Internet web sites. These sources will help you find stocks that interest you. In this lesson, you will begin to examine the specific detailed information you will need to evaluate these investment prospects and choose the ones you want for your portfolio.

WHERE TO GET INVESTMENT IDEAS

There are many good ways to identify stocks that you might like to purchase. You want to invest in growth companies, ones whose earnings per share and sales are growing at a rate higher than that of the economy as a whole.

TAKE A LOOK AROUND YOU

One of the best ways to come up with investment ideas is simply to keep your eyes open and observe what is going on all around you. Is there a product or service you really love? Have you noticed a new restaurant chain that offers great food at reasonable prices, with a fun atmosphere? Have you seen people using certain products or services that are growing in popularity? Are you aware of population or lifestyle trends that represent business opportunities? Are there problems that cry out for creative solutions—health problems, daily hassles, service gaps? Nearly every problem represents a business opportunity for somebody. Use your eyes and your ears. Sometimes a trip to the mall or a conversation with a friend can give you many investment ideas.

"BETTER INVESTING" MAGAZINE

This monthly magazine is a rich source for investment information and "stock to study" ideas. In the spring of each year, *Better Investing* lists names of the top 200 companies held by NAIC investment clubs. *Better Investing* can be obtained by subscription or through NAIC membership.

READ OTHER PUBLICATIONS

As you know from reading lesson 2.5, there are many excellent print and electronic sources of investment information. Let them stimulate your thinking. Learn what other investors are thinking. Use them to turn up more information on companies that interest you.

Read the financial section of your local newspaper, and consider companies in your own area. You will generally have an information edge on these companies compared with people in other parts of the country. If there are stocks that you are interested in buying or selling, watch their performance on the stock tables of your newspaper.

Check out the *Wall Street Journal* at your local library. It is the granddaddy of all business newspapers. Watch for information—hard numbers and written comments—on the companies that interest you.

USE "VALUE LINE" AND "STANDARD & POOR'S" STOCK REPORTS

Two other sources of investment information recommended by the NAIC are *Value Line* and *Standard & Poor's*, which are found in most libraries. In lesson 6.1 you will be introduced to the Stock Selection Guide and Report (SSG), a four-page form which millions of investors have used to analyze stocks. *Value Line* and *Standard & Poor's* stock reports will provide the information you need to fill out the SSG and evaluate stocks for your portfolio.

Sample *Value Line* and *Standard & Poor's* reports on Tootsie Roll Industries, Inc. are shown on the next two pages. Read the descriptions on these pages and familiarize yourself with the information they contain. The items listed below are numbered in the reports to help you find them. Don't worry about what the terms mean. Definitions and explanations will be provided in the next few lessons.

ROCK SOLID

Don't invest in anything you don't understand. Always research the company, the company's product and the investment tool you select. You should always understand the level of risk you are taking.

On the *Standard & Poor's* sheets find:

1. Total sales/revenues (different terms used in different industries)
2. Earnings per share
3. Quarterly sales
4. Quarterly earnings
5. Quarterly dividends
6. Yearly prices
7. Number of shares outstanding
8. Net before taxes
9. Book Value
10. P/E ratio
11. Beta
12. Percent return on equity
13. Percent long term debt of capitalization
14. Institutional holdings
15. Dividends

Tootsie Roll Industries

NYSE Symbol **TR**

30-OCT-99

Industry: Foods

Summary: This company is a major manufacturer and distributor of candy, sold primarily under the Tootsie Roll brand name, and is the largest U.S. confectioner of lollipops.

Quantitative Evaluations

Outlook (1 Lowest—5 Highest)
- **NA**

Fair Value
- **NA**

Risk
- **Low**

Earn./Div. Rank
- **A+**

Technical Eval.
- **Bearish** since 10/99

Rel. Strength Rank (1 Lowest—99 Highest)
- **44**

Insider Activity
- **NA**

Recent Price • 30
52 Wk Range • 46⅞-29⅜

Yield • 0.8%
12-Mo. P/E • 20.5

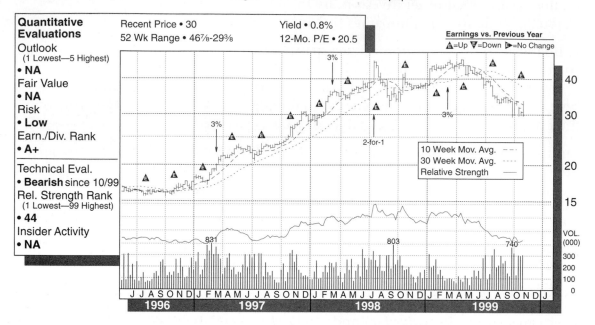

Earnings vs. Previous Year
▲=Up ▼=Down ▶=No Change

10 Week Mov. Avg. – – –
30 Week Mov. Avg. ·······
Relative Strength ——

Business Profile - 24-AUG-99

Tootsie Roll continues to make capital investments and improve operations to support growth, increase efficiency and improve quality. TR added production capacity and reengineered several key processes in its manufacturing operations to increase productivity. The company's strong balance sheet continues to improve. Future growth is expected to come from product line extensions, acquisitions, and expansion in the Far East and other international markets. During 1998, TR launched the company's first website on the internet. Directors and officers own about 83% of the voting power of the company's stock.

Operational Review - 24-AUG-99

Net sales for the 26 weeks ended July 3, 1999, advanced 4.4%, reflecting successful marketing and promotional programs, as well as new products and product line extensions. Despite higher ingredient costs and greater labor and related fringe benefits, profitability improved, due to cost control programs and significantly higher other income on decreased foreign exchange translation losses related to the company's Mexican operations. Pretax income rose 7.7%. After taxes at 36.3% in both periods, net earnings increased 7.8%, to $27.1 million ($0.55 a share), from $25.1 million ($0.51).

Stock Performance - 29-OCT-99

In the past 30 trading days, TR's shares have declined 5%, compared to a 2% rise in the S&P 500. Average trading volume for the past five days was 25,720 shares, compared with the 40-day moving average of 63,113 shares.

Key Stock Statistics

Dividend Rate/Share	0.25	Shareholders	9,500
Shs. outstg. (M)	49.0	Market cap. (B)	$ 1.1
Avg. daily vol. (M)	0.055	Inst. holdings	21%
Tang. Bk. Value/Share	6.55		
Beta	0.58		

Value of $10,000 invested 5 years ago: $ 22,093

Fiscal Year Ending Dec. 31

	1999	1998	1997	1996	1995	1994
Revenues (Million $)						
1Q	74.20	69.70	66.26	63.27	60.27	56.37
2Q	88.27	85.93	82.28	72.51	68.77	62.89
3Q	152.7	144.2	140.7	128.7	116.5	111.0
4Q	—	88.80	86.40	76.48	67.15	66.66
Yr.	—	388.7	375.6	340.9	312.7	296.9
Earnings Per Share ($)						
1Q	0.25	0.23	0.19	0.16	0.15	0.14
2Q	0.30	0.28	0.25	0.18	0.17	0.16
3Q	0.60	0.55	0.50	0.38	0.32	0.31
4Q	—	0.31	0.28	0.21	0.17	0.15
Yr.	—	1.37	1.21	0.94	0.80	0.75

Next earnings report expected: NA

Dividend Data (Dividends have been paid since 1943.)

Amount ($)	Date Decl.	Ex-Div. Date	Stock of Record	Payment Date
3%	Feb. 23	Mar. 05	Mar. 09	Apr. 21 '99
0.053	Feb. 23	Mar. 05	Mar. 09	Apr. 08 '99
0.063	Jun. 02	Jun. 17	Jun. 21	Jul. 12 '99
0.063	Sep. 13	Sep. 29	Oct. 01	Oct. 12 '99

Tootsie Roll Industries, Inc.

30-OCT-99

Business Summary - 24-AUG-99

Tootsie Roll Industries, Inc. continues to grow its core brands through successful targeted promotions and marketing. This conservatively managed candy producer is on a roll, having reported 21 consecutive annual sales increases, and having distributed an annual stock dividend for over 30 consecutive years.

TR has been engaged in the manufacture and sale of candy for more than 100 years. Some 100 candy and grocery brokers and the company itself service about 15,000 customers throughout the U.S. The company's flagship product is the Tootsie Roll, a chocolate-flavored candy of a chewy consistency, sold in several sizes, and also used as a center for other products in the line, including Tootsie Pops, a spherical fruit or chocolate-flavored shell of hard candy with a center of Tootsie Roll candy on a paper safety stick. Products also include Tootsie Roll Flavor Rolls and Tootsie Frooties. The company makes other candies under the Mason and Tootsie labels, including Mason Dots and Mason Crows, and produces a chocolate-covered cherry confection under the Cella's trademark.

In 1993, Cambridge Brands Inc., the chocolate and caramel confections business of Warner-Lambert Co., was acquired. Brands purchased included Junior Mints, Sugar Daddy, Sugar Babies and Charleston Chew. In 1988, the company acquired privately held Charms Co.,

a maker of lollipops and hard candy sold under the trademarks Charms, Blow-Pop, Blue Razz and Zip-A-Dee-Doo-Da-Pops.

TR's products are marketed in a variety of packages designed for display and sold in retail outlets and vending machines. The company has recently experienced a consumer trend toward larger sized bags and multi-packs that pack candy in 5 and 10 count lay-down packs.

The company's principal markets are in the U.S., Canada and Mexico. TR operates a Mexican manufacturing facility that supplies a very small percentage of the products marketed in the U.S. or Canada.

Tootsie Roll has found that its sales normally maintain a consistent level throughout the year, except for a substantial upsurge in the third quarter, reflecting sales associated with Halloween. In anticipation of this increase, TR generally ramps up inventory in the second quarter to build its inventory for Halloween. Revenues from a major customer accounted for 17.2%, 15.9% and 16.2% of total net sales in 1998, 1997 and 1996, respectively.

TR has advertised nationally for many years. Although most forms of advertising media have been used at one time or another in the past, presently most of TR's advertising expenditures are for the airing of network and syndicated TV and cable and spot television commercials in major markets throughout the country.

Per Share Data ($)

(Year Ended Dec. 31)	1998	1997	1996	1995	1994	1993	1992	1991	1990	1989
Tangible Bk. Val.	6.45	5.41	4.50	3.50	2.82	2.21	2.71	2.11	1.63	1.20
Cash Flow	1.67	1.52	1.22	1.02	2.07	0.85	0.76	0.65	0.55	0.50
Earnings	1.37	1.21	0.94	0.81	0.76	0.70	0.64	0.53	0.45	0.40
Dividends	0.18	0.16	0.13	0.11	0.09	0.07	0.06	0.05	0.04	0.04
Payout Ratio	13%	13%	14%	14%	12%	11%	9%	9%	10%	11%
Prices - High	46$^{1}/_{2}$	30$^{3}/_{4}$	18$^{1}/_{2}$	18$^{1}/_{4}$	16$^{1}/_{8}$	17$^{1}/_{2}$	17$^{1}/_{8}$	14$^{7}/_{8}$	9$^{5}/_{8}$	7$^{1}/_{8}$
- Low	27$^{3}/_{8}$	17	15$^{1}/_{2}$	12$^{7}/_{8}$	11$^{5}/_{8}$	13$^{1}/_{2}$	12$^{1}/_{8}$	7	6	4$^{1}/_{2}$
P/E Ratio - High	34	25	20	23	21	25	27	28	21	18
- Low	20	14	17	16	15	19	19	13	13	11

Income Statement Analysis (Million $)

	1998	1997	1996	1995	1994	1993	1992	1991	1990	1989
Revs.	389	376	341	313	297	260	245	208	194	179
Oper. Inc.	114	103	83.6	72.2	70.5	61.0	53.9	47.2	40.7	37.4
Depr.	12.8	12.8	12.1	10.8	10.5	7.5	6.0	6.0	5.2	4.8
Int. Exp.	0.8	0.5	1.5	1.5	1.6	0.6	0.4	0.2	0.5	1.2
Pretax Inc.	106	95.4	75.1	64.0	61.2	57.7	51.9	44.2	37.1	33.2
Eff. Tax Rate	36%	36%	37%	37%	38%	39%	38%	40%	39%	39%
Net Inc.	67.5	60.7	47.2	40.4	37.9	35.4	32.0	26.5	22.6	20.2

Balance Sheet & Other Fin. Data (Million $)

	1998	1997	1996	1995	1994	1993	1992	1991	1990	1989
Cash	80.7	60.4	144	104	62.4	56.2	88.9	65.3	36.8	18.5
Curr. Assets	229	207	202	165	119	112	130	102	78.0	54.0
Total Assets	487	437	391	354	310	304	222	184	160	136
Curr. Liab.	53.4	53.6	48.2	55.0	26.3	50.9	22.5	21.2	22.6	20.7
LT Debt	7.5	7.5	7.5	7.5	27.5	27.5	7.5	Nil	Nil	Nil
Common Eqty.	396	351	313	272	240	212	182	153	130	110
Total Cap.	413	367	330	289	276	246	193	158	136	114
Cap. Exp.	14.9	8.6	9.8	4.6	8.2	52.5	12.5	6.6	5.2	3.1
Cash Flow	80.3	73.5	59.3	51.2	48.4	43.0	38.0	32.5	27.7	25.0
Curr. Ratio	4.3	3.9	4.2	3.0	4.5	2.2	5.8	4.8	3.5	2.6
% LT Debt of Cap.	1.8	2.0	2.3	2.6	10.0	11.2	3.9	Nil	Nil	Nil
% Net Inc.of Revs.	17.4	16.2	13.8	12.9	12.8	13.7	13.1	12.8	11.6	11.3
% Ret. on Assets	14.6	14.7	12.7	6.1	12.4	13.5	15.7	15.4	15.2	15.2
% Ret. on Equity	18.1	18.3	16.1	12.2	16.8	18.0	19.2	18.8	18.8	20.1

Data as orig reptd.; bef. results of disc opers/spec. items. Per share data adj. for stk. divs. Bold denotes diluted EPS (FASB 128)-prior periods restated. E-Estimated. NA-Not Available. NM-Not Meaningful. NR-Not Ranked.

Office—7401 S. Cicero Ave., Chicago, IL 60629. **Tel**—(773) 838-3400. **Website**—http://www.tootsie.com. **Chrmn & CEO**—M. J. Gordon. **Pres & COO**—E. R. Gordon. **Treas**—B. P. Bowen. **VP-Fin**—G. H. Ember Jr. **Dirs**—L. J. Lewis-Brent, E. R. Gordon, M. J. Gordon, C. W. Seibert. **Transfer Agent & Registrar**—ChaseMellon Shareholder Services, Ridgefield Park, NJ. **Incorporated**—in Virginia in 1919. **Empl**— 1,750. **S&P Analyst:** A. Bensinger

On the *Value Line* page find:

1. Total sales/revenues
2. Earnings per share
3. Quarterly sales
4. Quarterly earnings
5. Quarterly dividends
6. Yearly prices
7. Number of shares outstanding
8. Tax rate
9. Net profit
10. Book value
11. Beta
12. Percent earned on net worth
13. Long term debt percent of capitalization
14. Insider holdings
15. Dividends

UTILIZE COMPANY INFORMATION

You can also find the above financial data in the annual reports of the companies you are researching. For beginners, however, the NAIC recommends using *Value Line* and *Standard & Poor's* because they summarize key information in easy-to-use formats.

You can usually get corporate information by calling the investor relations person at the company and asking for it. Both *Value Line* and *Standard & Poor's* provide company addresses and telephone numbers. Company annual reports are also available at many libraries and on the Internet.

inve$tor profile

Marcellus Wesley

Two years ago, Marcellus Wesley, a high school student, was interested in learning more about the stock market. A friend introduced Marcellus to his investment club, Saint George's Junior Investment Club. Marcellus has been a member of the club ever since, and he is now president. He is proud of the fact that the club's returns from November 1998 to November 1999 have increased an impressive 30%. The investment club's annual rate of return, though it is only three years old, exceeds 10%. The maximum age for active members is 21.

Marcellus continues to enjoy learning more about the stock market. He plans to go to college, however, he has yet to decide whether he will study to become a composer or work with the stock market in some capacity. Marcellus plays the French horn, cello, and piano. He is also interested in computers, enjoys keeping up with the latest technology, and is involved in community service activities.

Marcellus has become one of his family's investment advisors. His parents have learned that Marcellus' advice can bring great returns, and they regret not taking his advice from the beginning. His advice to new investors is to try the fantasy investing sites on the Web to introduce yourself to the stock market with minimal risk.

TOOTSIE ROLL NYSE-TR

RECENT PRICE	**34**	
P/E RATIO	**21.9** (Trailing: 24.1 / Median: 19.0)	
RELATIVE P/E RATIO	**1.30**	
DIV'D YLD	**0.7%**	
		VALUE LINE

TIMELINESS	**4** Lowered 8/6/99
SAFETY	**1** Raised 5/14/99
TECHNICAL	**3** Lowered 3/12/99
BETA	.65 (1.00 = Market)

High / Low (yearly):
High:	6.4	7.2	9.6	14.8	17.2	17.5	16.2	18.2	18.5	30.8	46.5	46.9
Low:	4.8	5.9	4.5	7.0	12.1	13.5	11.6	12.9	15.5	17.0	27.4	33.4

LEGENDS
— 16.0 x "Cash Flow" p sh
···· Relative Price Strength
3-for-2 split 7/86
2-for-1 split 5/87
2-for-1 split 7/95
2-for-1 split 7/98
Options: No
Shaded area indicates recession

Target Price Range 2002 | 2003 | 2004

2002-04 PROJECTIONS
	Price	Gain	Ann'l Total Return
High	50	(+45%)	10%
Low	40	(+20%)	4%

Insider Decisions
	S	O	N	D	J	F	M	A	M
to Buy	0	0	0	0	0	0	0	0	1
Options	0	0	0	0	0	0	0	0	0
to Sell	0	0	0	0	0	0	0	0	0

Institutional Decisions
	3Q1998	4Q1998	1Q1999
to Buy	40	37	35
to Sell	50	38	65
Hld's(000)	10162	11087	10741

Percent shares traded	4.5 / 3.0 / 1.5

% TOT. RETURN 7/99
	THIS STOCK	VL ARITH. INDEX
1 yr.	-14.4	15.0
3 yr.	118.7	73.5
5 yr.	165.4	128.5

	1983	1984	1985	1986	1987	1988	1989	1990	1991	1992	1993	1994	1995	1996	1997	1998	1999	2000	© VALUE LINE PUB., INC.	02-04
Sales per sh A	1.52	1.83	2.12	2.21	2.28	2.55	3.56	3.86	4.13	4.88	5.16	5.90	6.22	6.78	7.57	7.88	8.40	8.55		11.10
"Cash Flow" per sh	.14	.20	.25	.30	.34	.40	.50	.56	.63	.76	.88	1.02	1.02	1.18	1.48	1.63	1.80	1.95		2.50
Earnings per sh A B	.11	.17	.22	.25	.29	.33	.40	.45	.53	.64	.70	.75	.80	.94	1.22	1.37	1.55	1.65		2.20
Div'ds Decl'd per sh C	.02	.02	.03	.03	.04	.04	.04	.04	.05	.06	.08	.09	.12	.14	.16	.19	.24	.28		.43
Cap'l Spending per sh	.03	.06	.13	.08	.05	.09	.06	.10	.08	.25	.56	.16	.09	.19	.17	.30	.30	.30		.30
Book Value per sh D	.74	.88	1.06	1.28	1.53	1.82	2.18	2.58	3.04	3.61	4.22	4.78	5.41	6.22	7.07	8.04	9.00	10.05		13.95
Common Shs Outst'g E	51.34	50.88	50.41	50.38	50.37	50.36	50.35	50.34	50.33	50.33	50.31	50.30	50.29	50.27	49.65	49.30	48.80	48.30		46.80
Avg Ann'l P/E Ratio	7.8	7.3	11.4	14.5	17.7	16.6	14.4	16.3	19.9	23.5	22.1	18.4	19.1	17.7	19.1	26.6				20.0
Relative P/E Ratio	.66	.68	.93	.98	1.18	1.38	1.09	1.21	1.27	1.43	1.31	1.21	1.28	1.11	1.10	1.41				1.15
Avg Ann'l Div'd Yield	2.4%	1.8%	1.1%	.9%	.8%	.7%	.7%	.6%	.5%	.4%	.5%	.6%	.7%	.8%	.7%	.7%				1.0%

Bold figures are Value Line estimates

CAPITAL STRUCTURE as of 4/3/99
Total Debt $7.5 mill. **Due in 5 Yrs** Nil
LT Debt $7.5 mill. **LT Interest** $.5 mill.
Capitalized leases $7.5 mill.
(2% of Cap'l)

Leases, Uncapitalized None
Pension Liability None

Pfd Stock None
Common Stock 49,293,098 shs.
Includes 15,846,841 Class B shs. (10 votes a sh.)
As of 4/3/99 (98% of Cap'l)

MARKET CAP: $1.7 billion (Mid Cap)

	1983	1984	1985	1986	1987	1988	1989	1990	1991	1992	1993	1994	1995	1996	1997	1998	1999	2000		02-04
Sales ($mill) A							179.3	194.3	207.9	245.4	259.6	296.9	312.7	340.9	375.6	388.7	410	435		520
Operating Margin							21.1%	21.2%	22.3%	22.3%	24.0%	24.6%	24.0%	25.3%	27.4%	29.4%	29.5%	30.0%		31.0%
Depreciation ($mill)							5.1	5.7	5.2	6.1	8.8	13.2	10.8	12.1	12.8	12.8	12.0	13.0		15.0
Net Profit ($mill)							20.2	22.6	26.5	32.0	35.4	37.9	40.4	47.2	60.7	67.5	75.0	80.0		105.0
Income Tax Rate							39.1%	39.2%	39.9%	38.3%	38.6%	38.0%	37.0%	37.1%	36.4%	36.3%	35.0%	35.0%		35.0%
Net Profit Margin							11.3%	11.6%	12.8%	13.1%	13.7%	12.8%	12.9%	13.8%	16.2%	17.4%	18.5%	18.5%		20.0%
Working Cap'l ($mill)							33.5	55.3	80.5	107.2	61.0	92.6	109.7	153.3	153.4	175.1	215	260		425
Long-Term Debt ($mill)							--	--	--	7.5	27.5	27.5	7.5	7.5	7.5	7.5	7.5	7.5		7.5
Shr. Equity ($mill)							109.6	129.8	152.8	181.7	212.3	240.5	272.2	312.9	351.2	396.5	440	485		655
Return on Total Cap'l							18.4%	17.4%	17.4%	16.9%	14.8%	14.3%	14.6%	14.8%	17.0%	16.8%	17.0%	16.5%		16.0%
Return on Shr. Equity							18.4%	17.4%	17.4%	17.6%	16.7%	15.8%	14.8%	15.1%	17.3%	17.0%	17.0%	16.5%		16.0%
Retained to Com Eq							16.5%	15.6%	15.7%	16.0%	15.0%	13.9%	12.9%	13.1%	15.2%	14.7%	14.5%	14.0%		12.0%
All Div'ds to Net Prof							11%	10%	9%	9%	10%	12%	13%	13%	12%	14%	16%	17%		22%

CURRENT POSITION ($MILL.)
	1997	1998	4/3/99
Cash Assets	142.3	163.9	150.8
Receivables	23.3	22.4	26.3
Inventory (LIFO)	36.7	36.5	44.4
Other	4.7	5.7	8.7
Current Assets	207.0	228.5	230.2
Accts Payable	11.6	12.5	12.7
Debt Due	--	--	--
Other	42.0	40.9	44.1
Current Liab.	53.6	53.4	56.8

ANNUAL RATES
of change (per sh)	Past 10 Yrs.	Past 5 Yrs.	Est'd '96-'98 to '02-'04
Sales	12.0%	9.5%	8.5%
"Cash Flow"	15.5%	13.5%	10.0%
Earnings	15.0%	13.5%	11.0%
Dividends	15.5%	20.5%	18.0%
Book Value	16.5%	14.5%	12.0%

QUARTERLY SALES ($ mill.) A
Calendar	Mar.31	Jun.30	Sep.30	Dec.31	Full Year
1996	63.3	72.5	128.6	76.5	340.9
1997	66.3	82.3	140.6	86.4	375.6
1998	69.7	86.0	144.2	88.8	388.7
1999	74.2	88.3	155	92.5	410
2000	80.0	90.0	170	95.0	435

EARNINGS PER SHARE A B
Calendar	Mar.31	Jun.30	Sep.30	Dec.31	Full Year
1996	.16	.19	.38	.21	.94
1997	.19	.25	.50	.28	1.22
1998	.23	.28	.55	.31	1.37
1999	.25	.30	.65	.35	1.55
2000	.25	.32	.70	.38	1.65

GROSS QUARTERLY DIV'DS PAID C
Calendar	Mar.31	Jun.30	Sep.30	Dec.31	Full Year
1995	.025	.03	.03	.03	.12
1996	.03	.035	.035	.035	.14
1997	.035	.04	.04	.04	.16
1998	.04	.05	.05	.05	.19
1999	.05	.05			.06

BUSINESS: Tootsie Roll Industries, Inc. produces candy. Products include: *Tootsie Roll, Tootsie Pop, Tootsie Bubble Pop, Tootsie Pop Drops, Tootsie Roll Flavor Rolls,* and *Mason Dots.* Acquired Warner-Lambert's former chocolate/caramel brands (*Junior Mints, Sugar Daddy, Sugar Babies, Charleston Chew,* and *Pom Poms*) 10/93; *Charms* Co. (*Charms, Blow Pops*), 9/88; and Cella's Con-fections (chocolate covered cherries), 7/85. Has four plants in U.S.; one in Mexico. Int'l ops. (Mexico and Canada): 8% of '98 sales, 7% of earnings. Has about 1,750 employees. M.J. and E.R. Gordon control 43% of voting power; L.R. Weiner, 12% (4/99 Proxy). Chairman & C.E.O.: M.J. Gordon. Pres. & C.O.O.: E.R. Gordon. Inc.: VA. Add.: 7401 S. Cicero Ave., Chicago, IL 60629. Tel.: 773-838-3400.

Tootsie Roll continues to hoard its cash while it looks for acquisitions. With free cash flow likely to reach $70 million this year, and cash & marketable securities totaling $151 million ($3.05 a share), management is actively seeking acquisitions. But the company continues to believe that candy companies are commanding excessive prices. Thus, Tootsie Roll will likely wait for prices to become "more reasonable". The company's most recent purchase (in 1993) demonstrates management's disciplined approach: Cambridge Brands (the company's first acquisition since 1988) was purchased for $81.3 million and generated $36.6 million in earnings the same year (equating to a 2.2 Price/Earnings multiple). Because potential deal terms are unknown, our estimates do not reflect any acquisitions. **Continued product introductions and international expansion will keep capital spending at elevated levels.** Excluding years with acquisitions or unusual expenditures, capital spending has historically run between $5 million and $10 million a year. Going forward, though, we project $15 million a year to support regular capital spending, international expansion in Australia and the Philippines, and new product introductions.

Stock dividends and share repurchases will likely continue. Each April, Tootsie Roll issues a 3% stock dividend along with an increase in its quarterly dividend payout. We expect both plans to continue. Meanwhile, share repurchases should somewhat offset increases in shares outstanding. The company's future repurchases are limited by the decreasing availability of large blocks of shares. In the short term, average daily volume of 30,000 shares should support a moderate repurchase plan approaching 1.5 million shares a year. However, we have modeled a more conservative 500 thousand share-a-year plan, which reflects the company's recent share repurchase trend.

Despite their recent decline, shares of Tootsie Roll do not represent a compelling value. At current levels, Tootsie Roll shares discount the company's future growth. These untimely shares are expected to underperform the market over the coming 3 to 5 years.

David H. Kurzman   *August 13, 1999*

(A) Fiscal year ends Dec. 31. First three quarters end on Sat. closest to end of month. (B) Based on average shares through 1996, diluted thereafter. Next earnings report due about Oct. 27. (C) Next dividend declared about Sept. 25. Next ex date about Oct. 1. Dividends paid about Jan. 9, Apr. 9, July 9, and Oct. 9. stock div'd paid each year about Apr. 21, since 1966. (D) Includes intangibles. In '98: $87.8 million ($1.84/share). (E) In millions, adjusted for stock splits and dividends. 3% stock div'd paid each year about Apr. 21, since 1966.

Company's Financial Strength	A+
Stock's Price Stability	95
Price Growth Persistence	65
Earnings Predictability	95

To subscribe call 1-800-833-0046.

UNDERSTAND TERMS AND IDEAS

1. Write to a corporation and ask for the last two annual reports and any subsequent quarterly reports.

    _____

    _____

    _____

2. Take a look around your hometown or your state for companies you might want to study. Compile a list.

    _____

    _____

    _____

3. List some of the key data found in *Value Line* which are used in filling out the SSG.

    _____

    _____

    _____

4. Take your list of hometown or state companies (question 2) to the library and see how many you can find in *Value Line* or *Standard & Poor's*.

    _____

    _____

    _____

5. What are some of the major trends (lifestyles, recreation, technology, demographics) which are visible in the United States right now?

    _____

    _____

    _____

6. Identify some companies which are taking advantage of these trends.

    _____

    _____

    _____

The Annual Report

*A*ccounting is the language of business, and before you begin to use the Stock *Selection Guide (SSG),* you need to become acquainted with some of the most frequently used accounting terms. This lesson will examine the content of a company's annual report, which is the primary source of financial information about the corporation. You do not have to become an accountant to invest in stocks, but some knowledge of accounting terminology is very helpful.

THE COMPANY REPORT CARD

Just like your school, which issues periodic reports on your progress, public companies must send out "report cards" to their shareholders. The **annual report** is a yearly record summarizing the financial condition of a corporation that must be distributed to shareholders.

You can obtain an annual report from a company by calling and asking for investor's information. You can also access annual reports for some companies on the Internet. Annual reports can be quite lengthy, almost the size of a small magazine. Some are filled with color pictures and graphics and are very attractive. Public companies are required by law to send out annual reports to their shareholders. The reports provide "bundles" of information about the company, its products or services, its employees, its customers, and its future outlook. While all annual reports are not alike, you will find the following major sections in most of them:

- Corporate Profile
- Financial Highlights
- Letter to the Shareholders
- Operational Overview
- Independent Auditors' Report
- Financial Statements
- Notes to Financial Statements
- Management's Discussion and Analysis
- Description of the Company's Business
- Business Segment Information
- Company Directors and Executive Officers
- Five-year Historical Financial Data Summary

GOALS

- Discuss what an Annual Report is all about.
- Describe the major sections of an Annual Report.

Many companies publish their annual reports or financial statements on the Internet. Enter keywords or phrases such as annual report, income statement, or balance sheet. Several web sites contain links to annual reports. This provides a central location where you can find annual reports for companies you may be interested in analyzing as investment opportunities.

CORPORATE PROFILE

This section, usually little more than a paragraph, describes the company's business, what it makes or sells. This section may also include information about where the company does business—for example, in the United States, Canada, Europe, etc.

FINANCIAL HIGHLIGHTS

One of the more important parts of the annual report is the financial highlights section, which has a brief summary of the "numbers" for the year. Here are many of the numbers that are especially important to shareholders such as profit and loss data. Remember that this is only a summary. More detailed information is contained in the financial statement section. Below is the financial highlights section from the 1998 annual report for Tootsie Roll Industries, Inc.

Financial Highlights

	December 31,	
	1998	1997
	(in thousands except per share data)	
Net Sales	$388,659	$375,594
Net Earnings	67,526	60,682
Working Capital	175,155	153,355
Net Property, Plant and Equipment	83,024	78,364
Shareholders' Equity	396,457	351,163
Average Shares Outstanding*	48,051	48,294
Per Share Items*		
Net Earnings	$1.41	$1.26
Shareholders' Equity	8.29	7.29
Cash Dividends Paid	.20	.16

*Based on average shares outstanding adjusted for stock dividends and 2-for-1 stock split.

LETTER TO THE SHAREHOLDERS

A letter to shareholders (owners of the company) from one of the leaders of the corporation is usually found in the first few pages in the annual report. Sometimes this section is called a "report from management." The person who writes the letter may be the Chief Executive Officer (the CEO), the Chairman of the Board of Directors, or the President. Sometimes, one person holds two or more of these titles, for example, President and CEO. The letter to the shareholders gives the corporate leader a chance to communicate with the company owners about the business and its future.

OPERATIONAL OVERVIEW

This is also a highlights section. It discusses the company's products or services, as well as significant events or accomplishments during the year. For example, the overview may mention that the company opened 200 new stores or two new manufacturing plants.

INDEPENDENT AUDITORS' REPORT

The auditors are certified public accountants (CPAs) who are responsible for inspecting the company's records (their "books") and offering an opinion on how well these records comply with generally accepted accounting rules. The auditors must be independent, and may not be company employees. If the auditors find the accounting records in order, they issue what is known as a "clean opinion." If they find deviations from acceptable accounting practices, they issue a "qualified opinion." The auditors' opinion is critical to shareholders.

FINANCIAL STATEMENTS

This is the heart of the annual report. As preparation for learning to use the SSG, we shall discuss the two major parts of the financial statement section, (a) the balance sheet and (b) income statement, in the next lesson.

Operating Report

"Tootsie Caramel Apple Pops — so good, only the stick will remain."

Marketing and Sales

Sales reached a new record high in 1998, driven by continued growth in our core brands. These increases resulted from successfully targeted promotions such as shipper displays, combo packs and bonus bags.

Sales growth was also realized from a shift to larger sized bags which reflect a continuing trend in the trade toward a higher "ring" or selling price per item. This trend meshes well with our products which continue to offer quality, branded confections that are attractive values.

Another trend that emerged recently is the popularity of multi-packs which feature popular bars or boxed goods in 5 and 10 count lay-down packs. Incremental sales were realized by launching snack-size Tootsie Roll and Charleston Chew bars and mini-boxes of Junior Mints and Dots in this new format. We also extended our popular Caramel Apple Pop to several new pack configurations, including a unique bulk display that incorporates a real wooden apple basket!

As is customary for our company, the third quarter was again our highest selling period due to Halloween and back-to-school programs. Halloween was led by continuing strength in our bagged goods, particularly in the larger sized assortments that have become well established consumer favorites during the past several years. We also experienced Halloween growth from the introduction of several new and larger pack sizes for existing items that we felt could become even more popular among trick-or-treaters.

New product growth included Wicked Red-berry Blow Pop, a mouth-watering strawberry-kiwi flavored Blow Pop in a bold, eye catching wrapper and Caramel-A-Lot, a blend of luscious caramel and chewy nougat wrapped in chocolaty goodness. In addition, several promising new items were developed for introduction in early 1999.

Advertising and Public Relations

Television was again the chief medium used to advertise our products to broad audiences of children and adults in 1998. Numerous placements in selected spot and cable markets featured our classic "How Many Licks?" theme, as well as two new commercials that were developed and introduced during the year.

The first of these new commercials, "Caramel Apple Pops," tempts consumers with the message that this remarkable pop is "so good only the stick will remain," while "Chocolate Attack" encourages mothers to quell their youngsters' chocolate cravings with delicious, low-fat Tootsie Rolls and Tootsie Pops. Both of these messages were economically delivered in ten and fifteen second formats on popular talk, game and adventure shows to maximize their reach.

Also in 1998 we launched the company's first web site on the internet. Both children and adults can now enhance their cyber travels by visiting "tootsie.com" to learn interesting facts about Tootsie Roll Industries, its history and its products in an enjoyable, user friendly environment. Whether curious about Clara Hirshfield (the original "Tootsie"), looking for our latest financial release or seeking an answer to the famous question "How many licks does it take to get to the Tootsie Roll center of a Tootsie Pop?," "tootsie.com" has something of interest for every Tootsie Roll fan.

The introduction of our web site was but one of the many positive mentions we received in the press and on television news programs last year. The company was also favorably reviewed in Forbes' Annual Report on American Industry.

We again received thousands of positive letters from our loyal consumers during the year. These serve as a constant reminder that each of the millions of Tootsie Rolls, Tootsie Pops and other popular confections we produce each day can make a life-long impression.

3

"Oh-oh, another chocolate attack! Better reach for a Tootsie Roll or chocolatey center Tootsie Pop! Delicious and always low in fat."

Manufacturing and Distribution

Continuing capital investments and operating improvements were made throughout the company in 1998 to support growth, increase efficiency or improve quality.

We added production capacity to meet growing demand for the products we make in Chicago, Illinois and Covington, Tennessee. We also reengineered several key processes at these plants to increase efficiency and reduce cost, and began the first of several infrastructure enhancements that are needed to support expanding production.

Also in support of our continued growth, we acquired land adjacent to our Covington, Tennessee plant and have commenced construction of a new regional distribution center there. This center will incorporate the automated inventory tracking systems that we have successfully implemented in Chicago, utilizing advanced technology to maximize control and minimize out of stock situations.

Purchasing

Markets for the key commodities and ingredients we use remained stable or declined slightly in 1998 as adverse economic conditions in many markets continued to dampen world-wide demand. Further, our ongoing hedging program and fixed price contracts helped to insulate us from those price fluctuations that did occur in spot markets.

The cost of the various packaging materials we use remained stable during the year. Also, leveraging the high volume of annual purchases we make of these items, competitive bidding was again successfully utilized to further control cost.

Information Technology

During 1998 we completed an extensive review of the information systems we utilize throughout the company and determined that the vast majority of these systems—indeed those most critical to our operations—are "Y2K" compliant by design. Our initial testing has confirmed this, and final testing is scheduled for completion by the middle of 1999.

Y2K issues were identified in our systems in Mexico and the necessary corrective programming changes have been written and implemented. Final testing of these changes is scheduled to be completed by mid year, as are the other minor program corrections that were identified in several secondary domestic systems.

We view information technology as an indispensable tool with which we can streamline an ever-expanding variety of functions and tasks. In this regard, during 1998 we completed the initial phases of automating a number of operations that had previously been handled manually. Completion of the final phases of these projects is scheduled for 1999, and we expect that these and other information technology applications will yield ongoing efficiencies.

International

Our Canadian subsidiary reported increased sales and profits in 1998, both due to growth in seasonal sales at Halloween and to distribution gains throughout the year. Also, the Super Blow Pop was introduced in that market during the year with promising results.

Our Mexican operations had a difficult year due to currency devaluations and increased competitive pressures on top of generally soft local market conditions for confectionery. On the positive side, the latest phase of our plant modernization program was completed there, which will increase productivity and enhance our competitive position in Mexico. These improvements will enable us to respond more quickly to local competition with efficiently produced, high quality products. Our Tutsi Pop still remains the local favorite.

Sales trends in other international markets were positive as we continue to export our well known items to many markets throughout the world.

4

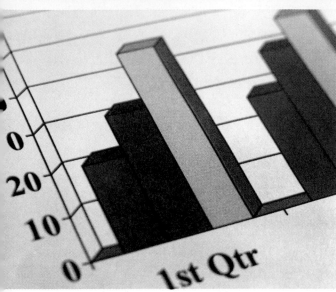

NOTES TO FINANCIAL STATEMENTS

For beginners, this section is difficult to understand. As you become more familiar with accounting terminology, the notes will become more relevant.

MANAGEMENT'S DISCUSSION AND ANALYSIS

This is a detailed section that discusses different segments of the business and how money was made (or lost). It is geared toward money issues.

DESCRIPTION OF THE COMPANY'S BUSINESS

This is a brief description of the nature of the company's business.

BUSINESS SEGMENT INFORMATION

It is not unusual for a corporation to be engaged in a number of different businesses. This section is important because it lets you know what percentage of the company is dedicated to each business segment. For example, the company may derive 60% of its revenues from Industry A and 40% from Industry B.

COMPANY DIRECTORS AND EXECUTIVE OFFICERS

The leaders of the corporation are listed in the annual report. They include (a) the members of the board of directors and (b) the top level officers. Shareholders elect the board of directors. The directors make broad strategy and policy decisions for the company. The corporate officers, however, run the business from day to day.

FIVE-YEAR HISTORICAL FINANCIAL DATA SUMMARY

This required section summarizes key financial data for the past five years, usually in a table format.

There is a wealth of information in an annual report, and it reveals a great deal about the management of a firm. All sections of the annual report are important in evaluating a company's future prospects.

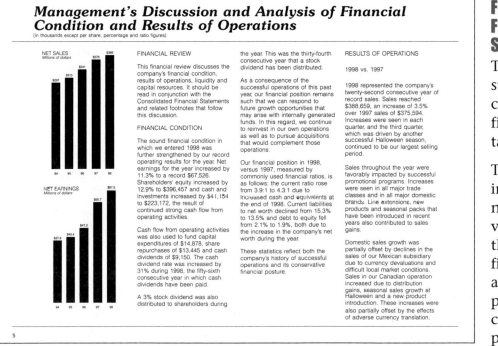

Management's Discussion and Analysis of Financial Condition and Results of Operations

(in thousands except per share, percentage and ratio figures)

FINANCIAL REVIEW

This financial review discusses the company's financial condition, results of operations, liquidity and capital resources. It should be read in conjunction with the Consolidated Financial Statements and related footnotes that follow this discussion.

FINANCIAL CONDITION

The sound financial condition in which we entered 1998 was further strengthened by our record operating results for the year. Net earnings for the year increased by 11.3% to a record $67,526. Shareholders' equity increased by 12.9% to $396,457 and cash and investments increased by $41,154 to $223,172, the result of continued strong cash flow from operating activities.

Cash flow from operating activities was also used to fund capital expenditures of $14,878, share repurchases of $13,445 and cash dividends of $9,150. The cash dividend rate was increased by 31% during 1998, the fifty-sixth consecutive year in which cash dividends have been paid.

A 3% stock dividend was also distributed to shareholders during the year. This was the thirty-fourth consecutive year that a stock dividend has been distributed.

As a consequence of the successful operations of this past year, our financial position remains such that we can respond to future growth opportunities that may arise with internally generated funds. In this regard, we continue to reinvest in our own operations as well as to pursue acquisitions that would complement those operations.

Our financial position in 1998, versus 1997, measured by commonly used financial ratios, is as follows: the current ratio rose from 3.9:1 to 4.3:1 due to increased cash and equivalents at the end of 1998. Current liabilities to net worth declined from 15.3% to 13.5% and debt to equity fell from 2.1% to 1.9%, both due to the increase in the company's net worth during the year.

These statistics reflect both the company's history of successful operations and its conservative financial posture.

RESULTS OF OPERATIONS

1998 vs. 1997

1998 represented the company's twenty-second consecutive year of record sales. Sales reached $388,659, an increase of 3.5% over 1997 sales of $375,594. Increases were seen in each quarter, and the third quarter, which was driven by another successful Halloween season, continued to be our largest selling period.

Sales throughout the year were favorably impacted by successful promotional programs. Increases were seen in all major trade classes and in all major domestic brands. Line extensions, new products and seasonal packs that have been introduced in recent years also contributed to sales gains.

Domestic sales growth was partially offset by declines in the sales of our Mexican subsidiary due to currency devaluations and difficult local market conditions. Sales in our Canadian operation increased due to distribution gains, seasonal sales growth at Halloween and a new product introduction. These increases were also partially offset by the effects of adverse currency translation.

NET SALES
Millions of dollars

$297 $313 $341 $376 $389
94 95 96 97 98

NET EARNINGS
Millions of dollars

$37.9 $40.4 $47.2 $60.7 $67.5
94 95 96 97 98

5

UNDERSTAND TERMS AND IDEAS

1. Get a copy of an annual report for one of the companies you are investigating. Read through the major sections. What does the report tell you about the company's products or services, its business segments, its most recent changes and accomplishments, its financial condition, its future plans, the quality of its management?

   _____

   _____

   _____

   _____

2. Take a ride on the Internet and find a company's web site. Look at the annual report online. How closely does it conform with the outline presented in this chapter?

   _____

   _____

   _____

   _____

3. What is the meaning of "independent auditors"?

   _____

   _____

   _____

   _____

4. What does the "business segments" section of the annual report tell you and why does this matter to you as an investor?

   _____

   _____

   _____

   _____

5. Why is a company's annual report so important?

   _____

   _____

   _____

   _____

Income Statement and Balance Sheet

In this lesson, you will examine two major accounting reports: the income statement and the balance sheet. As a beginning investor, you will want to understand the basic information and terminology used in these reports. You will also see what these two reports reveal about a company's operations and its financial health.

GOALS

■ **Distinguish between the time frames of an income statement and a balance sheet.**

■ **Identify terms found in income statements and balance sheets.**

INCOME STATEMENT

The **income statement** reports financial information over a specific period of time, indicating the financial progress of a business in earning a net income or a net loss. **Revenues** are the earnings of a business from business activities. **Expenses** are the amounts a business pays to operate the business and earn the revenue. The revenue earned and the expenses incurred to earn that revenue are reported in the same time period. The time period is often one year or one quarter.

The income statement shows a "flow" of sales and expenses over time. Sometimes the income statement is called the *profit and loss statement*, since it shows how much profit or loss was generated by the business.

Look at the income statement of XYZ Corporation on the next page. Find each item that is discussed below.

NET SALES OR REVENUES

The **top line** of the income statement is net sales or revenues. It represents total sales during the accounting time period minus products returned and allowances. The sales or revenues are from the primary businesses or core operations of the corporation. Often, companies set goals to meet a particular number for the top line.

Gross Sales – Returns and Allowances = Net Sales

COST OF GOODS SOLD (CGS)

Cost of goods sold (or cost of sales) refers to the operating expenses directly involved in producing the company's products/services: labor, raw materials, and other related expenses.

GROSS PROFIT

This is the company's profit after the cost of goods sold is subtracted from company revenues.

Revenues – CGS = Gross Profit

SELLING, GENERAL, AND ADMINISTRATIVE EXPENSES (SG&A)

These are operating expenses not directly associated with making the product. These expenses include sales commissions, legal expenses, accounting expenses, advertising, and executive compensation.

OPERATING INCOME (PROFIT)

Operating income or profit is what remains from revenues (net sales) after both CGS and SG&A expenses have been subtracted. Operating income is an important figure for evaluating the success or failure of the company's operations.

Net Sales – CGS – SG&A = Operating Income

OTHER INCOME (EXPENSES)

Other income, which is not derived from operations, includes interest and dividends on securities owned by the company, other investment-related activities, and gains from selling assets. Other expenses are non-operating expenses such as interest paid on the company's debts and miscellaneous expenses.

INCOME BEFORE TAXES

Income before taxes, also called pre-tax income or earnings, is simply operating income plus any non-operating income or minus any non-operating expenses before corporate income taxes.

XYZ CORPORATION (fictitious)

December 31, 1999
CONSOLIDATED STATEMENT OF INCOME
(In millions except for per share data)

	1997	1998	1999
Net Sales	$850.5	$947.3	$1,075.1
Cost of Goods Sold	620.1	710.3	820.5
Gross Profit	230.4	237.0	254.6
Selling, General, and Admin. Expenses	95.2	89.4	85.7
Operating Income	135.2	147.6	168.9
Other Income (Expenses)	3.0	(1.5)	2.6
Income Before Taxes	138.2	146.1	171.5
Income Taxes	55.3	58.4	68.6
Net Income	82.9	87.7	102.9
Earnings per Share	$1.02	$1.12	$1.31

NET INCOME

This is often called the **bottom line**, and is an important goal in companies. It is net income or net income after taxes.

Net Sales – Expenses and Taxes = Net Income

EARNINGS PER SHARE (EPS)

This is a very significant figure for investors, and one you will use in filling out the Stock Selection Guide (SSG). Earnings per share is the company's net income divided by the number of common stock shares outstanding.

Net Income ÷ Outstanding Common Shares = Earnings Per Share

The story of a business is told in numbers. The numbers tell the difference between a successful business and a failure, between an investment opportunity and an investment nightmare. The basic flow of a company's money can be tracked and combined to give an accurate picture of the company's history, current status, and possible future. For example, Small Family Business Corporation (fictional) is owned by only five family members. It recorded the following figures. From this information, find the net sales, the operating income, the net income and the earnings per share.

Gross Sales	$152,000
Returns and Allowances	$2,000
Cost of Goods Sold (CGS)	$75,000
Selling, General, and Administrative Expenses (SG&A)	$45,000
Other Expenses	$10,000
Taxes	$5,000
Outstanding Common Shares	5

Solution

Calculate the net sales.

Gross Sales − Returns and Allowances = Net Sales
$152,000 − $2,000 = $150,000

Calculate the operating income.

Net Sales − CGS − SG&A = Operating Income
$150,000 − $75,000 − $45,000 = $30,000

Calculate the net income.

Operating Income − Other Expenses − Taxes = Net Income
$30,000 − $10,000 − $5,000 = $15,000

Calculate the earnings per share.

Net Income ÷ Outstanding Common Shares = Earnings Per Share
$15,000 ÷ 5 = $3,000

BALANCE SHEET

The **balance sheet** shows what the company owns (assets) and what it owes (liabilities) plus the shareholders' equity at a particular time.

Assets = Liabilities + Stockholders' Equity

Assets are the items of value the company owns, including items such as cash, equipment, and inventory. **Liabilities** are debts that a business owes to others. **Stockholders' equity** is the difference between assets and liabilities, and consists of capital supplied by stockholders and net profits which were "plowed back" (or retained) into the company for future growth.

The name "balance sheet" refers to the fact that it shows both sides of a company's financial condition. As the accounting equation shows, on one side are the assets and on the other side are the liabilities and the shareholders' equity. These two sides should always be equal.

The balance sheet represents a single point in time while the income statement shows a flow of sales and expenses over time. The balance sheet is a "snapshot" of the company's financial condition taken on a certain date. That snapshot will look one way on March 31 and another way on December 31. The balance sheet on page 153 shows you the basic format of a balance sheet. You can evaluate a company's solvency, or ability to pay its debts, by studying the balance sheet.

ASSETS

Companies usually separate assets into *current assets* and *fixed assets*.

CURRENT ASSETS

Assets that could be converted into cash within a year are current assets. They are considered very "liquid," meaning they can be liquidated into cash relatively quickly. Current assets are short-term assets, as opposed to longer-term (fixed) assets. In the category of current assets, you will find cash, marketable securities, accounts receivable, inventories, and miscellaneous assets.

Marketable Securities Includes Treasury bills or notes and other securities with ready markets.

Accounts Receivable Dollars owed to the corporation by customers from the sale of goods or services.

Inventories Includes raw material inventories (to be used to manufacture goods) and finished product inventories (already manufactured and awaiting sale).

FIXED ASSETS

Fixed assets are longer-term assets such as land, buildings, and equipment. All of these assets, with the exception of land, are depreciable. Because these assets age, wear out, and decline in value, their original cost is "written off" or "depreciated" over a number of years. Remember that fixed assets are recorded on the corporate records at cost, and that, after a period of time, these figures do not necessarily reflect actual market values.

OTHER ASSETS

There are other assets that may show up on the balance sheet. Prepaid expenses or deferred charges are items the company has paid for in advance, such as a couple months' rent paid ahead of time and prepaid insurance. Some companies list "intangible" assets, assets you can't see or touch, such as patents or copyrights and goodwill. Goodwill is created when one company acquires another company and pays a sum of money over and above the value the company's tangible assets.

TOTAL ASSETS

The total assets are the sum of the current assets, the fixed assets and any other assets.

Total assets = Current Assets + Fixed Assets + Other Assets

LIABILITIES

Liabilities are amounts of money the corporation owes its creditors. Companies usually separate liabilities into *current liabilities* and *long-term liabilities*.

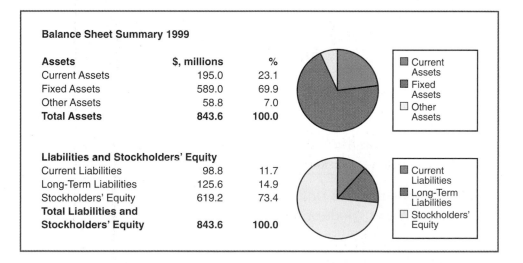

Balance Sheet Summary 1999

Assets	$, millions	%
Current Assets	195.0	23.1
Fixed Assets	589.0	69.9
Other Assets	58.8	7.0
Total Assets	**843.6**	**100.0**

Liabilities and Stockholders' Equity	$, millions	%
Current Liabilities	98.8	11.7
Long-Term Liabilities	125.6	14.9
Stockholders' Equity	619.2	73.4
Total Liabilities and Stockholders' Equity	**843.6**	**100.0**

ZZZ CORPORATION (fictitious)

December 31, 1999
CONSOLIDATED BALANCE SHEET
(In millions)

ASSETS	1998	1999
Current Assets		
Cash	$ 1.8	$ 2.0
Marketable Securities	1.0	1.2
Accounts Receivable	82.0	83.0
Inventories	95.6	107.2
Other	1.4	1.6
Total Current Assets	$181.8	$195.0
Fixed Assets		
Buildings	300.7	320.1
Machinery and Equipment	550.2	580.1
Less Accumulated Depreciation	(340.2)	(350.4)
Land	40.0	40.0
Total Fixed Assets	$550.7	$589.8
Other Assets	55.2	58.8
Total Assets	**$787.7**	**$843.6**
LIABILITIES AND STOCKHOLDERS' EQUITY		
Current Liabilities		
Accounts Payable	$ 78.0	$85.0
Current Maturities on Long-term Debt	4.0	4.3
Income Taxes Payable	8.1	9.5
Total Current Liabilities	$ 90.1	$ 98.8
Long-Term Liabilities		
Long-term Debt	$120.5	$125.6
Stockholders' Equity		
Common Stock	81.2	81.8
Retained Earnings	495.9	537.4
Total Stockholders' Equity	$577.1	$619.2
Total Liabilities and Stockholder's Equity	**$787.7**	**$843.6**

CURRENT LIABILITIES

Current liabilities include debts or claims due within one year. The next 12 months' payments on a long-term debt are also included as current liabilities. Current liabilities include accounts payable, notes payable (current portion), accrued expenses, income taxes payable, and other liabilities.

Accounts Payable Bills the company must pay. These include materials, supplies, and services the company has contracted for and usually pays for within 30 days.

Notes Payable The amount due on notes (promissory notes or promises to pay) within the next 12 months.

Accrued Expenses Expenses already incurred, but not yet paid. For example, at the end of an accounting period (i.e. a month), the company may owe money to its employees for days worked, but not yet paid. In other words, the accounting date does not coincide with the end of a pay period. Accrued expenses include wages and salaries, interest on debt, and miscellaneous debt.

Income Taxes Payable Taxes due on corporate income, but not yet paid.

LONG-TERM LIABILITIES

This section of the balance sheet summarizes all long-term liabilities, or debts due after one year. You will see such items as notes payable, bonds (also called debentures), and mortgages.

STOCKHOLDERS' EQUITY

The stockholders' equity section represents the amount of money invested by equity owners (both common stock and preferred stockholders) and the amount of net income that was retained in the business. The "retained earnings" are profits "plowed back" into the corporation to invest in future growth. Other terms you will hear used interchangeably with stockholders' equity are *book value* and *net worth*.

TOTAL LIABILITIES AND STOCKHOLDERS' EQUITY

This is the sum of the total current liabilities, long-term liabilities, and the stockholders' equity.

A company's income statement and balance sheet measure its financial health. The income statement has key data such as sales (revenues) and earnings (operating, pre-tax, and net) for the latest fiscal year. The balance sheet reports the company's assets and liabilities.

These accounting reports are tools that help you understand a company's operations and performance. Don't be afraid of the accounting terms. With a little experience, you will feel more comfortable with the language of accounting.

UNDERSTAND TERMS AND IDEAS

1. Explain why a balance sheet is a "snapshot or photo" of a company.

   _____

   _____

2. What are the key terms found on the income statement?

   _____

   _____

   _____

3. If a company is said to have a "negative net worth," what does this mean? What would cause such a situation?

   _____

   _____

4. List six major terms found on a balance sheet and explain each.

   _____

   _____

   _____

   _____

   _____

5. Using the annual report you obtained from a company of interest to you, list the following:

   Total assets _____

   Total liabilities _____

   Stockholders' Equity _____

   Revenues _____

   Pre-tax profits _____

   Net Income _____

   Earnings per share _____

SUMMARY

LESSON 5.1 INVESTMENT PRINCIPLES
The NAIC has developed a long-term approach to investing. The goal is to double the value of your investments every five years.

LESSON 5.2 SEARCH FOR COMPANIES TO BUY
Investing wisely requires information. You must evaluate a potential investment before selecting it for your portfolio.

LESSON 5.3 THE ANNUAL REPORT
A company's annual report is the primary source of financial information about the corporation.

LESSON 5.4 INCOME STATEMENT AND BALANCE SHEET
The income statement and balance sheet reveal much to investors about a company's operations and financial health.

REVIEW INVESTING TERMS

Write the letter of the term that matches each definition. Some terms may not be used.

1. ___i___ debts that a business owes to others

2. ___e___ invest in different companies of various sizes from a variety of industries to reduce the risk of your overall portfolio

3. ___h___ reports financial information over a specific period of time, indicating the financial progress of a business in earning a net income or a net loss

4. ___j___ the earnings of a business from business activities

5. ___b___ items of value the company owns, including items such as cash, equipment, and inventory

6. ___a___ yearly record summarizing the financial condition of a corporation that must be distributed to shareholders

7. ___f___ investing roughly equal amounts of money at regular intervals

a. annual report
b. assets
c. balance sheet
d. bottom line
e. diversification
f. dollar cost averaging
g. expenses
h. income statement
i. liabilities
j. revenue
k. stockholders' equity
l. top line

UNDERSTAND TERMS AND IDEAS

8. List the NAIC's four basic investment principles.

Invest in a regular basis on a long period of time
Reinvest all earnings
Invest in good quality growth companies
Diversify your portfolio

9. Why is an annual report similar to a report card for a company? List the 12 sections you will find in most annual reports.

Letter of investors   Operation overview
Balance sheet   financial statement
EPS   " highlits
current Asset

10. Describe the two major parts of the financial statement section.

Income statement
Balance sheet

11. Explain the difference between a current asset and a fixed asset. Give examples of both.

Inventory, stocks / equipment

Chapter 5 REVIEW

SHARPEN YOUR RESEARCH SKILLS

12. What toy is currently the most popular? Look up the manufacturer on the Internet or at the library. Does it manufacture other items? Examine the company's annual report. Does this company look like a good investment? Why or why not?

_____

_____

_____

13. Think of a sit-down restaurant chain (not fast food) that has recently opened in your area. Look at the annual report for the company. Is this company a good investment? Why or why not?

_____

_____

_____

THINK CRITICALLY

14. Your friend Tim describes his current stock portfolio. He lists seven stocks, all in the area of computer and Internet technology. The value of his portfolio has risen 20% in the last 4 weeks. What, if any, advice would you give him?

_____

_____

_____

_____

15. Your friend Susanne has been saving for months. She wants to have $2,500 to invest in the stock market at one time. How would you advise her?

_____

_____

_____

_____

PROSPECTIVE PORTFOLIO PROJECT

In this chapter, you learned to use a company's annual report to evaluate the company as a potential investment. Use the annual reports to analyze your current portfolio. Write comments in each column for every stock in your portfolio. Some companies may move up in your portfolio. Others may be eliminated. You also learned about the NAIC's principle of diversification. Do you think that your portfolio is diversified?

Company	Financial Highlights	Letter to Shareholders	Operational Overview	Financial Statements	Management's Analysis	5-Year Financial Statement Summary

Chapter 6

PLOTTING THE PAST

LESSON 6.1

STOCK SELECTION GUIDE OVERVIEW

LESSON 6.2

PLOT THE DATA

LESSON 6.3

TREND LINES AND GROWTH RATES

INDUSTRY INDICATORS

FINANCE

American Express Company

Founded in 1850

By the early 1900s, American Express had emerged as a credit and tourist service firm, providing credit and access to funds for business and pleasure travelers alike. Since that time, American Express has widened its travel, financial, and network service offerings, allowing it to become the world leader not only in charge and credit cards, but also in Traveler's Cheques, financial planning, and international banking.

Probably best known for its credit card services, American Express is the largest issuer of credit cards in the world and maintains offices in over 150 countries. Its Travel Related Services (TRS) division includes travel agencies worldwide and specializes in organized travel packages. The income of the TRS exceeded $1 billion in 1998. Other divisions of American Express include its Financial Advisors, a global division helping clients meet their financial objectives; and American Express Bank, which provides commercial banking services in other countries and Traveler's Cheques globally.

American Express has many plans for further expansion. The number of financial institutions with the ability to issue American Express cards increases as the company establishes new partnerships. By investing in online firms, American Express electronic commerce capabilities will grow, and it will be able to use the Internet as a venue for product and service distribution. Internationally, American Express expands by continually offering new proprietary card products to its customers worldwide. By maintaining a global presence, American Express has the ability to grow in importance both in the U.S. and internationally, making it a company of worldwide significance.

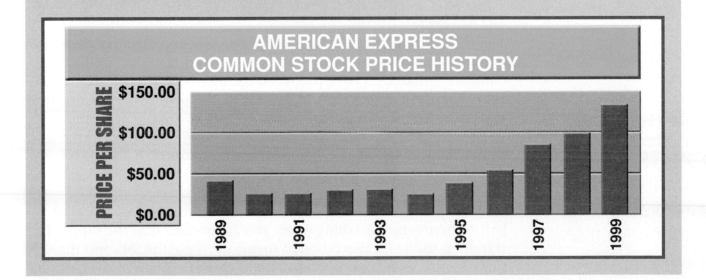

AMERICAN EXPRESS COMMON STOCK PRICE HISTORY

Stock Selection Guide Overview

You do not rely simply on outward appearance to judge a person's health. You also want to know what the doctor says based on a whole battery of tests and diagnostic procedures. The Stock Selection Guide (SSG), which you will begin to use in this lesson, will help you extract hard data on a company and examine it in a systematic way so that you can do your own diagnosis of that company and its prospects for future growth.

GOALS

- **State the two main objectives of the Stock Selection Guide.**

- **Explain the reasoning behind the SSG.**

- **Describe the major sections of the SSG.**

WHAT IS THE STOCK SELECTION GUIDE?

The Stock Selection Guide (SSG) was created in the early 1950's, soon after the founding of the NAIC. Since that date, the SSG has been shown to be a powerful tool for helping investors make informed stock investment decisions. The SSG approach is systematic. It walks you through the process of evaluating companies from sales, earnings, and profit margin trends to the use of price/earnings ratios. The SSG was not designed for short-term trading action or for highly cyclical stocks. It was designed primarily for growth stocks and long-term investors.

OBJECTIVES

The Stock Selection Guide has two clear objectives:

1. to help you find companies with a record of consistent growth
2. to help you determine a reasonable price to pay for the stock of such a company

THE REASONING BEHIND THE SSG

The NAIC knows that a past record of revenue and earnings growth does not guarantee future growth, but it is a good indicator. If a company's managers have produced consistent growth for five to ten years, there is a strong probability that such growth will continue into the future. In forecasting future stock prices, the SSG relies on past relationships between stock prices and earnings (P/E ratio), and it assumes that similar relationships will continue into the future.

USE JUDGEMENT

Despite the SSG's usefulness, it should not be considered a "crystal ball." There is no sure thing when you are peering into the future. It is quite possible for two different investors to use the SSG and the same historical data on a company and come to different conclusions about that company and its stock. The stock market has thousands of investors—buyers and sellers—and many different expectations about the future. This is part of what makes the stock market work. Remember that the SSG is an effective tool for sharpening the stock selection process, but you must learn its strengths and limitations. You must add your own judgment.

Additional information on the SSG may be found in NAIC's Official Guide, *Starting And Running A Profitable Investment Club*, by Thomas E. O'Hara and Kenneth S. Janke, Sr.

HOW IS THE SSG ORGANIZED?

The Stock Selection Guide and Report contains four pages to be filled out by the potential investor.

Page one

- General information on the company (at top of the page)
- Recent quarterly sales and earning figures (in box)
- Section 1: Visual Analysis—graph for charting sales, earnings per share, and price

Page two

- Section 2: Evaluating Management—gives trends in two key financial ratios
- Section 3: Price-Earnings History—to help you calculate the price to earnings ratio
- Section 4: Evaluating Risk and Reward—critical to determining whether you should buy a particular stock
- Section 5: 5-Year Potential—for estimating the potential 5-year return in the future

Pages three and four

- Contain eight questions to help you determine whether a stock is an appropriate purchase based on your goals

USE ONLY ONE SOURCE

When you are transferring data to the SSG, you should rely on only one investment information source, and should not mix sources such as *Value Line* and *Standard & Poor's*. There are small differences in how they calculate certain figures.

NOT A RECOMMENDATION

For illustration purposes, we shall use information on a real company that produces candy, Tootsie Roll Industries, Inc. This company is being used to illustrate how to complete the Stock Selection Guide and we are not making a recommendation to purchase stock in this company.

Market analysts constantly rate stocks. They advise investors to buy, sell, or hold. Sometimes they even make it sound urgent by using terms like "strong buy." If all the analysts agreed and the stock market followed their ratings, investing would be easy. Unfortunately, even though analysts look at the same information, they rarely agree. Look at ratings by different analysts for the same stock. Enter key words or phrases such as *stock rating* or *market analyst*.

GENERAL INFORMATION

First complete the general information about the company you are evaluating. The information is numbered in red on the Tootsie Roll Value Line report to correspond to the numbers on the SSG.

Enter the date you prepared the report in case you want to compare it with a new study of the same stock. Be sure to note the source of your data. You may use a corporate annual report, *Value Line*, *Standard & Poor's*, or a source downloaded from an online computer service. For consistency purposes, your data should come from one source only.

PERCENT INSIDERS

The box entitled "% Insiders" refers to the percentage of common stock owned by officers and directors of the company. This figure is found in Value Line in the paragraph in the middle of the page entitled "BUSINESS." It is a good sign when insiders own shares because they are risking some of their own money on the future of the company.

PERCENT INSTITUTION

The amount of stock held by institutional investors (mutual funds, banks, pension funds, etc.) is found in Value Line under "Institutional Decisions." For Tootsie Roll as of 1Q1999 (1st quarter 1999), institutions held 10,741,000 of the 49,293,098 shares outstanding. Find the percentage: 10,741,000 ÷ 49,293,098 = 0.218 = 21.8%. So institutions hold 21.8% of the outstanding shares.

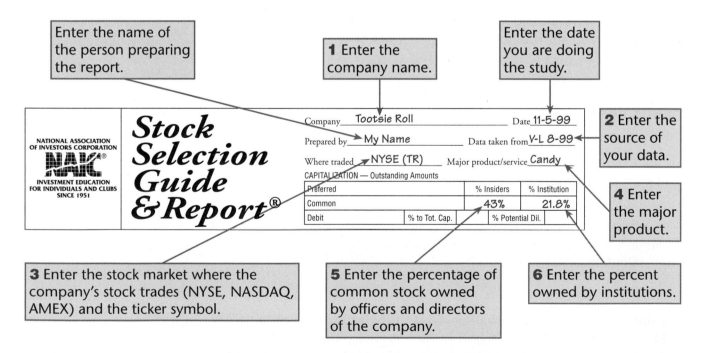

TOOTSIE ROLL NYSE-TR

RECENT PRICE	**34**	P/E RATIO	**21.9**	(Trailing: 24.1 Median: 19.0)	RELATIVE P/E RATIO	**1.30**	DIV'D YLD	**0.7%**	VALUE LINE	**1502**

TIMELINESS	**4**	Lowered 8/6/99
SAFETY	**1**	Raised 5/14/99
TECHNICAL	**3**	Lowered 3/12/99
BETA	.65	(1.00 = Market)

High/Low: 6.4/4.8 · 7.2/4.5 · 9.6/5.9 · 14.8/7.0 · 17.2/12.1 · 17.5/13.5 · 16.2/11.6 · 18.2/12.9 · 18.5/15.5 · 30.8/17.0 · 46.5/27.4 · 46.9/33.4

Target Price Range 2002 | 2003 | 2004

LEGENDS
— 16.0 x "Cash Flow" p sh
···· Relative Price Strength
3-for-2 split 7/86
2-for-1 split 5/87
2-for-1 split 7/95
2-for-1 split 7/98
Options: No
Shaded area indicates recession

2002-04 PROJECTIONS

	Price	Gain	Ann'l Total Return
High	50	(+45%)	10%
Low	40	(+20%)	4%

Insider Decisions

	S	O	N	D	J	F	M	A	M
to Buy	0	0	0	0	0	0	0	0	1
Options	0	0	0	0	0	0	0	0	0
to Sell	0	0	0	0	0	0	0	0	0

Institutional Decisions

	3Q1998	4Q1998	1Q1999
to Buy	40	37	35
to Sell	50	38	65
Hld's(000)	10162	11087	10741

Percent shares traded: 4.5 / 3.0 / 1.5

	1983	1984	1985	1986	1987	1988	1989	1990	1991	1992	1993	1994	1995	1996	1997	1998	1999	2000	© VALUE LINE PUB., INC.	02-04
Sales per sh A	1.52	1.83	2.12	2.21	2.28	2.55	3.56	3.86	4.13	4.88	5.16	5.90	6.22	6.78	7.57	7.88	8.40	8.55		11.10
"Cash Flow" per sh	.14	.20	.25	.30	.34	.40	.50	.56	.63	.76	.88	1.02	1.02	1.18	1.48	1.63	1.80	1.95		2.50
Earnings per sh A B	.11	.17	.22	.25	.29	.33	.40	.45	.53	.64	.70	.75	.80	.94	1.22	1.37	1.55	1.65		2.20
Div'ds Decl'd per sh C	.02	.02	.03	.03	.04	.04	.04	.04	.05	.06	.08	.09	.12	.14	.16	.19	.24	.28		.43
Cap'l Spending per sh	.03	.06	.13	.08	.05	.09	.06	.10	.08	.25	.56	.16	.09	.19	.17	.30	.30	.30		.30
Book Value per sh D	.74	.88	1.06	1.28	1.53	1.82	2.18	2.58	3.04	3.61	4.22	4.78	5.41	6.22	7.07	8.04	9.00	10.05		13.95
Common Shs Outst'g E	51.34	50.88	50.41	50.38	50.37	50.36	50.35	50.34	50.33	50.33	50.31	50.30	50.29	50.27	49.65	49.30	48.80	48.30		46.80
Avg Ann'l P/E Ratio	7.8	7.3	11.4	14.5	17.7	16.6	14.4	16.3	19.9	23.5	22.1	18.4	19.1	17.7	19.1	26.6	Bold figures are			20.0
Relative P/E Ratio	.66	.68	.93	.98	1.18	1.38	1.09	1.21	1.27	1.43	1.31	1.21	1.28	1.11	1.10	1.41	Value Line estimates			1.15
Avg Ann'l Div'd Yield	2.4%	1.8%	1.1%	.9%	.8%	.7%	.7%	.6%	.5%	.4%	.5%	.6%	.7%	.8%	.7%	.7%				1.0%
Sales ($mill) A							179.3	194.3	207.9	245.4	259.6	296.9	312.7	340.9	375.6	388.7	410	435		520
Operating Margin							21.1%	21.2%	22.3%	22.3%	24.0%	24.6%	24.0%	25.3%	27.4%	29.4%	29.5%	30.0%		31.0%
Depreciation ($mill)							5.1	5.7	5.2	6.1	8.8	13.2	10.8	12.1	12.8	12.8	12.0	13.0		15.0
Net Profit ($mill)							20.2	22.6	26.5	32.0	35.4	37.9	40.4	47.2	60.7	67.5	75.0	80.0		105.0
Income Tax Rate							39.1%	39.2%	39.9%	38.3%	38.6%	38.0%	37.0%	37.1%	36.4%	36.3%	35.0%	35.0%		35.0%
Net Profit Margin							11.3%	11.6%	12.8%	13.1%	13.7%	12.8%	12.9%	13.8%	16.2%	17.4%	18.5%	18.5%		20.0%
Working Cap'l ($mill)							33.5	55.3	80.5	107.2	61.0	92.6	109.7	153.3	153.4	175.1	215	260		425
Long-Term Debt ($mill)							--	--	--	7.5	27.5	27.5	7.5	7.5	7.5	7.5	7.5	7.5		7.5
Shr. Equity ($mill)							109.6	129.6	152.8	181.7	212.3	240.5	272.2	312.9	351.2	396.5	440	485		655
Return on Total Cap'l							18.4%	17.4%	17.4%	16.9%	14.8%	14.3%	14.6%	14.8%	17.0%	16.8%	17.0%	16.5%		16.0%
Return on Shr. Equity							18.4%	17.4%	17.4%	17.6%	16.7%	15.8%	14.8%	15.1%	17.3%	17.0%	17.0%	16.5%		16.0%
Retained to Com Eq							16.5%	15.6%	15.7%	16.0%	15.0%	13.9%	12.9%	13.1%	15.2%	14.7%	14.5%	14.0%		12.0%
All Div'ds to Net Prof							11%	10%	9%	9%	10%	12%	13%	13%	12%	14%	16%	17%		22%

CAPITAL STRUCTURE as of 4/3/99

Total Debt $7.5 mill. — Due in 5 Yrs Nil
LT Debt $7.5 mill. — LT Interest $.5 mill.
Capitalized leases $7.5 mill.

(2% of Cap'l)

Leases, Uncapitalized None
Pension Liability None

Pfd Stock None
Common Stock 49,293,098 shs.
Includes 15,846,841 Class B shs. (10 votes a sh.)
As of 4/3/99 — (98% of Cap'l)

MARKET CAP: $1.7 billion (Mid Cap)

CURRENT POSITION ($MILL.)

	1997	1998	4/3/99
Cash Assets	142.3	163.9	150.8
Receivables	23.3	22.4	26.3
Inventory (LIFO)	36.7	36.5	44.4
Other	4.7	5.7	8.7
Current Assets	207.0	228.5	230.2
Accts Payable	11.6	12.5	12.7
Debt Due	--	--	--
Other	42.0	40.9	44.1
Current Liab.	53.6	53.4	56.8

ANNUAL RATES

of change (per sh)	Past 10 Yrs.	Past 5 Yrs.	Est'd '96-'98 to '02-'04
Sales	12.0%	9.5%	8.5%
"Cash Flow"	15.5%	13.5%	10.0%
Earnings	15.0%	13.5%	11.0%
Dividends	15.5%	20.5%	18.0%
Book Value	16.5%	14.5%	12.0%

QUARTERLY SALES ($ mill.) A

Calendar	Mar.31	Jun.30	Sep.30	Dec.31	Full Year
1996	63.3	72.5	128.6	76.5	340.9
1997	66.3	82.3	140.6	86.4	375.6
1998	69.7	86.0	144.2	88.8	388.7
1999	74.2	88.3	155	92.5	410
2000	80.0	90.0	170	95.0	435

EARNINGS PER SHARE A B

Calendar	Mar.31	Jun.30	Sep.30	Dec.31	Full Year
1996	.16	.19	.38	.21	.94
1997	.19	.25	.50	.28	1.22
1998	.23	.28	.55	.31	1.37
1999	.25	.30	.65	.35	1.55
2000	.25	.32	.70	.38	1.65

GROSS QUARTERLY DIV'DS PAID C

Calendar	Mar.31	Jun.30	Sep.30	Dec.31	Full Year
1995	.025	.03	.03	.03	.12
1996	.03	.035	.035	.035	.14
1997	.035	.04	.04	.04	.16
1998	.04	.05	.05	.05	.19
1999	.05	.05	.06		

BUSINESS: Tootsie Roll Industries, Inc. produces candy. Products include: Tootsie Roll, Tootsie Pop, Tootsie Bubble Pop, Tootsie Pop Drops, Tootsie Roll Flavor Rolls, and Mason Dots. Acquired Warner-Lambert's former chocolate/caramel brands (Junior Mints, Sugar Daddy, Sugar Babies, Charleston Chew, and Pom Poms) 10/93; Charms Co. (Charms, Blow Pops), 9/88; and Cella's Confections (chocolate covered cherries), 7/85. Has four plants in U.S.; one in Mexico. Int'l ops. (Mexico and Canada): 8% of '98 sales, 6% of earnings. Has about 1,750 employees. M.J. and E.R. Gordon control 43% of voting power; L.R. Weiner, 12% (4/99 Proxy). Chairman & C.E.O.: M.J. Gordon. Pres. & C.O.O.: E.R. Gordon. Inc.: VA. Add.: 7401 S. Cicero Ave., Chicago, IL 60629. Tel.: 773-838-3400.

Tootsie Roll continues to hoard its cash while it looks for acquisitions. With free cash flow likely to reach $70 million this year, and cash & marketable securities totaling $151 million ($3.05 a share), management is actively seeking acquisitions. But the company continues to believe that candy companies are commanding excessive prices. Thus, Tootsie Roll will likely wait for prices to become "more reasonable". The company's most recent purchase (in 1993) demonstrates management's disciplined approach: Cambridge Brands (the company's first acquisition since 1988) was purchased for $81.3 million and generated $36.6 million in earnings the same year (equating to a 2.2 Price/Earnings multiple). Because potential deal terms are unknown, our estimates do not reflect any acquisitions.

Continued product introductions and international expansion will keep capital spending at elevated levels. Excluding years with acquisitions or unusual expenditures, capital spending has historically run between $5 million and $10 million a year. Going forward, though, we project $15 million a year to support regular capital spending, international expansion in Australia and the Philippines, and new product introductions.

Stock dividends and share repurchases will likely continue. Each April, Tootsie Roll issues a 3% stock dividend along with an increase in its quarterly dividend payout. We expect both plans to continue. Meanwhile, share repurchases should somewhat offset increases in shares outstanding. The company's future repurchases are limited by the decreasing availability of large blocks of shares. In the short term, average daily volume of 30,000 shares should support a moderate repurchase plan approaching 1.5 million shares a year. However, we have modeled a more conservative 500 thousand share-a-year plan, which reflects the company's recent share repurchase trend.

Despite their recent decline, shares of Tootsie Roll do not represent a compelling value. At current levels, Tootsie Roll shares discount the company's future growth. These untimely shares are expected to underperform the market over the coming 3 to 5 years.
David H. Kurzman — August 13, 1999

% TOT. RETURN 7/99

	THIS STOCK	VL ARITH. INDEX
1 yr.	-14.4	15.0
3 yr.	118.7	73.5
5 yr.	165.4	128.5

(A) Fiscal year ends Dec. 31. First three quarters end on Sat. closest to end of month. (B) Based on average shares through 1996; diluted thereafter. Next earnings report due about Oct. 27. (C) Next dividend declared about Sept. 25. Next ex date about Oct. 1. Dividends paid about Jan. 9, Apr. 9, July 9, and Oct. 9. 3% stock div'd paid each year about Apr. 21, since 1966. (D) Includes intangibles. In '98: $87.8 million, $1.84/share. (E) In millions, adjusted for stock splits and dividends.

Company's Financial Strength	A+
Stock's Price Stability	95
Price Growth Persistence	65
Earnings Predictability	95

To subscribe call 1-800-833-0046.

CAPITALIZATION AND DEBT

The term **capitalization** means how the corporation is financed, through common stock, preferred stock, long-term debt, or a combination of them. There are spaces for both common stock and preferred stock (if any). This information is found Capital Structure block on the middle left side.

> **CAPITAL STRUCTURE as of 4/3/99**
> **Total Debt** $7.5 mill.   **Due in 5 Yrs** Nil
> **LT Debt** $7.5 mill.   **LT Interest** $.5 mill.
> Capitalized leases $7.5 mill.
> (2% of Cap'l)
>
> **Leases, Uncapitalized** None
> **Pension Liability** None
>
> **Pfd Stock** None
> **Common Stock** 49,293,098 shs.
> Includes 15,846,841 Class B shs. (10 votes a sh.)
> **As of 4/3/99**   (98% of Cap'l)
>
> **MARKET CAP: $1.7 billion (Mid Cap)**

"Debt" can mean either total debt or long-term debt. Value Line reports total debt amounts, including long-term debt. S&P reports current liabilities and long-term debt on separate lines. The sum of these two equals total debt.

Company debt adds risk to a company's earnings performance because the interest payments on that debt must be paid whether a company has a good year or not. More meaningful than the amount of debt in dollars is the debt percentage, which is the ratio of debt to total capitalization. At Tootsie Roll, the 1998 long-term debt as a percentage of total capitalization was 2%, a relatively low number.

Although there are exceptions, the debt should generally not be more than 33% (1/3) of capitalization. Some industries, such as utilities, will always have a larger debt. To determine if a larger debt is acceptable, you should check the historical debt of that company and compare it with the debt of other companies in the same industry.

Dilution means reducing the value of the shares held by existing shareholders by issuing additional shares. In other words, net earnings are divided by more shares outstanding. Dilution is a negative for existing shareholders. Any potential dilution would be noted in the Capital Structure box or in the footnotes.

7 Enter the amount of preferred shares.

8 Enter the amount of common shares, in millions.

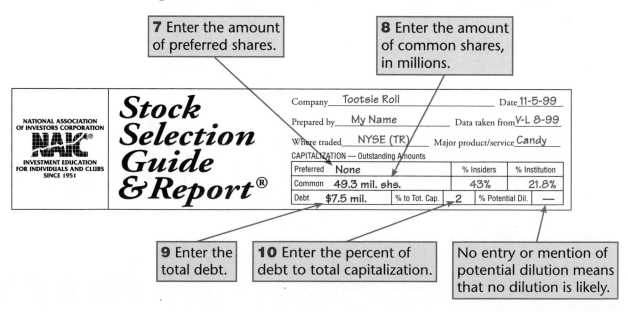

9 Enter the total debt.

10 Enter the percent of debt to total capitalization.

No entry or mention of potential dilution means that no dilution is likely.

RECENT QUARTERLY FIGURES

"Wall Street" (that is, the institutional investor) is obsessed with quarterly data and buys and sells based on quarterly expectations. This stimulates short-term fluctuations in the stock prices and creates buying opportunities. Quarterly financial information is available when the company releases this information, and it can be found in the financial press (*The Wall Street Journal*, etc.) and on the Internet. Some companies will even send this information to your email address, if you request it.

Cal-endar	QUARTERLY SALES ($ mill.) A				Full Year
	Mar.31	Jun.30	Sep.30	Dec.31	
1996	63.3	72.5	128.6	76.5	340.9
1997	66.3	82.3	140.6	86.4	375.6
1998	69.7	86.0	144.2	88.8	388.7
1999	74.2	88.3	*155*	*92.5*	*410*
2000	*80.0*	*90.0*	*170*	*95.0*	*435*

Cal-endar	EARNINGS PER SHARE A B				Full Year
	Mar.31	Jun.30	Sep.30	Dec.31	
1996	.16	.19	.38	.21	.94
1997	.19	.25	.50	.28	1.22
1998	.23	.28	.55	.31	1.37
1999	.25	.30	*.65*	*.35*	*1.55*
2000	*.25*	*.32*	*.70*	*.38*	*1.65*

Cal-endar	GROSS QUARTERLY DIV'DS PAID C				Full Year
	Mar.31	Jun.30	Sep.30	Dec.31	
1995	.025	.03	.03	.03	.12
1996	.03	.035	.035	.035	.14
1997	.035	.04	.04	.04	.16
1998	.04	.05	.05	.05	.19
1999	.05	.05	.06		

The Recent Quarterly Figures section on page 1 of the SSG is used to record the latest quarterly revenues and earnings per share figures, compared to the same quarter one year ago. This gives you the latest performance data and keeps you up to date on the company's current environment. It also alerts you to a possible change in direction. You will find the quarterly sales and earnings per share data on the lower left side of the Value Line report.

First, record the date of the most recent quarterly data. The numbers in italics on Value Line are projected data, so be sure to use the latest real data. For Tootsie Roll the latest real data is for June 30, 1999, Quarter 2. To calculate percentage change:

$$\frac{\text{Latest quarter} - \text{Year ago quarter}}{\text{Year ago quarter}} \times 100 = \text{Percent change}$$

11 Enter date of most recent data.

12 Enter quarterly sales data.

2nd qtr. RECENT QUARTERLY FIGURES
6-30-99

	SALES	EARNINGS PER SHARE
Latest Quarter	88.3	0.30
Year Ago Quarter	86.0	0.28
Percentage Change	2.7%	7%

See Chapter 8, 9, and 10 of the NAIC Official Guide for complete instructions. Use this Guide as working section NAIC Stock Selection Guide & Report.

13 Enter earnings per share.

$$\frac{88.3 - 86.0}{86.0} = 0.027 = 2.7\%$$

$$\frac{0.30 - 0.28}{0.28} = 0.07 = 7\%$$

First-time investors are often confused about the factors needed to select appropriately priced common stocks for their portfolio. The Stock Selection Guide offers a systematic approach to finding and selecting good growth companies at reasonable prices.

UNDERSTAND TERMS AND IDEAS

1. List the five major sections of the SSG.

   _____

   _____

   _____

   _____

2. On the blank SSG provided in Appendix E, fill in the top right corner with the necessary information for Home Depot using the Value Line report in Appendix D.

   _____

   _____

   _____

3. Fill in the "Recent Quarterly Results" box for Home Depot.

   _____

   _____

4. Is it permissible to mix data from different investment sources (i.e. Value Line and S&P) when completing the SSG?

   _____

   _____

   _____

5. The SSG was designed primarily for investing long term in growth-oriented stocks. (True or False) Why or why not?

   _____

   _____

6. The SSG will aid an investor who is trying to determine short-term trading ranges of a stock. (True or False) Why or why not?

   _____

   _____

7. What are the major reasons for completing the SSG?

   _____

   _____

   _____

   _____

Plot The Data

Growth rates are the primary drivers behind common stock prices. The primary function of the SSG graph is to estimate historical and future growth rates for revenues and earnings per share. You will quickly see that this complicated-looking graph is easy to use as you plot data. It will become one of your principal investment tools.

THE SSG GRAPH

You are probably scratching your head right now, and asking, "What in the world is this crazy graph with all the lines?" You will use the graph to plot a company's sales (revenues), earnings per share, and common stock prices for the past ten years. The Stock Selection Guide graph is on semi-logarithmic graph paper (also called semi-log paper or a ratio chart). The beauty of semi-log paper is that it allows you to record dollar amounts, and to plot and study them as percentages of change over a period of time. This means you can compare the rate of change of companies, even if they are different sizes.

You will plot three key kinds of corporate data.

1. Total sales (revenues)
2. Earnings per share
3. High and low annual common stock prices for the past ten years

Once plotted, these data are used to estimate the historical growth rates of the revenues and earnings per share. The historical growth rates, along with the recent quarterly growth rates, will help you project future growth rates for the next five years.

WHY DO YOU CHART DATA ON THE SSG GRAPH?

Sales and earnings are plotted in order to find the average rate (percentage) of growth over the past ten years. This will help you make a reasonable growth projection for the next five years. Revenue and earnings have a significant influence on common stock prices. So, you will carry the projected earnings figures over to page 2 of the SSG, and use them to help you forecast the high price of the company's stock in the next five years. Growth is the principal determinant of stock price increases. Where consistent growth is present, an increase in price over time is almost certain to follow.

GOALS

- Discuss why you plot sales, earnings, and price data on the SSG graph.

- Explain sales and EPS trends.

- Visualize a company's performance.

Also plotted on the graph are the high and low prices of the company's common stock for each year. You can see how well the company's stock has done in the past 10 years. If it has done well, it will probably continue to do so in the next five years.

EVALUATE THE FUTURE

You chart the past because you want to evaluate the possible future growth of the company. You are not buying the past. You are buying the future. It just so happens that looking back is often one of the best ways of looking ahead. Of course, there are other factors to weigh—the future of the industry the company is in, the competition in that industry, and the condition of the economy as a whole. Studying the past is only one way of sizing up the future. At one time, buggy whips and ice boxes were great industries and they probably had excellent track records, but something came along and changed everything.

VISUAL ANALYSIS OF SALES, EARNINGS, AND PRICES

When the SSG graph is filled in, you will have a picture of a company's sales, earnings per share, and stock price trends—and a good overview of management's accomplishments. If you have less than 10 years' data to work with, you should give more attention to the present state of the business cycle. Be more conservative. At least a five-year history is needed to produce a true evaluation on the SSG and a representative picture of management's accomplishments.

HOW TO READ THE GRAPH

On the graph, the vertical lines represent years. The horizontal lines represent dollar amounts. The shrinking spaces between numbers in the left margin reflect that, as the numbers increase, it takes a greater numerical change to produce the same percentage of change. For example: If you start with a dollar, it only takes a dollar to double your money. But if your start with ten dollars, you will need 10 dollars to produce the same percentage of gain!

VERTICAL SCALE (Horizontal lines)	HORIZONTAL SCALE (Vertical lines)
Represents dollar amounts.	Represents years.
When ten lines are between numbers, the value of each line is one.	The first ten years show historical data (the bold vertical line and the nine lines to the left of it).
When five lines are between numbers, value of each line is two.	Last five years (to the right of the bold vertical line) project future growth.
Cycles on graph: 1-10, 10-100, 100-200	

NUMBER THE YEARS

Corporations base their financial data on a fiscal year, which often does not correspond to a calendar year. The fiscal year may run, for example, from July 1 to June 30. When deciding which years to use, note when the fiscal year ends. You can find this in the quarterly information. This will help you determine the most recent year to plot at the bold vertical line. For Tootsie Roll, the fiscal year ends Dec. 31.

If the company has already issued three quarterly reports in the current year, add the estimated fourth quarter to complete the year. Recent information is important. If only one quarterly report is out for the current year, use the last fully reported year. It may also be best to use the last given year if two quarterly reports are out, but note if increases are expected in the next two quarters. For Tootsie Roll, use 1998.

PLOT HISTORICAL SALES

On the Value Line report, find and highlight the Sales information as shown on page 174. Scan the row to see how the sales numbers vary. Sales for Tootsie Roll from 1989 to 1998 vary from 179.3 M to 388.7 M. Use the cycle between 10 and 100 by reformatting 179.3 M as 17.93 ten millions. Plot 17.93 between 10 and 20 on the left scale by counting up seven lines and putting a dot just below line 8. (Think

You can represent numbers on the vertical scale of a semi-log graph by reformatting them. To arrive at workable numbers, move the decimal over as many places as you need. For example, to represent 90 million, you can write 90 M which means $90 \times 1,000,000$. You can use this principle to write numbers with the decimal wherever you want, just remember what the number means.

Number	95,000,000	950,000,000	2,950,000,000
Millions 1,000,000	95	950	2,950
Ten millions 10,000,000	9.5	95	295
Hundred millions 100,000,000	0.95	9.5	29.5
Billions 1,000,000,000	0.095	0.95	2.95
Hundred thousands 100,000	950	9,500	29,500

17.93 is close to 18.) Distinguish sales from earnings (which you will plot next) by using a colored pencil. Plot the sales figures for the remaining years as shown on the SSG graph on page 175.

Remember to move the decimal the same number of places for all similar numbers. You may plot sales in the 1-10 cycle or the 10-100 cycle. The graph of the changes will be the same in either cycle.

REASONS FOR SALES TREND CHANGES

Notice the sales trend changes on the graph. Read the paragraphs in the Value Line report to see whether some of the following may be reasons for sales trends. You can also read the company's annual report or other information about the company in newspapers, magazines, or on the Internet.

- New or improved products or services.
- An upturn from a recession.
- Purchase of another company. If so, check to see whether the company has made any successful purchases in the past. That success indicates that this purchase will probably succeed, too.
- A stagnating market for products or services, with little possibility of future expansion, causing sales to level off.
- An expanding market for products or services, causing sales to rise.
- A market that has expanded geographically.

PLOT HISTORICAL EARNINGS PER SHARE

Earnings per share are given in dollars and cents. If earnings were $0.46 per share, you could represent this amount on the graph by making a mark at the third line above 4—which is like moving the decimal one point to the right. Operating in this way, $0.40 is at the 4, and $1.00 is at 10 on the graph.

On the Value Line report find and highlight the Earnings per share information. You can plot earnings in either cycle, however, it is best to plot earnings in the lower cycle to have enough space to plot the price bars above earnings. Scan the earnings per share row on the Value Line report to see how the earnings per share numbers vary. Be sure to use earnings figures for the same years you used for sales. For Tootsie Roll from 1989 to 1998, earnings per share vary from $0.40 to $1.37.

When possible, plot sales and earnings in different cycles. If you avoid merging lines, the graph will be easier to read. For Tootsie Roll, plot earnings in the cycle from 1 to 10, using a different color. If you are graphing a fast growing company, start sales and earnings in the lower cycle to fit the data on the graph.

COMPARE SALES AND EARNINGS

Past earnings per share growth should be parallel to sales growth. Because earnings come from sales, the two lines should move up and down together. When they do not, you should try to figure out why.

Some reasons earnings might be growing more slowly than sales are:

1. Declining profit margins.
2. Increasing number of shares of stock outstanding, dividing earnings among more shares (dilution).
3. Special (non-recurring) situations such as:
   - A strike
   - Cost of opening new plants
   - Lawsuits against the corporation
   - A loss on sales of assets—perhaps a plant

Some reasons earnings might be growing faster than sales are:

1. Increasing profit margins because management is reducing expenses.
2. Decrease in number of shares of stock outstanding, so that earnings are divided among fewer shares (that is, a company stock repurchase plan).
3. Reductions in the size of the workforce, so fewer workers to pay.

The longer you hold an investment in a quality growth company, the better your chances of making money. An investment of $3,000 in Tootsie Roll on 12/30/88 would have grown to $22,305 by 12/31/98, a 22.2% annual return with dividends reinvested over the ten-year period. However, it is hard to judge what an investment may do over a short period, even for a quality company. The price of Tootsie Roll on 12/31/98 was $37.99 (adjusted for a stock dividend) but was down to $32.00 by 11/30/99, a decrease of 15.8% in 11 months.

PLOT HISTORICAL PRICE BARS

On the Value Line report, highlight the high and low price information at the top of the report. Use the same years as for sales and earnings. Always plot price bars in the same cycle as earnings. Price bars in relation to earnings gives a visual picture of the P/E ratio. The further the price is from the earnings line, the higher the P/E. The closer the price bar is to the earnings line, the smaller the P/E.

PLOT THE PRICE BARS

1. Find the low price for each year. Represent this low price on the graph with a short mark.
2. Find the high price for each year. Represent this high price on the graph with a short mark.
3. Connect these two marks to form the price bars.

Price bars show how much movement or **volatility** there is in the price each year. This could be an indicator of risk in future years.

TOOTSIE ROLL NYSE-TR

RECENT PRICE	**34**	
P/E RATIO	**21.9**	(Trailing: 24.1 / Median: 19.0)
RELATIVE P/E RATIO	**1.30**	
DIV'D YLD	**0.7%**	
VALUE LINE	**1502**	

TIMELINESS **4** Lowered 8/6/99
SAFETY **1** Raised 5/14/99
TECHNICAL **3** Lowered 3/12/99
BETA .65 (1.00 = Market)

2002-04 PROJECTIONS

	Price	Gain	Ann'l Total Return
High	50	(+45%)	10%
Low	40	(+20%)	4%

Insider Decisions

	S	O	N	D	J	F	M	A	M
to Buy	0	0	0	0	0	0	0	0	1
Options	0	0	0	0	0	0	0	0	0
to Sell	0	0	0	0	0	0	0	0	0

Institutional Decisions

	3Q1998	4Q1998	1Q1999
to Buy	40	37	35
to Sell	50	38	65
Hld's(000)	10162	11087	10741

Percent shares traded: 4.5 / 3.0 / 1.5

Chart legends:
- 16.0 x "Cash Flow" p sh
- Relative Price Strength
- 3-for-2 split 7/86
- 2-for-1 split 5/87
- 2-for-1 split 7/95
- 2-for-1 split 7/98
- Options: No
- Shaded area indicates recession

High: 6.4 7.2 9.6 14.8 17.2 17.5 16.2 18.2 18.5 30.8 46.5 46.9
Low: 4.8 4.5 5.9 7.0 12.1 13.5 11.6 12.9 15.5 17.0 27.4 33.4

Target Price Range 2002 2003 2004

% TOT. RETURN 7/99

	THIS STOCK	VL ARITH. INDEX
1 yr.	-14.4	15.0
3 yr.	118.7	73.5
5 yr.	165.4	128.5

	1983	1984	1985	1986	1987	1988	1989	1990	1991	1992	1993	1994	1995	1996	1997	1998	1999	2000	© VALUE LINE PUB., INC.	02-04
Sales per sh A	1.52	1.83	2.12	2.21	2.28	2.55	3.56	3.86	4.13	4.88	5.16	5.90	6.22	6.78	7.57	7.88	8.40	8.55		11.10
"Cash Flow" per sh	.14	.20	.25	.30	.34	.40	.50	.56	.63	.76	.88	1.02	1.02	1.18	1.48	1.63	1.80	1.95		2.50
Earnings per sh A B	.11	.17	.22	.25	.29	.33	.40	.45	.53	.64	.70	.75	.80	.94	1.22	1.37	1.55	1.65		2.20
Div's Decl'd per sh C	.02	.02	.03	.03	.04	.04	.04	.04	.05	.06	.08	.09	.12	.14	.16	.19	.24	.28		.43
Cap'l Spending per sh	.03	.06	.13	.08	.05	.09	.06	.10	.08	.25	.56	.16	.09	.19	.17	.30	.30	.30		.30
Book Value per sh D	.74	.88	1.06	1.28	1.53	1.82	2.18	2.58	3.04	3.61	4.22	4.78	5.41	6.22	7.07	8.04	9.00	10.05		13.95
Common Shs Outst'g E	51.34	50.88	50.41	50.38	50.37	50.36	50.35	50.34	50.33	50.33	50.31	50.30	50.29	50.27	49.65	49.30	48.80	48.30		46.80
Avg Ann'l P/E Ratio	7.8	7.3	11.4	14.5	17.7	16.6	14.4	16.3	19.9	23.5	22.1	18.4	19.1	17.7	19.1	26.6	Bold figures are Value Line estimates			20.0
Relative P/E Ratio	.66	.68	.93	.98	1.18	1.38	1.09	1.21	1.27	1.43	1.31	1.21	1.28	1.11	1.10	1.41				1.15
Avg Ann'l Div'd Yield	2.4%	1.8%	1.1%	.9%	.8%	.7%	.7%	.6%	.5%	.4%	.5%	.6%	.7%	.8%	.7%	.7%				1.0%

CAPITAL STRUCTURE as of 4/3/99
Total Debt $7.5 mill. Due in 5 Yrs Nil
LT Debt $7.5 mill. LT Interest $.5 mill.
Capitalized leases $7.5 mill.
(2% of Cap'l)

Leases, Uncapitalized None
Pension Liability None

Pfd Stock None
Common Stock 49,293,098 shs.
Includes 15,846,841 Class B shs. (10 votes a sh.)
As of 4/3/99 (98% of Cap'l)

MARKET CAP: $1.7 billion (Mid Cap)

	1989	1990	1991	1992	1993	1994	1995	1996	1997	1998	1999	2000		02-04
Sales ($mill) A	179.3	194.3	207.9	245.4	259.6	296.9	312.7	340.9	375.6	388.7	410	435		520
Operating Margin	21.1%	21.2%	22.3%	22.3%	24.0%	24.6%	24.0%	25.3%	27.4%	29.4%	29.5%	30.0%		31.0%
Depreciation ($mill)	5.1	5.7	5.2	6.1	8.8	13.2	10.8	12.1	12.8	12.8	12.0	13.0		15.0
Net Profit ($mill)	20.2	22.6	26.5	32.0	35.4	37.9	40.4	47.2	60.7	67.5	75.0	80.0		105.0
Income Tax Rate	39.1%	39.2%	39.9%	38.3%	38.6%	38.0%	37.0%	37.1%	36.4%	36.3%	35.0%	35.0%		35.0%
Net Profit Margin	11.3%	11.6%	12.8%	13.1%	13.7%	12.8%	12.9%	13.8%	16.2%	17.4%	18.5%	18.5%		20.0%
Working Cap'l ($mill)	33.5	55.3	80.5	107.2	61.0	92.6	109.7	153.3	153.4	175.1	215	260		425
Long-Term Debt ($mill)	--	--	--	7.5	27.5	27.5	7.5	7.5	7.5	7.5	7.5	7.5		7.5
Shr. Equity ($mill)	109.6	129.8	152.8	181.7	212.3	240.5	272.2	312.9	351.2	396.5	440	485		655
Return on Total Cap'l	18.4%	17.4%	17.4%	16.9%	14.8%	14.3%	14.6%	14.8%	17.0%	16.8%	17.0%	16.5%		16.0%
Return on Shr. Equity	18.4%	17.4%	17.4%	17.6%	16.7%	15.8%	14.8%	15.1%	17.3%	17.0%	17.0%	16.5%		16.0%
Retained to Com Eq	16.5%	15.6%	15.7%	16.0%	15.0%	13.9%	12.9%	13.1%	15.2%	14.7%	14.5%	14.0%		12.0%
All Div'ds to Net Prof	11%	10%	9%	9%	10%	12%	13%	13%	12%	14%	16%	17%		22%

CURRENT POSITION ($MILL.)

	1997	1998	4/3/99
Cash Assets	142.3	163.9	150.8
Receivables	23.3	22.4	26.3
Inventory (LIFO)	36.7	36.5	44.4
Other	4.7	5.7	8.7
Current Assets	207.0	228.5	230.2
Accts Payable	11.6	12.5	12.7
Debt Due	--	--	--
Other	42.0	40.9	44.1
Current Liab.	53.6	53.4	56.8

ANNUAL RATES of change (per sh)

	Past 10 Yrs.	Past 5 Yrs.	Est'd '96-'98 to '02-'04
Sales	12.0%	9.5%	8.5%
"Cash Flow"	15.5%	13.5%	10.0%
Earnings	15.0%	13.5%	11.0%
Dividends	15.5%	20.5%	18.0%
Book Value	16.5%	14.5%	12.0%

QUARTERLY SALES ($ mill.) A

Calendar	Mar.31	Jun.30	Sep.30	Dec.31	Full Year
1996	63.3	72.5	128.6	76.5	340.9
1997	66.3	82.3	140.6	86.4	375.6
1998	69.7	86.0	144.2	88.8	388.7
1999	74.2	88.3	155	92.5	410
2000	80.0	90.0	170	95.0	435

EARNINGS PER SHARE A B

Calendar	Mar.31	Jun.30	Sep.30	Dec.31	Full Year
1996	.16	.19	.38	.21	.94
1997	.19	.25	.50	.28	1.22
1998	.23	.28	.55	.31	1.37
1999	.25	.30	.65	.35	1.55
2000	.25	.32	.70	.38	1.65

GROSS QUARTERLY DIV'DS PAID C

Calendar	Mar.31	Jun.30	Sep.30	Dec.31	Full Year
1995	.025	.03	.03	.03	.12
1996	.03	.035	.035	.035	.14
1997	.035	.04	.04	.04	.16
1998	.04	.05	.05	.05	.19
1999	.05	.06			

BUSINESS: Tootsie Roll Industries, Inc. produces candy. Products include: Tootsie Roll, Tootsie Pop, Tootsie Bubble Pop, Tootsie Pop Drops, Tootsie Roll Flavor Rolls, and Mason Dots. Acquired Warner-Lambert's former chocolate/caramel brands (Junior Mints, Sugar Daddy, Sugar Babies, Charleston Chew, and Pom Poms) 10/93; Charms Co. (Charms, Blow Pops), 9/88; and Cella's Confections (chocolate covered cherries), 7/85. Has four plants in U.S.; one in Mexico. Int'l ops. (Mexico and Canada): 8% of '98 sales, 0% of earnings. Has about 1,750 employees. M.J. and E.R. Gordon control 43% of voting power; L.R. Weiner, 12% (4/99 Proxy). Chairman & C.E.O.: M.J. Gordon. Pres. & C.O.O.: E.R. Gordon. Inc.: VA. Add.: 7401 S. Cicero Ave., Chicago, IL 60629. Tel.: 773-838-3400.

Tootsie Roll continues to hoard its cash while it looks for acquisitions. With free cash flow likely to reach $70 million this year, and cash & marketable securities totaling $151 million ($3.05 a share), management is actively seeking acquisitions. But the company continues to believe that candy companies are commanding excessive prices. Thus, Tootsie Roll will likely wait for prices to become "more reasonable". The company's most recent purchase (in 1993) demonstrates management's disciplined approach: Cambridge Brands (the company's first acquisition since 1988) was purchased for $81.3 million and generated $36.6 million in earnings the same year (equating to a 2.2 Price/Earnings multiple). Because potential deal terms are unknown, our estimates do not reflect any acquisitions.

Continued product introductions and international expansion will keep capital spending at elevated levels. Excluding years with acquisitions or unusual expenditures, capital spending has historically run between $5 million and $10 million a year. Going forward, though, we project $15 million a year to support regular capital spending, international expansion in Australia and the Philippines, and new product introductions.

Stock dividends and share repurchases will likely continue. Each April, Tootsie Roll issues a 3% stock dividend along with an increase in its quarterly dividend payout. We expect both plans to continue. Meanwhile, share repurchases should somewhat offset increases in shares outstanding. The company's future repurchases are limited by the decreasing availability of large blocks of shares. In the short term, average daily volume of 30,000 shares should support a moderate repurchase plan approaching 1.5 million shares a year. However, we have modeled a more conservative 500 thousand share-a-year plan, which reflects the company's recent share repurchase trend.

Despite their recent decline, shares of Tootsie Roll do not represent a compelling value. At current levels, Tootsie Roll shares discount the company's future growth. These untimely shares are expected to underperform the market over the coming 3 to 5 years.

David H. Kurzman August 13, 1999

(A) Fiscal year ends Dec. 31. First three quarters end on Sat. closest to end of month. (B) Based on average shares through 1996, diluted thereafter. Next earnings report due about Oct. 27. (C) Next dividend declared about Sept. 25. Next ex date about Oct. 1. Dividends paid about Jan. 9, Apr. 9, July 9, and Oct. 9. 3% stock div'd paid each year about Apr. 21, since 1966. (D) Includes intangibles. In '98 $87.8 million, $1.84/share. (E) In millions, adjusted for stock splits and dividends.

Company's Financial Strength A+
Stock's Price Stability 95
Price Growth Persistence 65
Earnings Predictability 95

To subscribe call 1-800-833-0046.

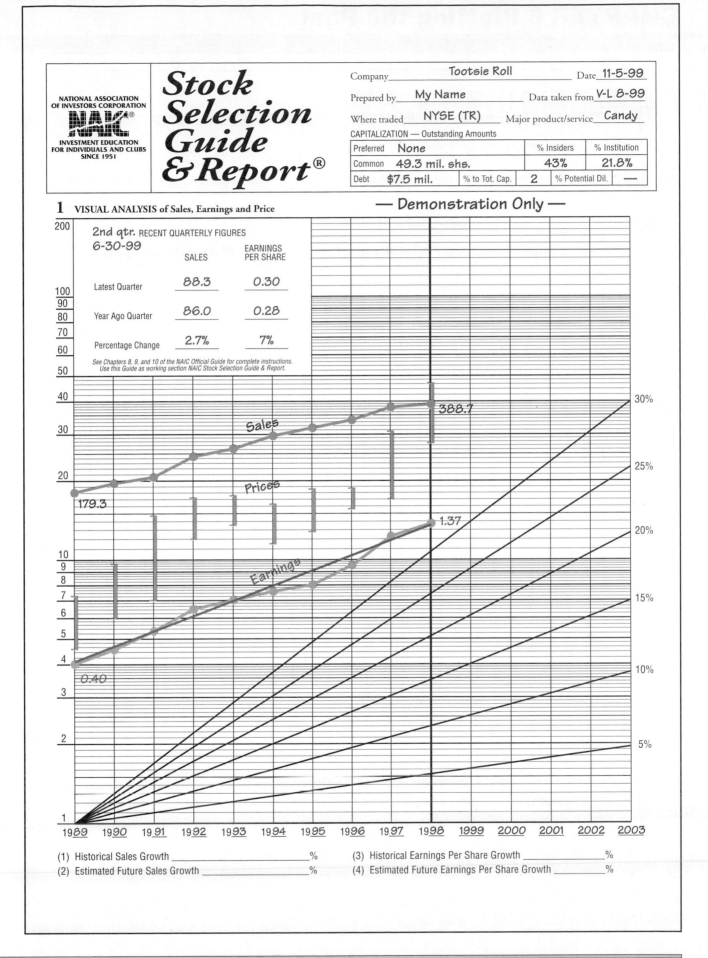

Stock Selection Guide & Report®

NATIONAL ASSOCIATION OF INVESTORS CORPORATION
NAIC®
INVESTMENT EDUCATION FOR INDIVIDUALS AND CLUBS SINCE 1951

Company	Tootsie Roll
Date	11-5-99
Prepared by	My Name
Data taken from	V-L 8-99
Where traded	NYSE (TR)
Major product/service	Candy

CAPITALIZATION — Outstanding Amounts

		% Insiders	% Institution
Preferred	None		
Common	49.3 mil. shs.	43%	21.8%

Debt	$7.5 mil.	% to Tot. Cap.	2	% Potential Dil.	—

1 VISUAL ANALYSIS of Sales, Earnings and Price

— Demonstration Only —

2nd qtr. RECENT QUARTERLY FIGURES
6-30-99

	SALES	EARNINGS PER SHARE
Latest Quarter	88.3	0.30
Year Ago Quarter	86.0	0.28
Percentage Change	2.7%	7%

See Chapters 8, 9, and 10 of the NAIC Official Guide for complete instructions.
Use this Guide as working section NAIC Stock Selection Guide & Report.

Sales — 388.7 — 179.3

Prices

Earnings — 1.37 — 0.40

(1) Historical Sales Growth _____ %
(2) Estimated Future Sales Growth _____ %
(3) Historical Earnings Per Share Growth _____ %
(4) Estimated Future Earnings Per Share Growth _____ %

UNDERSTAND TERMS AND IDEAS

1. Explain why the graph is on semi-log paper.

_____

_____

_____

2. How many years of a company's history must you have to produce a meaningful evaluation on the SSG?

_____

_____

3. Give some reasons why a company's sales may have increased in the past. Can you think of reasons other than the ones listed?

_____

_____

_____

4. Give some reasons why earnings might grow more slowly than sales. Can you think of reasons not in the list?

_____

_____

5. Why are you looking at the past when you are really buying the future?

_____

_____

6. On the SSG graph in Appendix E, plot sales, earnings, and price bar data for Home Depot using the Value Line report in Appendix D.

_____

_____

7. Notice the sales trend changes on your Home Depot graph. What may be some reasons for the changes?

_____

8. Compare sales and earnings for Home Depot. What may be some reasons earnings are growing more slowly than sales or sales are growing more slowly than earnings?

_____

Trend Lines and Growth Rates

*N*ow that you have plotted historical sales, earnings per share, and stock prices, the next step is to use these data to estimate growth rates. You'll look at four methods of drawing trend lines and estimating historical growth rates. Remember, the objective here is to determine the company's past performance in terms of revenues and EPS, and then use judgment to estimate a future growth rate. Once again, you'll be working on the SSG graph.

GOALS

■ Explain the importance of historical trends lines on the SSG graph.

■ Describe the four methods used to draw trend lines.

DRAW HISTORICAL TREND LINES

You have plotted the data for sales, earnings, and price in Section 1 of the Stock Selection Guide. This section is called *Visual Analysis of Sales, Earnings, and Price* because you can view the trends of these three variables. This visual analysis is a crucial step in the SSG approach to stock selection. The main objective is to identify consistent trends in a company's sales, earnings, and stock price.

LOOK FOR OUTLIERS

First, inspect the graph to see whether there is a year where a data point seems to be out of line—an **outlier**. An outlier looks abnormal in relationship to the rest of the data. It may be a year where earnings were up or down significantly, probably due to an unusual (non-recurring) event. Although there are no outliers in Tootsie Roll example, be sure to watch for them so you can evaluate them.

When you find an outlier, do some research to see if you can find the reason for the year's abnormal data. Was there a strike by a labor union? A gain resulting from the sale of a subsidiary? And you certainly want to know whether there were any significant changes in the company's operations at the time in question. Or was it due to a down economic cycle?

FOUR BASIC TREND LINES

With the data plotted on the graph, you can identify trends by drawing trend lines which represent an average of the data points for each variable. There are four different methods for drawing trend lines. You should know when to use each method, but typically, you will select only one. Your historical trend line is drawn from the vertical line on the far left (10-year-old data) to the bold line (current year). The four basic methods of drawing trend lines are shown on page 179. Be sure to use a ruler.

ROCK SOLID

The value of your stock doesn't have to increase every day in order to meet your investment goals. If you follow the NAIC guidelines, you will buy quality stocks with a history of growth. It doesn't matter if you buy a stock on Monday and the price drops on Tuesday. It is important for the value of your stock to trend upward over time.

Inspection or Best Judgment Method This is the most commonly used method. You look at the historical data for one variable (sales or earnings), and (excluding outliers) draw a line that best represents the overall trend. In other words, you are "eyeballing" the data and using your best judgment to draw a representative trend line.

Peak Period Method This method should be used only when deep peaks and valleys have appeared on the graph. You have what is known as a cyclical pattern, and the company you are evaluating is a cyclical company. Place your ruler at the most recent peak (most current years) and drop down to the next peak (earlier years). Draw a line that connects these points.

Midpoint Method This method uses mathematical averages and is fairly easy to calculate.

1. Calculate the average of the most recent five data points for sales and earnings, respectively. For Tootsie Roll,

$$\text{Sales: } \frac{296.9 + 312.7 + 340.9 + 375.6 + 388.7}{5} = 342.96, \text{ or } 343$$

$$\text{Earnings: } \frac{0.75 + 0.80 + 0.94 + 1.22 + 1.37}{5} = 1.016, \text{ or } 1.02$$

2. With an ×, plot these numbers on the graph at the midpoint (the third year) of the most recent five-year period. For Tootsie Roll, 1996 is the midpoint of the most recent five-year period.

3. Calculate the average for the previous five years.

$$\text{Sales: } \frac{179.3 + 194.3 + 207.9 + 245.4 + 259.6}{5} = 217.3, \text{ or } 217$$

$$\text{Earnings: } \frac{0.40 + 0.45 + 0.53 + 0.64 + 0.70}{5} = 0.544, \text{ or } 0.54$$

4. With an ×, plot these numbers at the midpoint (the third year) of that five-year period. For Tootsie Roll, 1991 is the midpoint of that five-year period.

5. Draw a trend line through the two points for earnings going from the left margin to the current year (bold line). Draw a trend line for sales.

6. If you are working with fewer than 10 years, find the averages for the first half of those years and the last half and use those two averages to plot on the middle years and draw the trend line.

The Area Method The objective of this method is to draw a trend line through the middle of the data points and divide the area they cover in half. The area enclosed by data points above the line is roughly equal to the area enclosed by data points below the line.

CHOOSING A METHOD

You will use one of these four methods to represent the growth rate of the data you have plotted. After a little experience, you will quickly recognize which method to use. The purpose of the trend line is to show the average growth rate of the data points you have plotted. If the points follow a consistent upward pattern, you will have more confidence in your trend line. But if the data points are scattered "all over the board," your trend line will be more difficult to draw, and you will not have as much confidence in it. The trend line represents an average, and the slope of the line shows an estimated historical growth rate. A line that is steeper than another line reflects faster growth.

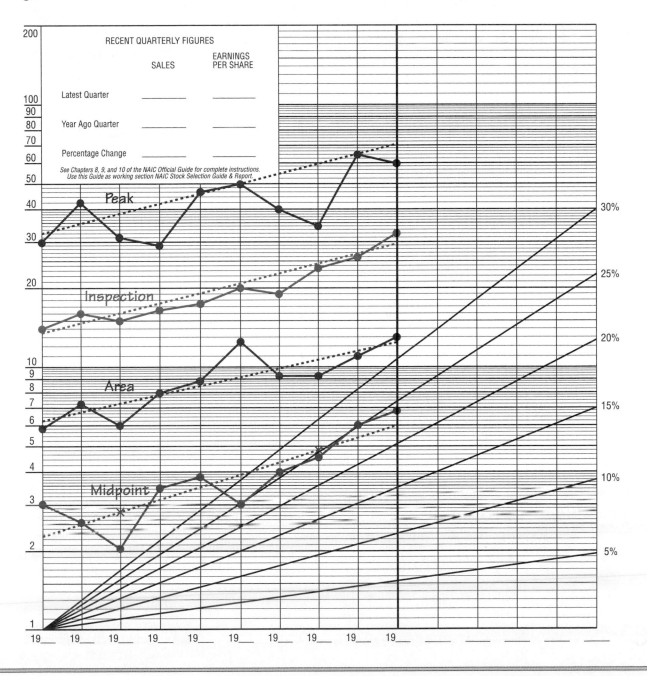

RECENT QUARTERLY FIGURES

	SALES	EARNINGS PER SHARE
Latest Quarter	_____	_____
Year Ago Quarter	_____	_____
Percentage Change	_____	_____

See Chapters 8, 9, and 10 of the NAIC Official Guide for complete instructions.
Use this Guide as working section NAIC Stock Selection Guide & Report.

TOOTSIE ROLL NYSE-TR

| RECENT PRICE | 34 | P/E RATIO | 21.9 | (Trailing: 24.1 / Median: 19.0) | RELATIVE P/E RATIO | 1.30 | DIV'D YLD | 0.7% | VALUE LINE | 1502 |

TIMELINESS **4**	Lowered 8/6/99	
SAFETY **1**	Raised 5/14/99	
TECHNICAL **3**	Lowered 3/12/99	
BETA .65 (1.00 = Market)		

| High: | 6.4 | 7.2 | 9.6 | 14.8 | 17.2 | 17.5 | 16.2 | 18.2 | 18.5 | 30.8 | 46.5 | 46.9 |
| Low: | 4.8 | 4.5 | 5.9 | 7.0 | 12.1 | 13.5 | 11.6 | 12.9 | 15.5 | 17.0 | 27.4 | 33.4 |

LEGENDS
— 16.0 x "Cash Flow" p sh
···· Relative Price Strength
3-for-2 split 7/86
2-for-1 split 5/87
2-for-1 split 7/95
2-for-1 split 7/98
Options: No
Shaded area indicates recession

2002-04 PROJECTIONS

	Price	Gain	Ann'l Total Return
High	50	(+45%)	10%
Low	40	(+20%)	4%

Insider Decisions

	S	O	N	D	J	F	M	A	M
to Buy	0	0	0	0	0	0	0	0	1
Options	0	0	0	0	0	0	0	0	0
to Sell	0	0	0	0	0	0	0	0	0

Institutional Decisions

	3Q1998	4Q1998	1Q1999
to Buy	40	37	35
to Sell	50	38	65
Hld's(000)	10162	11087	10741

Percent shares traded: 4.5 / 3.0 / 1.5

Target Price Range 2002 | 2003 | 2004

% TOT. RETURN 7/99

	THIS STOCK	VL ARITH. INDEX
1 yr.	-14.4	15.0
3 yr.	118.7	73.5
5 yr.	165.4	128.5

	1983	1984	1985	1986	1987	1988	1989	1990	1991	1992	1993	1994	1995	1996	1997	1998	1999	2000	© VALUE LINE PUB., INC.	02-04
Sales per sh A	1.52	1.83	2.12	2.21	2.28	2.55	3.56	3.86	4.13	4.88	5.16	5.90	6.22	6.78	7.57	7.88	8.40	8.55		11.10
"Cash Flow" per sh	.14	.20	.25	.30	.34	.40	.50	.56	.63	.76	.88	1.02	1.02	1.18	1.48	1.63	1.80	1.95		2.50
Earnings per sh A B	.11	.17	.22	.25	.29	.33	.40	.45	.53	.64	.70	.75	.80	.94	1.22	1.37	1.55	1.65		2.20
Div'ds Decl'd per sh C	.02	.02	.03	.03	.04	.04	.04	.04	.05	.06	.08	.09	.12	.14	.16	.19	.24	.28		.43
Cap'l Spending per sh	.03	.06	.13	.08	.05	.09	.06	.10	.08	.25	.56	.16	.09	.19	.17	.30	.30	.30		.30
Book Value per sh D	.74	.88	1.06	1.28	1.53	1.82	2.18	2.58	3.04	3.61	4.22	4.78	5.41	6.22	7.07	8.04	9.00	10.05		13.95
Common Shs Outst'g E	51.34	50.88	50.41	50.38	50.37	50.36	50.35	50.34	50.33	50.33	50.31	50.30	50.29	50.27	49.46	49.30	48.80	48.30		46.80
Avg Ann'l P/E Ratio	7.8	7.3	11.4	14.5	17.7	16.6	14.4	16.3	19.9	23.5	22.1	18.4	19.1	17.7	19.1	26.6	Bold figures are			20.0
Relative P/E Ratio	.66	.68	.93	.98	1.18	1.38	1.09	1.21	1.27	1.43	1.31	1.21	1.28	1.11	1.10	1.41	Value Line estimates			1.15
Avg Ann'l Div'd Yield	2.4%	1.8%	1.1%	.9%	.8%	.7%	.7%	.6%	.5%	.4%	.5%	.6%	.7%	.8%	.7%	.7%				1.0%

CAPITAL STRUCTURE as of 4/3/99

Total Debt $7.5 mill. **Due in 5 Yrs** Nil
LT Debt $7.5 mill. **LT Interest** $.5 mill.
Capitalized leases $7.5 mill.
(2% of Cap'l)

Leases, Uncapitalized None
Pension Liability None

Pfd Stock None
Common Stock 49,293,098 shs.
Includes 15,846,841 Class B shs. (10 votes a sh.)
As of 4/3/99 (98% of Cap'l)

MARKET CAP: $1.7 billion (Mid Cap)

	179.3	194.3	207.9	245.4	259.6	296.9	312.7	340.9	375.6	388.7	410	435	Sales ($mill) A	520
	21.1%	21.2%	22.3%	22.3%	24.0%	24.6%	24.0%	25.3%	27.4%	29.4%	29.5%	30.0%	Operating Margin	31.0%
	5.1	5.7	5.2	6.1	8.8	13.2	10.8	12.1	12.8	12.8	12.0	13.0	Depreciation ($mill)	15.0
	20.2	22.6	26.5	32.0	35.4	37.9	40.4	47.2	60.7	67.5	75.0	80.0	Net Profit ($mill)	105.0
	39.1%	39.2%	39.9%	38.3%	38.6%	38.0%	37.0%	37.1%	36.4%	36.3%	35.0%	35.0%	Income Tax Rate	35.0%
	11.3%	11.6%	12.8%	13.1%	13.7%	12.8%	12.9%	13.8%	16.2%	17.4%	18.5%	18.5%	Net Profit Margin	20.0%
	33.5	55.3	80.5	107.2	61.0	92.6	109.7	153.3	153.4	175.1	215	260	Working Cap'l ($mill)	425
	--	--	--	7.5	27.5	27.5	7.5	7.5	7.5	7.5	7.5	7.5	Long-Term Debt ($mill)	7.5
	109.6	129.8	152.8	181.7	213.2	240.5	272.2	312.9	351.2	396.5	440	485	Shr. Equity ($mill)	655
	18.4%	17.4%	17.4%	16.9%	14.8%	14.3%	14.6%	14.8%	17.0%	16.8%	17.0%	16.5%	Return on Total Cap'l	16.0%
	18.4%	17.4%	17.4%	17.6%	16.7%	15.8%	14.8%	15.1%	17.3%	17.0%	17.0%	16.5%	Return on Shr. Equity	16.0%
	16.5%	15.6%	15.7%	16.0%	15.0%	13.9%	12.9%	13.1%	15.2%	14.7%	14.5%	14.0%	Retained to Com Eq	12.0%
	11%	10%	9%	9%	10%	12%	13%	13%	12%	14%	16%	17%	All Div'ds to Net Prof	22%

CURRENT POSITION ($MILL.)

	1997	1998	4/3/99
Cash Assets	142.3	163.9	150.8
Receivables	23.3	22.4	26.3
Inventory (LIFO)	36.7	36.5	44.4
Other	4.7	5.7	8.7
Current Assets	207.0	228.5	230.2
Accts Payable	11.6	12.5	12.7
Debt Due	--	--	--
Other	42.0	40.9	44.1
Current Liab.	53.6	53.4	56.8

ANNUAL RATES

of change (per sh)	Past 10 Yrs.	Past 5 Yrs.	Est'd '96-'98 to '02-'04
Sales	12.0%	9.5%	8.5%
"Cash Flow"	15.5%	13.5%	10.0%
Earnings	15.0%	13.5%	11.0%
Dividends	15.5%	20.5%	18.0%
Book Value	16.5%	14.5%	12.0%

QUARTERLY SALES ($ mill.) A

Cal-endar	Mar.31	Jun.30	Sep.30	Dec.31	Full Year
1996	63.3	72.5	128.6	76.5	340.9
1997	66.3	82.3	140.6	86.4	375.6
1998	69.7	86.0	144.2	88.8	388.7
1999	74.2	88.3	155	92.5	410
2000	80.0	90.0	170	95.0	435

EARNINGS PER SHARE A B

Cal-endar	Mar.31	Jun.30	Sep.30	Dec.31	Full Year
1996	.16	.19	.38	.21	.94
1997	.19	.25	.50	.28	1.22
1998	.23	.28	.55	.31	1.37
1999	.25	.30	.65	.35	1.55
2000	.25	.32	.70	.38	1.65

GROSS QUARTERLY DIV'DS PAID C

Cal-endar	Mar.31	Jun.30	Sep.30	Dec.31	Full Year
1995	.025	.03	.03	.03	.12
1996	.03	.035	.035	.035	.14
1997	.035	.04	.04	.04	.16
1998	.04	.05	.05	.05	.19
1999	.05	.05	.06		

BUSINESS: Tootsie Roll Industries, Inc. produces candy. Products include: Tootsie Roll, Tootsie Pop, Tootsie Bubble Pop, Tootsie Pop Drops, Tootsie Roll Flavor Rolls, and Mason Dots. Acquired Warner-Lambert's former chocolate/caramel brands (Junior Mints, Sugar Daddy, Sugar Babies, Charleston Chew, and Pom Poms) 10/93; Charms Co. (Charms, Blow Pops), 9/88; and Cella's Con-fections (chocolate covered cherries), 7/85. Has four plants in U.S.; one in Mexico. Int'l ops. (Mexico and Canada): 8% of '98 sales, 0% of earnings. Has about 1,750 employees. M.J. and E.R. Gordon control 43% of voting power; L.R. Weiner, 12% (4/99 Proxy). Chairman & C.E.O.: M.J. Gordon. Pres. & C.O.O.: E.R. Gordon. Inc.: VA. Add.: 7401 S. Cicero Ave., Chicago, IL 60629. Tel.: 773-838-3400.

Tootsie Roll continues to hoard its cash while it looks for acquisitions. With free cash flow likely to reach $70 million this year, and cash & marketable securities totaling $151 million ($3.05 a share), management is actively seeking acquisitions. But the company continues to believe that candy companies are commanding excessive prices. Thus, Tootsie Roll will likely wait for prices to become "more reasonable". The company's most recent purchase (in 1993) demonstrates management's disciplined approach: Cambridge Brands (the company's first acquisition since 1988) was purchased for $81.3 million and generated $36.6 million in earnings the same year (equating to a 2.2 Price/Earnings multiple). Because potential deal terms are unknown, our estimates do not reflect any acquisitions.

Continued product introductions and international expansion will keep capital spending at elevated levels. Excluding years with acquisitions or unusual expenditures, capital spending has historically run between $5 million and $10 million a year. Going forward, though, we project $15 million a year to support regular capital spending, international expansion in Australia and the Philippines, and new product introductions.

Stock dividends and share repurchases will likely continue. Each April, Tootsie Roll issues a 3% stock dividend along with an increase in its quarterly dividend payout. We expect both plans to continue. Meanwhile, share repurchases should somewhat offset increases in shares outstanding. The company's future repurchases are limited by the decreasing availability of large blocks of shares. In the short term, average daily volume of 30,000 shares should support a moderate repurchase plan approaching 1.5 million shares a year. However, we have modeled a more conservative 500 thousand share-a-year plan, which reflects the company's recent share repurchase trend.

Despite their recent decline, shares of Tootsie Roll do not represent a compelling value. At current levels, Tootsie Roll shares discount the company's future growth. These untimely shares are expected to underperform the market over the coming 3 to 5 years.

David H. Kurzman   August 13, 1999

(A) Fiscal year ends Dec. 31. First three quarters end on Sat. closest to end of month. (B) Based on average shares through 1996, diluted thereafter. Next earnings report due about Oct. 27. (C) Next dividend declared about Sept. 25. Next ex date about Oct. 1. Dividends paid about Jan. 9, Apr. 9, July 9, and Oct. 9. 3% stock div'd paid each year about Apr. 21, since 1966. (D) Includes intangibles. In '98: $87.8 million/share. (E) In millions, adjusted for stock splits and dividends.

Company's Financial Strength	A+
Stock's Price Stability	95
Price Growth Persistence	65
Earnings Predictability	95

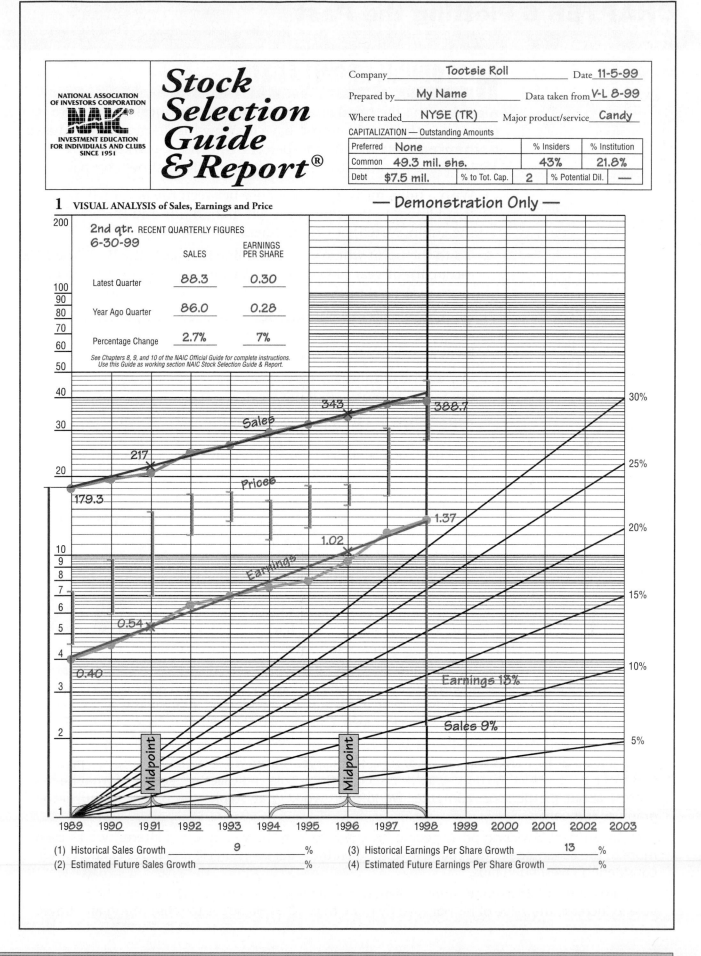

HISTORICAL GROWTH RATE

After drawing the trend line, determine the historical growth rate by comparing the trend line you have drawn with the graph's pre-drawn **percentage growth lines**—percent guidelines, marked 5%, 10%, 15%, 20%, 25%, and 30%. Here's what you do as shown on page 181.

1. With a ruler, measure the distance between the point where your trend line for sales crosses the left margin line and the bottom of the graph. Note that measurement.

2. Go to the point where your trend line intersects the bold line (the most current year). Measure down from that point the same distance measured in step 1. Mark that point on the graph.

3. Estimate where this point is located between the guidelines. For Tootsie Roll sales this point is between 5% and 10%. Estimating gives approximately 9% annual growth rate for sales.

4. Record the number for sales on line (1) at the bottom of page 1 of the SSG. For Tootsie Roll, it's 9%.

5. Repeat steps 1-4 for earnings and record the number for earnings on line (3) at the bottom of page 1 of the SSG. For Tootsie Roll earnings, this point is between 10% and 15%, or approximately 13% annual growth for earnings per share.

inve$tor profile

Eric Olson

At 13, Eric started taking control of the stock portfolio that his dad had set up for him. His dad, John, is a Certified Financial Planner. Eric has obtained investing information from his dad, from reading books and from researching on the Internet.

Eric enjoys researching stock on the Internet when he is not busy making good grades, playing in various school bands, and working part-time at Staples. Working with his own portfolio has opened Eric's eyes to the world of finance. Now he plans to pursue a degree and a career in finance, thanks in part to his teacher and mentor, Frank Damelio. One day, Eric hopes to manage a mutual fund.

In the meantime, Eric prefers to invest in companies with a long track record of growth and companies that he thinks will still be around twenty years from now. He investigates companies that make the products he uses every day, such as Coca-Cola and Gillette. Because of what he has learned about the personal computer world from working at Staples, he is researching silicon graphics companies.

Eric's investment advice to other people his age is to learn how compound interest works even more to the advantage of the young investor than the older investor. He also urges caution when considering investing in fads.

He invests at least $25 a month from his earnings at Staples, and in the last three years, he has been able to increase the value of his portfolio by more than 10%! He hopes to retire young and travel.

UNDERSTAND TERMS AND IDEAS

1. Explain why you draw trend lines on the SSG graph.

   _____

   _____

   _____

   _____

   _____

2. What are outliers? What should you do with them? Explain.

   _____

   _____

   _____

   _____

3. Explain each of the four methods for drawing trend lines.

   _____

   _____

   _____

   _____

   _____

   _____

   _____

   _____

   _____

   _____

4. On the SSG provided in Appendix E, draw the most appropriate trend lines for sales and earnings per share for Home Depot using the Value Line report in Appendix D.

5. Determine the historical growth rates for sales and earning per share for Home Depot.

   Historical Sales Growth _____

   Historical Earnings Per Share Growth _____

SUMMARY

LESSON 6.1 **STOCK SELECTION GUIDE OVERVIEW**
The Stock Selection Guide (SSG) created by the NAIC is a tool to help investors evaluate and choose stocks for their investment portfolios. It was designed primarily for growth stocks and long-term investors. The SSG walks you through collecting and analyzing data about potential stock investments.

LESSON 6.2 **PLOT THE DATA**
Use the SSG graph to estimate historical and future growth rates for revenues and earnings per share. Plot sales and earnings on the graph to find the average rate (percentage) of growth over the past ten years.

LESSON 6.3 **TREND LINES AND GROWTH RATES**
Trend lines for the historical sales and earnings per share represent an average. The slope of the line shows an estimated historical growth rate. This will help you make a reasonable growth projection for the next five years.

REVIEW INVESTING TERMS

Write the letter of the term that matches each definition. Some terms may not be used.

1. _____ a data point that seems to be out of line

2. _____ reducing the value of the shares held by existing shareholders by issuing additional shares at less than the current market price

3. _____ identifies how the corporation is financed, through common stock, preferred stock, long-term debt, or a combination of them

4. _____ movement in stock price

5. _____ pre-drawn percent guidelines on the Stock Selection Guide

a. capitalization

b. dilution

c. outlier

d. percentage growth lines

e. volatility

UNDERSTAND TERMS AND IDEAS

6. What are the objectives of the Stock Selection Guide?

_____

_____

_____

7. Are officers and directors able to own stock in their own company? What does this mean to a potential investor?

_____

_____

_____

_____

8. Describe the importance of a company's debt. What is an acceptable debt level?

_____

_____

_____

_____

_____

_____

9. List the three key kinds of corporate data plotted on the Stock Selection Guide graph.

_____

_____

10. List the four methods used to draw trend lines. Which is the most common?

_____

_____

_____

_____

SHARPEN YOUR RESEARCH SKILLS

11. What do the analysts say about Home Depot? Locate recommendations by two different stock analysts. What rating do they give to Home Depot? Did the analysts agree? If not, why do you think each analyst gave a different rating?

_____

_____

_____

12. Identify one of Tootsie Roll's competitors. How did you find this information?

_____

_____

_____

THINK CRITICALLY

13. Your friend Dave has started buying and selling stocks. He prefers to make a quick profit, so he never holds a stock for more than a few days. Unfortunately, he has been losing money on stocks lately. He asks you if the Stock Selection Guide will help him choose better stocks. What do you tell him?

_____

_____

_____

_____

14. A local company began selling stock last year. You have heard good things about the company and you think it might be a good investment. Can you analyze the stock with the help of the Stock Selection Guide? Explain your answer.

_____

_____

_____

_____

PROSPECTIVE PORTFOLIO PROJECT

In this chapter, you began to learn how to use the Stock Selection Guide to analyze stocks as potential investments. It is time again to analyze your current portfolio. Begin a SSG for each of the stocks in your portfolio. As you fill in the data for Section 1 of the SSG, write comments in each column below for every stock in your portfolio. This will help you compare the stocks to each other. Again, some companies may move up in your portfolio. Others may be eliminated.

Company	% Insiders and % Institution	Total Debt and Debt %	% Change in Sales and Earnings	Historical Sales Trends	Historical Earnings per Share Trend	Historical Price Trend

Compare the data for the stocks in your portfolio. Are some companies starting to look better than others?

PROJECTING THE FUTURE

INDUSTRY INDICATORS
CONSUMER PRODUCTS

Newell Rubbermaid
Founded in 1902

Newell began as a small company, manufacturing curtain rods for variety stores. With the evolution of the mass market and the consolidation of the retail industry in the 1960s, it became necessary for Newell to change so that its products would become more important to emerging large retailers. How could a small curtain rod manufacturer become a company whose products were necessary for large retailers? Newell had to begin merchandizing a more broad-based, multi-product offering of everyday consumer products.

Over the past thirty years, Newell expanded its consumer offerings by acquiring various product lines in the United States and around the globe. From hardware and home furnishings to office products and art supplies, Newell's assortment of products has gradually expanded, allowing Newell to grow into a multi-billion dollar company. You are probably familiar with many of Newell's product lines—WearEver®, Calphalon®, and Mirro® cookware, Levolor® and Kirsch® window treatments, Anchor Hocking® glass, Goody® hair accessories, Rolodex® office products, and Sharpie®, Eberhard Faber® and Uni-Ball® writing instruments.

In 1999, Newell acquired Rubbermaid®, one of the most well-known brand names for home products in the United States. Rubbermaid is not only a maker of organizational and storage products (which may be found in any basement or college dorm room), but is also associated with infant, juvenile, and commercial products.

Rubbermaid makes car seats, strollers, and playpens under the Graco® and Century® brands, and children's toys and playground equipment under the Little Tikes® brand name. Newell's strategy of gradually acquiring popular consumer brands like Rubbermaid has increased its number of product offerings. As a result, Newell has become a company of great significance to large retailers and consumers alike.

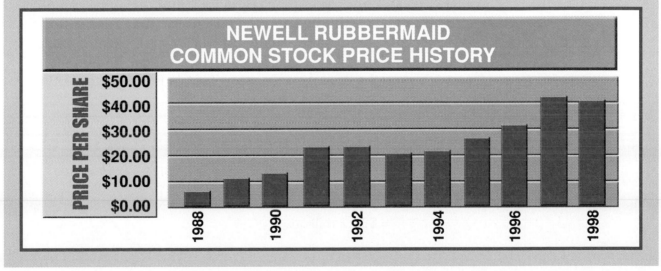

NEWELL RUBBERMAID
COMMON STOCK PRICE HISTORY

LESSON 7.1

Evaluate Management

S ection 2 of the Stock Selection Guide is a tool to help you evaluate a company's management by examining two key ratios: (1) the ratio of pre-tax profit to sales (revenue) and (2) the ratio of net earnings to equity. A good profit margin and a good return on the equity capital invested in the company are both signs that the company is well managed.

GOALS

■ **Determine if the pre-tax profit on sales is growing.**

■ **Determine if management is controlling costs.**

■ **Analyze the percent earned on equity for a company.**

SSG SECTION 2

The first thing to do in this section is to fill in the years you are examining. Use the same years as you used on the graph—SSG Section 1. For Tootsie Roll, use 1989 to 1998 as shown on page 192.

2A • PROFIT MARGIN: RATIO OF PRE-TAX PROFIT TO SALES

The **ratio of pre-tax profit to sales** is an indicator of how well management is controlling costs and revenues and producing stable or increasing pre-tax profit margins. The reason for focusing on pre-tax profit rather than after-tax profit is the fact that management exercises more control over pre-tax profit. After all, the government sets corporate tax rates and plays an important role in determining net (after tax) profit.

Where do you get the information to calculate these ratios? S&P reports the "pre-tax income" for up to ten years for each of the companies it analyzes. All you have to do is divide this number by the sales figure for the same year and multiply by 100.

Value Line does not report pre-tax profits, but it does give you net profit (after taxes) and the tax rate. You can use that information to calculate profit before taxes. Highlight the rows for Net Profit and Income Tax Rate on Value Line as shown for Tootsie Roll on page 191. Then calculate the pre-tax profit using Tootsie Roll figures for 1989.

$$\text{Pre-Tax Profit} = \frac{\text{Net Profit}}{(1 - \text{Tax Rate})}$$

$$= \frac{\$20.2 \text{ million}}{1 - 0.391} \quad \longleftarrow \text{Net Profit from Value Line}$$
$$\longleftarrow \text{39.1\% Income Tax Rate from Value Line as a decimal}$$

$$= \frac{\$20.2 \text{ million}}{0.609}$$

$$= \$33.2 \text{ million}$$

Next calculate the pre-tax profit as a percent of sales, that is, the ratio of the pre-tax profit (net before taxes) to sales, or profit margin.

$$\text{Ratio of Pre-Tax Profit to Sales} = \frac{\text{Pre-Tax Profit}}{\text{Sales}}$$

$$= \frac{\$33.2 \text{ million}}{\$179.3 \text{ million}} \longleftarrow \text{Sales from Value Line}$$

$$= 0.185, \text{ or } 18.5\%$$

You may use a table like that shown below to do your calculations. Then record the results in Section 2A as shown on page 192.

Calculations for Section 2A Form

Year	1989	1990	1991	1992	1993	1994	1995	1996	1997	1998
Net Profit (from Value Line)	20.2	22.6	26.5	32.0	35.4	37.9	40.4	47.2	60.7	67.5
Tax Rate as a decimal (from Value Line)	0.391	0.392	0.399	0.383	0.386	0.380	0.370	0.371	0.364	0.363
1 – Tax Rate	0.609	0.608	0.601	0.617	0.614	0.620	0.630	0.629	0.636	0.637
Pre-Tax Profit $= \frac{\text{Net Profit}}{1 - \text{Tax Rate}}$	33.2	37.2	44.1	51.9	57.7	61.1	64.1	75.0	95.4	106.0
Sales (from Value Line)	179.3	194.3	207.9	245.4	259.6	296.9	312.7	340.9	375.6	388.7
$\frac{\text{Pre-Tax Profit}}{\text{Sales}}$	0.185	0.191	0.212	0.211	0.222	0.206	0.205	0.220	0.254	0.273
Pre-Tax Profits as a Percent of Sales	18.5	19.1	21.2	21.1	22.2	20.6	20.5	22.0	25.4	27.3

1989	1990	1991	1992	1993	1994	1995	1996	1997	1998	1999	2000	© VALUE LINE PUB., INC.	02-04
3.56	3.86	4.13	4.88	5.16	5.90	6.22	6.78	7.57	7.88	8.40	8.55	Sales per sh[A]	11.10
.50	.56	.63	.76	.88	1.02	1.02	1.18	1.48	1.63	1.80	1.95	"Cash Flow" per sh	2.50
.40	.45	.53	.64	.70	.75	.80	.94	1.22	1.37	1.55	1.65	Earnings per sh[A B]	2.20
.04	.04	.05	.06	.08	.09	.12	.14	.16	.19	.24	.28	Div'ds Decl'd per sh[C]	.43
.06	.10	.08	.25	.56	.16	.09	.19	.17	.30	.30	.30	Cap'l Spending per sh	.30
2.18	2.58	3.04	3.61	4.22	4.78	5.41	6.22	7.07	8.04	9.00	10.05	Book Value per sh[D]	13.95
50.35	50.34	50.33	50.33	50.31	50.30	50.29	50.27	49.65	49.30	48.80	48.30	Common Shs Outst'g[E]	46.80
14.4	16.3	19.9	23.5	22.1	18.4	19.1	17.7	19.1	26.6	Bold figures are		Avg Ann'l P/E Ratio	20.0
1.09	1.21	1.27	1.43	1.31	1.21	1.28	1.11	1.10	1.41	Value Line		Relative P/E Ratio	1.15
.7%	.6%	.5%	.4%	.5%	.6%	.7%	.8%	.7%	.7%	estimates		Avg Ann'l Div'd Yield	1.0%
179.3	194.3	207.9	245.4	259.6	296.9	312.7	340.9	375.6	388.7	410	435	Sales ($mill)[A]	520
21.1%	21.2%	22.3%	22.3%	24.0%	24.6%	24.0%	25.3%	27.4%	29.4%	29.5%	30.0%	Operating Margin	31.0%
5.1	5.7	5.2	6.1	8.8	13.2	12.0	12.1	12.8	12.8	12.0	13.0	Depreciation ($mill)	15.0
20.2	22.6	26.5	32.0	35.4	37.9	40.4	47.2	60.7	67.5	75.0	80.0	Net Profit ($mill)	105.0
39.1%	39.2%	39.9%	38.3%	38.6%	38.0%	37.0%	37.1%	36.4%	36.3%	35.0%	35.0%	Income Tax Rate	35.0%
11.3%	11.6%	12.8%	13.1%	13.7%	12.8%	12.9%	13.8%	16.2%	17.4%	18.5%	18.5%	Net Profit Margin	20.0%
33.5	55.3	80.5	107.2	61.0	92.6	109.7	153.3	153.4	175.1	215	260	Working Cap'l ($mill)	425
--	--	--	7.5	27.5	27.5	7.5	7.5	7.5	7.5	7.5	7.5	Long-Term Debt ($mill)	7.5
109.6	129.8	152.8	181.7	212.3	240.5	272.2	312.9	351.2	396.5	440	485	Shr. Equity ($mill)	655
18.4%	17.4%	17.4%	16.9%	14.8%	14.3%	14.6%	14.8%	17.0%	16.8%	17.0%	16.5%	Return on Total Cap'l	16.0%
18.4%	17.4%	17.4%	17.6%	16.7%	15.8%	14.8%	15.1%	17.3%	17.0%	17.0%	16.5%	Return on Shr. Equity	16.0%
16.5%	15.6%	15.7%	16.0%	15.0%	13.9%	12.9%	13.1%	15.2%	14.7%	14.5%	14.0%	Retained to Com Eq	12.0%
11%	10%	9%	9%	10%	12%	13%	13%	12%	14%	16%	17%	All Div'ds to Net Prof	22%

PROFIT MARGIN TREND

After you have completed the calculations of pre-tax profit as a percent of sales, examine the trend, called the **profit margin trend**, for the last five years. Average your percentage figures for the past five years and place that number in the Last 5-Year Average box. For Tootsie Roll, the last five-year average is:

$$\frac{20.6+20.5+22.0+25.4+27.3}{5}=23.2$$

Observe whether last year's profit margin figure is higher or lower than the five-year average. A higher number indicates that the company is continuing to increase profit margins and earnings. For Tootsie Roll the last year is higher than the average. Show this by placing an arrow or a check in the Up box.

2 EVALUATING MANAGEMENT   Company _Tootsie Roll_

	19_89_	19_90_	19_91_	19_92_	19_93_	1994	19_95_	19_96_	19_97_	19_98_	LAST 5 YEAR AVG.	TREND UP	TREND DOWN
A % Pre-tax Profits on Sales (Net Before Taxed ÷ Sales)	18.5	19.1	21.2	21.1	22.2	20.6	20.5	22.0	25.4	27.3	23.2	↑	
B % Earned on Equity (E/S ÷ Book Value)	18.4	17.4	17.4	17.6	16.7	15.8	14.8	15.1	17.3	17.0	16.0	↑	

SECTION 2B: PERCENT EARNED ON EQUITY

The **percent earned on equity** is an indicator of management's ability to earn an appropriate return on the capital supplied by common stockholders through skill in operating a business efficiently with superior marketing. Just to refresh your memory, the term equity is an accounting term used to mean stockholders' equity. It is found by subtracting total liabilities from total assets. Stockholders' equity is also called book value or net worth.

The numbers in Section 2B are calculated by dividing earnings per share by book value per share times 100. If you use S&P or Value Line, this calculation has already been done for you. S&P shows it as % Ret. on Equity, and Value Line as Return on Shr. Equity.

The calculation of the percent earned on equity may vary slightly among investment reporting services. When completing a SSG, remember to take all of your data from the same source. Do not mix and match data from different sources.

Highlight the row Return on Shr. Equity as shown on page 191. Use these numbers to fill in the percentage earned on equity for each year in the Section 2B as shown on this page. Then, as in Section 2A, take the average of the last five years. For Tootsie Roll, the last five-year average is:

$$\frac{15.8+14.8+15.1+17.3+17.0}{5}=16$$

Compare last year's figure to that average. What is the trend? Mark the result in the Trend box. It is desirable for the last year to be higher than the average of the last five years. For Tootsie Roll the last year is higher than the average. Show this by placing an arrow or a check in the Up box.

WHAT DO THE TRENDS TELL YOU?

As you review the 10-year data compiled in Section 2, look for patterns. Are 2A and 2B fairly stable, increasing, or declining? Or are the numbers all over the board? Good management attempts to control these key ratios, producing either stable patterns or slightly increasing trends.

As in Section 1 on page 1, you may want to eliminate "abnormal" or "atypical" data (outliers) from your trend consideration in this section. The most recent five-year period is generally more important to you than the earlier five-year period. The recent past carries more weight in an investor's decision.

You might want to note the last recessionary period and see how the company performed. How were the ratios affected? This might give a glimpse of how the company might be affected in the next down business cycle.

Pre-tax profit margins which are stable or increasing are positive indicators. Declining margins are "red flags" that should be studied to find out why. The same is true of the percent earned on equity. Decreasing pre-tax profits and percents earned on equity may be indicators that increasing competition, rising labor and raw material costs, or product quality problems are plaguing the company. You want to know what is going on.

The pre-tax profit margin and percent earned on equity ratios are critical in your evaluation of management. Pre-tax profit margin and percent earned on equity trends should be compared with trends among other companies in the same industry. The industry data are available in both S&P and Value Line. If the trends in the company you are studying are unfavorable compared with the industry as a whole, you may be justified in terminating your study of that particular stock.

ROCK SOLID

Companies frequently change management just before or after they change a critical business strategy. This allows them to put people that understand and support the new methods into key positions. Beware of buying stock in a company that has changed management frequently within the last few years. The company may be struggling to find a profitable direction.

DOLLAR SENSE
I've noticed that people who don't respect money don't have any.

—Paul Getty

2 EVALUATING MANAGEMENT   Company _____

	19___	19___	19___	19___	19___	19___	19___	19___	19___	19___	LAST 5 YEAR AVG.	TREND UP	TREND DOWN
A % Pre-tax Profits on Sales (Net Before Taxed ÷ Sales)													
B % Earned on Equity (E/S ÷ Book Value)													

3 PRICE-EARNING HISTORY as an indication of the future

This shows how stock prices have fluctuated with earnings and dividends. It is a building block for translating earnings into future stock prices.

PRESENT PRICE _____   HIGH THIS YEAR _____   LOW THIS YEAR _____

Year	A PRICE HIGH	B PRICE LOW	C Earnings Per Share	D Price Earnings Ratio HIGH A÷C	E Price Earnings Ratio LOW B÷C	F Dividend Per Share	G % Payout F÷C×100	H % High Yield F÷B×100
1								
2								
3								
4								
5								
6 TOTAL								
7 AVERAGE								
8 AVERAGE PRICE EARNINGS RATIO				9 CURRENT PRICE EARNINGS RATIO				

4 EVALUATING RISK and REWARD over the next 5 years

Assuming one recession and one business boom every 5 years, calculations are made of how high and how low the stock might sell. The upside-downside ratio is the key to evaluating risk and reward.

A HIGH PRICE — NEXT 5 YEARS

Avg. High P/E _____ (3D7 as adj.) × Estimated High Earnings Per Share _____ = Forecast High Price $ _____ (4A1)

B LOW PRICE — NEXT 5 YEARS

(a) Avg Low P/E _____ (3E7 as adj.) × Estimated Low Earnings Per Share _____ = Forecast Low Price $ _____

(b) Avg Low Price of Last 5 Years = _____ (3B7)

(c) Recent Severe Market Low Price = _____ (3B7)

(d) Price Dividend Will Support $\frac{\text{Present Divd.}}{\text{High Yield (H)}}$ = _____ = _____

Selected Estimated Low Price _____ = $ _____

C ZONING

_____ (4A1) High Forecast Price Minus _____ (4B1) Low Forecast Price Equals _____ (C) Range. 1/3 of Range = _____ (4CD)

(4C2) Lower 1/3 = _____ (4B1) to _____ (Buy)

(4C3) Middle 1/3 = _____ to _____ (Maybe)

(4C3) Upper 1/3 = _____ to _____ (4A1) (Sell)

Present Market Price of _____ is in the _____ (4C5) Range

D UPSIDE DOWNSIDE RATIO (Potential Gain vs. Risk of Loss)

$\frac{\text{High Price (4A1)} \_\_\_\_\_ \text{Minus Present Price} \_\_\_\_\_}{\text{Present Price} \_\_\_\_\_ \text{Minus Low Price (4B1)} \_\_\_\_\_}$ = _____ = _____ (4D) To 1

E PRICE TARGET (Note: This shows the potential market price appreciation over the next five years in simple interest terms.)

$\frac{\text{High Price (4A1)} \_\_\_\_\_}{\text{Present Market Price} \_\_\_\_\_}$ = (_____) × 100 = (_____) − 100 = _____ (4E) % Appreciation

5 5-YEAR POTENTIAL *This combines price appreciation with dividend yield to get an estimate of total return. It provides a standard for comparing income and growth stocks.*

A $\frac{\text{Present Full Year's Dividend \$} \_\_\_\_\_}{\text{Present Price of Stock \$} \_\_\_\_\_}$ = _____ × 100 = _____ (5A) Present Yield or % Returned on Purchase Price

B AVERAGE YIELD OVER NEXT FIVE YEARS

Avg. Earnings Per Share Next 5 Years _____ × Avg. % Payout (3G7) _____ = $\frac{\_\_\_\_\_}{\text{Present Price \$} \_\_\_\_\_}$ = _____ (5B) %

C ESTIMATED AVERAGE ANNUAL RETURN OVER NEXT 5 YEARS

$\frac{\text{5-Year Appreciation Potential (4E)} \_\_\_\_\_}{5}$ = _____ %

Average Yield (5B) .... _____ %

Average Total Return Over The Next 5 Years (5C) _____ %

Table to Convert From Simple to Compound Rate

Simple Rate 2 4 6 8 10 12 14 16 18 20 22 24 26 28 30 32 34 36 38 40

Compound Rate 2 4 6 8 10 12 14 16 18 20 22 24

UNDERSTAND TERMS AND IDEAS

1. On the blank SSG page 2 provided in Appendix E, fill in Section 2A using the Value Line for Home Depot in Appendix D. Use the Calculations for Section 2A Form at the bottom of this page for your calculations. Then fill in Section 2B.

2. What is your opinion of the management of Home Depot based on the data in 2A and 2B?

_____

3. Explain why the pre-tax profit margins and percents earned on equity are used to evaluate management.

_____

_____

_____

_____

4. What types of patterns for pre-tax profit margins and percents earned on equity are indicators of good management?

_____

_____

5. Why should you obtain all your SSG data from the same information source?

_____

Calculations for Section 2A Form										
Year										
Net Profit (from Value Line)										
Tax Rate as a decimal (from Value Line)										
1 – Tax Rate										
Pre-Tax Profit $= \dfrac{\text{Net Profit}}{1-\text{Tax Rate}}$										
Sales (from Value Line)										
$\dfrac{\text{Pre-Tax Profit}}{\text{Sales}}$										
Pre-Tax Profits as a Percent of Sales										

LESSON 7.2

Estimate Future Growth Rates

You have learned how to estimate a company's historical growth rates for sales (revenues) and earnings per share, and how to evaluate management by examining pre-tax profit margins and percents earned on equity. Historical growth rates and the two key ratios will be instrumental in the next step, estimating future growth rates for sales and earnings per share.

GOALS

- Explain the guidelines for making reasonable growth rate projections.

- List four major precautions when projecting future growth rates.

- Draw projection lines for sales and EPS growth.

ESTIMATING FUTURE GROWTH RATES

You now have a feel for a company's sales (revenues) and earnings per share (EPS) performance over a period of years. You can visualize the sales and earnings trends. Using the percentage growth lines, you have determined past growth rates for revenues and EPS. Now your judgment really comes into play! You need to form a picture of the company's future growth prospects. Here are some questions to ask yourself when you are trying to estimate future growth rates:

- Is growth likely to continue in the future at the same rate as in the past?

- Can a company growing at a very rapid rate (that is, over 20%) sustain that rate in the future?

- If pre-tax profit margins and percents earned on equity have been improving, should these be factored into the future growth rate of EPS?

HOW IS MANAGEMENT PRODUCING GROWTH?

Understanding how management is producing growth will help you develop a good impression of how fast and how long growth may continue. Some possible ways of producing growth:

- Introducing new products
- Developing new uses for an old product
- Developing variations of an established product
- Regional expansion
- International expansion
- Research and development on new products
- Acquisition (of other companies)

Determining how management is producing growth will come from research and from probing into the inner workings of the company and its industry. As companies get larger, it becomes more and more difficult to maintain very rapid growth rates. Thus, when you are looking to the future, it may be prudent to estimate a slowing down of growth rates.

JUDGMENT COMES INTO PLAY

Research the following areas before you estimate the future growth rates for EPS and sales for the company you are studying. Read *Value Line, Standard & Poor's*, annual reports (including footnotes), business magazines, online services. Tune in to business- and stock market-oriented radio and television programs. Take advantage of all sources of evaluation and forecasting information.

Economy

- Status of the national economy (the business cycle)
- How dependent is your company on the state of the overall economy?

As a company grows, it becomes more difficult to maintain a growth rate over 20%. Why does a company's growth seem to be slower as the company becomes larger? Let's look at the history of Little Sprouts (fictional), a garden supply company. Five years ago, they had 20 stores in different cities in Ohio. When Mr. Sprout retired, his daughter took over the business. She made it a company goal to open 10 new stores every year. This sounds like a solid business plan of steady growth. Is it really a steady rate of growth?

Solution Calculate the rate of growth using the following formula.

$$\text{Percent of Growth} = \frac{\text{New Stores}}{\text{Existing Stores}} \times 100$$

Year	Existing stores	New Stores	Total Stores	% Growth
1	20	10	30	50
2	30	10	40	33
3	40	10	50	25
4	50	10	60	20
5	60	10	70	17

As you can see, the rate of growth slowed, even though they opened the same number of stores every year.

Industry

- State of the industry your company is in
- How will the state of the industry affect your company?
- Is the industry growing or is it more like the buggy whip and the ice box?
- Debt ratio compared to other companies in the same industry

Products and Services

- The breadth of the company's products and services
- Is the company a one-product company?
- Are the products and services new, developing, or mature?
- Is the company researching and developing new products?
- How successful has it been with new products in the past?
- Luxury or "big ticket" products are the first to go in bad times.
- Necessity items are not cyclical.
- Government can quickly cancel defense orders.

Market

- What are the company's market shares for its products/services?
- Are new global markets coming into play?
- Is or will there be stiff competition that could affect profit margins?

The Directors

- Are they insiders or independents?
- What are their levels of experience?

The Management

- Are the managers responsible for the past track record?
- Is there new management? It usually takes new management two to three years to turn around a bad situation.

Sales

- Are fads producing the sales? Fads may go away.
- Are increased sales due to mergers? Has the company participated in profitable mergers in the past?
- If there are variations in the percent of growth of sales and earnings, determine the reasons.

Other conditions

- Are there any lawsuits which could affect the company?
- Labor disputes?

PROJECTIONS FOR SALES AND EPS

Projections are evaluations of a company's growth prospects for the next five years. They involve critical judgments. You should make the sales projection before the earnings projection because sales are the lifeblood of the company and earnings are derived from sales. Here are some guidelines to consider when you estimate future growth rates:

1. Err on the side of conservatism.

2. You should not project a growth rate over 20% and generally not over 15%. As a company grows, it becomes more difficult to maintain a growth rate over 20%.

3. Sales (revenues) are the source of earnings. You generally should not project that earnings per share will grow at a faster rate than past sales.

4. If the historical growth rate of EPS is less than the sales growth rate, project future earnings at the historical earnings rate or lower. It will be risky to estimate an improvement in earnings growth unless specifically justified.

5. The most recent five-year figures are much more important than the earlier five-year figures.

6. If there was a large aberration (variance) at the last data point, it will then be best to use the point where the trend line meets the bold 10-year line as the base for the projection line.

ESTIMATE FUTURE SALES GROWTH

In Lesson 6.3, the historical sales growth for Tootsie Roll was found to be 9%. Look at the Recent Quarterly Figures box on page 1 of the SSG. The sales growth for the last quarter was 2.7%, however, the company plans to grow in the future through new products and acquisitions. So for Tootsie Roll, a future growth rate of 9% seems achievable especially since the past growth rate has been so consistent. Record the estimated future growth rate for sales at the bottom of page 1 of the Stock Selection Guide as on page 201.

ESTIMATE FUTURE EARNINGS PER SHARE GROWTH

In Lesson 6.3, the historical earnings per share growth for Tootsie Roll was found to be a fairly consistent 13%. Although the last quarter earnings per share was only 7%, new products and acquisitions might favorably impact earnings and profit margins if expenses don't increase over the short term. Optimistically, you could project a future growth rate of 13%, or less optimistically you could project only 9% growth. Use 9% as the future growth rate for Tootsie Roll. Record the estimated future growth rate for sales at the bottom of page 1 of the Stock Selection Guide as on page 201.

If you encounter a situation where earnings per share are temporarily growing at a faster rate than sales, you might want to consider the following possible reasons:

- Company buying back stock so there are fewer shares outstanding.
- Company getting "lean and mean," downsizing by laying off personnel, or cutting other expenses.
- Sale of assets, such as plants and other facilities.

CAUTION FLAG! BE CAREFUL ABOUT...

1. Projecting sales higher in the future than in the past without clear knowledge of a major development.
2. Projecting sales or earnings growth over 20% or even over 15%.
3. Projecting earnings growth rates higher than sales unless justified.
4. Projecting earnings higher than they have been in the past unless you have strong reason to believe that pre-tax profit margins will increase.

DRAW EPS AND SALES PROJECTION LINES

After you have considered all the information and you have estimated future earnings and sales growth rate percentages, you are ready to draw the projection lines. Normally, trend lines are not used as projection lines. The five-year projection line is drawn from the last data point (on the bold line) out to the right margin of the graph. Here's how you draw projection lines for sales and for earnings per share.

1. Measure down the bold 10-year line from the last sales or earnings data points to the pre-drawn guideline for the percentage you have chosen. For Tootsie Roll, the estimated future sales growth is 9% and the estimated future earnings per share growth is 12%.
2. On the right margin, measure up that same distance from your growth percentage guideline. Mark that point.
3. Draw a line from the last data point (on the bold line) to this mark. This is your projection line.

Stock Selection Guide & Report®

Company	Tootsie Roll	Date	11-5-99

Prepared by	My Name	Data taken from	V-L 8-99

Where traded	NYSE (TR)	Major product/service	Candy

CAPITALIZATION — Outstanding Amounts

Preferred	None		% Insiders	% Institution
Common	49.3 mil. shs.		43%	21.8%
Debt	$7.5 mil.	% to Tot. Cap. 2	% Potential Dil.	—

1 VISUAL ANALYSIS of Sales, Earnings and Price

— Demonstration Only —

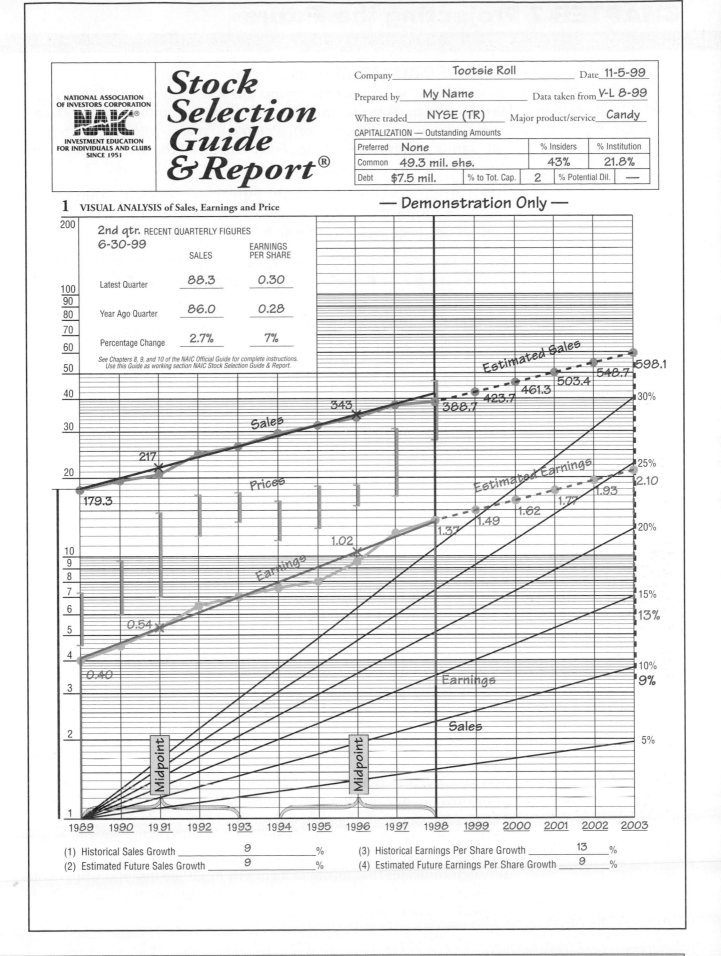

2nd qtr. RECENT QUARTERLY FIGURES 6-30-99

	SALES	EARNINGS PER SHARE
Latest Quarter	88.3	0.30
Year Ago Quarter	86.0	0.28
Percentage Change	2.7%	7%

See Chapters 8, 9, and 10 of the NAIC Official Guide for complete instructions.
Use this Guide as working section NAIC Stock Selection Guide & Report.

(1) Historical Sales Growth ___9___ %
(2) Estimated Future Sales Growth ___9___ %
(3) Historical Earnings Per Share Growth ___13___ %
(4) Estimated Future Earnings Per Share Growth ___9___ %

FIVE-YEAR DOLLAR PROJECTIONS

By observing where your projection line intersects the right margin line (five years in the future) and by noting the numerical value of the nearest horizontal line, you can assign dollar amounts to projected sales and earnings in five years. For Tootsie Roll the projected sales in five years is 598.1 and the projected earnings per share is 2.41.

Alternatively, you can calculate the estimated sales (and earnings). Simply multiply the last year's sales (or earnings) by 100 plus the percent of future growth. For Tootsie Roll, the calculations are:

Future Sales Growth	Future Earnings Growth
$388.7 \times 1.09 = 423.7$	$1.37 \times 1.09 = 1.49$
$423.7 \times 1.09 = 461.8$	$1.49 \times 1.09 = 1.62$
$461.8 \times 1.09 = 503.4$	$1.62 \times 1.09 = 1.77$
$503.4 \times 1.09 = 548.7$	$1.77 \times 1.09 = 1.93$
$548.7 \times 1.09 = 598.1$	$1.93 \times 1.09 = 2.10$

EVALUATING GROWTH PROJECTIONS

Now, armed with the projected growth rates for revenues and EPS, step back and analyze what you have. Some evaluation questions:

1. Do the company's projected sales and earnings meet your target growth rates?

2. Are earnings per share growing at a rate that is faster, slower, or about the same as sales?

3. Is the stock volatile?

4. Has the yearly price trend of the stock been similar to the growth rate of EPS? How has this growth been produced?

5. Can the future growth of sales, earnings, and prices be easily established? If growth has been steady over at least the last five years, it is reasonable to expect steady growth in the future.

6. Were any extraordinary items included in the earnings?

7. Should the study be discontinued or completed?

Estimating future growth of sales and earnings is a pivotal activity. You take the historical data into account, but you also weigh in with your own judgment. Ideally, sales and earnings will continue to grow at the same rate as in the past, but you have to decide whether these growth rates appear to be sustainable and whether there are any new conditions that would cause you to modify your projection. If your research indicates that future EPS growth might be disappointing, you can end the study right here and begin searching for another stock to study! It is your money and your call.

UNDERSTAND TERMS AND IDEAS

1. State some important criteria to be considered before making projections.

   _____

   _____

   _____

2. Explain why sales projections are made before earnings.

   _____

   _____

   _____

3. Name the four things you have to be careful about when you are making the projections.

   _____

   _____

   _____

   _____

4. What is a reasonable growth rate projection for sales for the stock you are studying?

   _____

   _____

   _____

5. What is a reasonable growth rate projection for earnings per share for the stock you are studying?

   _____

   _____

   _____

6. Note these estimated future growth rate percentages on lines 2 and 4 at the bottom of the SSG graph.

   _____

   _____

   _____

7. Draw projection lines based on these growth rates on your graph.

   _____

   _____

Price-Earnings History

*A*fter completing Sections 1 and 2 of the SSG, you have a pretty good idea whether the company you are studying has the kind of growth potential you want. If you are not satisfied with its growth prospects, it is time to drop the company and look for another candidate. If you are satisfied, then the big question is, "What should you be willing to pay (common stock price) for that future growth?" In this lesson, using Section 3 of the SSG, you will assemble some of the information needed to make that decision.

GOALS

- Determine the average five-year P/E.

- Determine the percentage of high yield during the last five years.

- Calculate the current P/E.

SECTION 3 OF THE SSG

You'll need some data from the stock table of your newspaper or from an online source. Enter this information in the row at the top of Section 3 on page 2 of the SSG. See page 207 for Tootsie Roll figures.

1. The stock's most recent price

2. The stock's high price for the current year (last 52 weeks)

3. The stock's low price for the current year (last 52 weeks)

Next enter the years in the first column, using the most recent five years you used on the front of the SSG. Then enter the following data for the past five years from Value Line as shown on page 207.

Column A High common stock prices

Column B Low common stock prices

Column C Earnings per share (EPS)

Column F Dividends per share

PRICE/EARNINGS RATIOS (P/E): COLUMNS D & E

The **price/earnings ratio (P/E)** is the price of a share divided by earnings per share. It is a way of measuring and comparing the value of stocks. The P/E is a gauge for judging what you are getting for your money when you buy a certain stock. You may sometimes find it written PE without the division sign. "Multiple" or "times" are other terms for P/E. You may hear that a stock is selling at a "multiple of 15". Or that it is selling at "15 times." In other words, investors are paying $15 for $1 worth of earnings. The stock's P/E is 15.

The P/E represents how people feel about a certain stock. If they think the company has strong growth potential, they will pay more for the stock, resulting in a higher P/E. A high P/E reflects expectations of rapid growth, and a low P/E reflects expectations of sluggish growth. A low P/E may be a warning sign that a stock probably will not meet your growth objectives. But when you find a company where the vital signs are strong (sales, earnings, profit margins, etc.), you want to get the stock at the lowest P/E possible.

Sometimes the entire stock market is down (a bear market), high quality stocks included. At these times, you can buy stock in a good company at a low P/E. The stock market is sensitive to all sorts of political and economic conditions—wars and other national catastrophes, interest and inflation rates, unemployment levels, etc. Many growth companies are less vulnerable to the cyclical ups and downs of the general economy. Their stocks will display consistent above-average growth, and generally, they will command higher P/E's than slower-growth or cyclical companies.

Column D To compute the high P/E, divide the high price (column A) by EPS (column C), and record the ratio in column D as shown on page 207.

Column E To compute the low P/E, divide the low price (column B) by EPS (column C), and record the ratio in column E as shown on page 207.

It is interesting to note the annual P/E ranges (high to low). The highs and lows indicate how much or how little investors were valuing the stock throughout the year.

PAYOUT AND HIGH YIELD

The percentage of net income that a company pays to shareholders in the form of cash dividends is called **payout**. Remember that growth companies typically do not pay out a large percentage of their net earnings. They prefer to reinvest the profits to help the business continue growing. The dollar amount paid out is the **dividend** and the dividend as a ratio to the price is called the **yield**.

Column G To compute the payout divide the dividend per share (column F) by the earnings per share (column C). Then multiply the result by 100 and record the percent in column G as shown on page 207.

Column H To compute the high yield divide the dividend per share (column F) by the low price (column B). Then multiply the result by 100 and record the percent in column H as shown on page 207.

Many small companies do not pay a dividend, but retain their earnings to support company growth. If the fundamentals are good, this is highly desirable. A well-managed company that is growing fast will need to invest in new activities and new facilities. The reward to stockholders will be a growth in the price of the stock they own (capital appreciation). A mature company tends to pay higher dividends. As it gets larger and larger, its growth rate slows, and more of the earnings can be paid out in dividends.

COMPUTE THE AVERAGES—LINES 6 & 7

With the data filled in on lines 1 through 5 for columns A-H, it's time to compute some averages. Start with column B. Add the 5 years of low prices, and record the sum in B6. Divide the sum by 5 to obtain the average low price. You record it in B7. Calculate the averages for columns D, E, and G the same way.

Note that an unusually high or low P/E should be considered an outlier and excluded from the averaging. Just remember to divide by 4 instead of 5. A P/E dropped from a high or low column does not require dropping the corresponding number from the other column.

AVERAGE PRICE/EARNINGS RATIO

The next step is to compute the average price/earnings ratio for the past five years. You simply add the average high P/E (7D) and average low P/E (7E) and divide by 2. Enter this figure, the average P/E, into 8. For Tootsie Roll, 24.6 + 16.4 = 41 and 41 ÷ 2 = 20.5. Note that neither S&P nor Value Line provides a five-year average P/E.

CURRENT P/E

Finally, calculate the current P/E by dividing the most recent price of the stock, as recorded at the top of Section 3, by the total of the earnings per share for the most recent 4 quarters. For Tootsie Roll:

$$\frac{32}{0.55+0.31+0.25+0.30} = \frac{32}{1.41} = 22.7$$

You can use the P/E you find in the newspaper from which you took the stock price. Sometimes, you will see this P/E calculated on the estimated EPS for the next 12 months. This is called the projected P/E.

WHAT DOES IT ALL MEAN?

Section 3 is entirely historical information. By looking at these price and earnings trends and averages, you have important new information about the stock you are studying.

Price Trends In columns A and B, you have an overview of common stock price trends for the past five years. Ideally, you want to see both the high and the low prices trending higher from year to year.

This indicates a growing company. If the common stock price has been relatively stagnant, you have to ask why—and what it will take to change this pattern.

Price Volatility Look at the differences between high and low prices for each year. If stock A had a high of $50 and a low of $45, and stock B had a high of $50 and a low of $20, what would you say about the

TOOTSIE ROLL NYSE-TR RECENT PRICE **34** P/E RATIO **21.9** (Trailing: 24.1 / Median: 19.0) RELATIVE P/E RATIO **1.30** DIV'D YLD **0.7%** VALUE LINE **1502**

	1989	1990	1991	1992	1993	1994	1995	1996	1997	1998	1999	2000	© VALUE LINE PUB., INC.	02-04
	3.56	3.86	4.13	4.88	5.16	5.90	6.22	6.78	7.57	7.88	8.40	8.55	Sales per sh A	11.10
	.50	.56	.63	.76	.88	1.02	1.02	1.18	1.48	1.63	1.80	1.95	"Cash Flow" per sh	2.50
	.40	.45	.53	.64	.70	.75	.80	.94	1.22	1.37	1.55	1.65	Earnings per sh A B	2.20
	.04	.04	.05	.06	.08	.09	.12	.14	.16	.19	.24	.28	Div'ds Decl'd per sh C	.43
	.06	.10	.08	.25	.56	.16	.09	.19	.17	.30	.30	.30	Cap'l Spending per sh	.30
	2.18	2.58	3.04	3.61	4.22	4.78	5.41	6.22	7.07	8.04	9.00	10.05	Book Value per sh D	13.95
	50.35	50.34	50.33	50.33	50.31	50.30	50.29	50.27	49.65	49.30	48.80	48.30	Common Shs Outst'g E	46.80
	14.4	16.3	19.9	23.5	22.1	18.4	19.1	17.7	19.1	26.6	Bold figures are Value Line estimates		Avg Ann'l P/E Ratio	20.0
	1.09	1.21	1.27	1.43	1.31	1.21	1.28	1.11	1.10	1.41			Relative P/E Ratio	1.15
	.7%	.6%	.5%	.4%	.5%	.6%	.7%	.8%	.7%	.7%			Avg Ann'l Div'd Yield	1.0%

TIMELINESS **4** Lowered 8/6/99
SAFETY **1** Raised 5/14/99
TECHNICAL **3** Lowered 3/12/99
BETA .65 (1.00 = Market)

2002-04 PROJECTIONS
	Price	Gain	Ann'l Total Return
High	50	(+45%)	10%
Low	40	(+20%)	4%

Insider Decisions
	S	O	N	D	J	F	M	A	M
to Buy	0	0	0	0	0	0	0	0	1
Options	0	0	0	0	0	0	0	0	0
to Sell	0	0	0	0	0	0	0	0	0

Institutional Decisions
	3Q1998	4Q1998	1Q1999
to Buy	40	37	35
to Sell	50	38	65
Hld's(000)	10162	11087	10741

Percent shares traded: 4.5 / 3.0 / 1.5

% TOT. RETURN 7/99
	THIS STOCK	VL ARITH. INDEX
1 yr.	-14.4	15.0
3 yr.	118.7	73.5
5 yr.	165.4	128.5

Cal-endar	EARNINGS PER SHARE A B				Full Year
	Mar.31	Jun.30	Sep.30	Dec.31	
1996	.16	.19	.38	.21	.94
1997	.19	.25	.50	.28	1.22
1998	.23	.28	.55	.31	1.37
1999	.25	.30	.65	.35	1.55
2000	.25	.32	.70	.38	1.65

2 EVALUATING MANAGEMENT   Company _Tootsie Roll_

	19**89**	19**90**	19**91**	19**92**	19**93**	19**94**	19**95**	19**96**	19**97**	19**98**	LAST 5 YEAR AVG.	TREND UP	DOWN
A % Pre-tax Profits on Sales (Net Before Taxed ÷ Sales)	18.5	19.1	21.2	21.1	22.2	20.6	20.5	22.0	25.4	27.3	23.2	↑	
B % Earned on Equity (E/S ÷ Book Value)	18.4	17.4	17.4	17.6	16.7	15.8	14.8	15.1	17.3	17.0	16.0	↑	

3 PRICE-EARNING HISTORY as an indication of the future

This shows how stock prices have fluctuated with earnings and dividends. It is a building block for translating earnings into future stock prices.

PRESENT PRICE ___32___   HIGH THIS YEAR ___46 15/16___   LOW THIS YEAR ___29 3/8___

	Year	A PRICE HIGH	B PRICE LOW	C Earnings Per Share	D Price Earnings Ratio HIGH A ÷ C	E Price Earnings Ratio LOW B ÷ C	F Dividend Per Share	G % Payout F ÷ C × 100	H % High Yield F ÷ B × 100
1	94	16.2	11.6	0.75	21.6	15.5	0.09	12.0	0.8
2	95	18.2	12.9	0.80	22.8	16.1	0.12	15.0	0.9
3	96	18.5	15.5	0.94	19.7	16.5	0.14	14.9	0.9
4	97	30.8	17.0	1.22	25.2	13.9	0.16	13.1	0.9
5	98	46.5	27.4	1.37	33.9	20.0	0.19	13.9	0.7
6	TOTAL		84.4		123.2	82.0		68.9	
7	AVERAGE		16.9		24.6	16.4		13.8	
8	AVERAGE PRICE EARNINGS RATIO 20.5				9 CURRENT PRICE EARNINGS RATIO 22.7				

volatility of these two stocks? Look for patterns in the range of high and low stock prices. Remember that the price patterns are nice to know, but the NAIC approach is grounded in the underlying fundamentals of the company (growth in revenues and earnings). If the fundamentals are solid, that will be reflected in the price of the stock!

Earnings per Share Column C is another record of the company's EPS. (There is also one on the first page of the SSG.) This is crucial information. Your goal is to find companies that can grow sufficiently so your investment can at least double in five years.

P/E Ratios The high and low P/E ratios should be reviewed for trends. It is considered a good sign when the P/E's have increased at a steady rate or remained fairly stable. If the P/E ratios have been going down steadily, it is not a healthy signal.

Dividends The dividend per share column has no significance for many smaller, growth companies which pay no dividends.

Payout The payout ratio tells you whether a company's management is growth minded. Companies that pay out a large percentage of net earnings (say, over 50%) are considered "income stocks" with high dividend yields. Growth stocks tend to have minimal dividend payouts.

High Yield The "% high yield" calculation will be used in estimating a low price in the next lesson.

Anne Uno

Anne Uno's interest in investing philosophy started with a college assignment in the mid-1960's. Her professor asked students to research various investing philosophies, choose some for themselves, and invest a fictional $10,000 using their new philosophy. Anne remembers two tenets of her investing philosophy, which she still uses today: get rich slowly and use the magic of compounding.

Remembering her own advice, she started investing regularly as soon as she graduated from college. In 1976, she joined NAIC, and she has been a member of three investment clubs. Her current investment club is made up of six other professional Asian-American women. She is a Certified Financial Planner, a tax preparer, a small business owner, and a single mother of two.

Because she started investing early and planned for her children's education, Anne was able to put her two children through private colleges. Her advice to them: max out your 401(k), not your credit cards! She is on target with her financial plans for retirement earning an average annual return of 12-16%, but she has no plans to slow down just yet. She enjoys working with her clients, investing with the NAIC, and giving seminars to professional women.

UNDERSTAND TERMS AND IDEAS

1. Complete Section 3 for the company you are studying.

   _____

2. Explain the importance of P/E ratios. What does a high P/E indicate?

   _____

   _____

   _____

   What does a low P/E indicate?

   _____

   _____

   _____

3. What other two terms are sometimes used for P/E?

   _____

   _____

   _____

4. Define the term "payout."

   _____

   _____

   _____

5. Why don't some small companies pay a dividend? Is that necessarily bad for a stockholder?

   _____

   _____

   _____

   _____

6. What kind of pattern should you look for in P/Es? Should you ever shop for a low P/E?

   _____

   _____

   _____

   _____

LESSON 7.4

Evaluate Risk and Reward

Let's look at what you have accomplished so far. You have created a visual analysis of trends for a company's revenues, earnings per share, and common stock price, and you have drawn future projections. You have evaluated the company's management based on pre-tax profit margins and on percent earned on equity ratios. In Section 3, you examined the company's five-year price-earnings history as an indicator of the future. All of this information leads to Section 4, which will help you decide whether the stock in question is attractive for purchase or appears overvalued and should not be purchased. In this lesson, you will estimate high and low prices for the next five years to establish buy, sell, and maybe price ranges, and learn how to achieve a positive balance between reward and risk in making a stock-purchasing decision.

GOALS

■ **Forecast high and low prices the company's stock might reach in the next five years.**

■ **Establish buy, maybe, and sell price ranges.**

■ **Use the upside/ downside ratio.**

■ **Estimate future price appreciation.**

SECTION 4A: FORECAST A HIGH PRICE

In Section 4A, you estimate the high price the stock might reach within the next 5 years. First enter the average high P/E from D7 in Section 3. For Tootsie Roll, the estimated average high P/E is 24.6 as shown on page 215.

Next, enter the estimated high earnings per share generated from the earnings projection line you drew on the graph on page 201 in Lesson 7.2. For Tootsie Roll, the estimated high EPS is 2.10.

Then compute the estimated high price by multiplying the average high P/E by the estimated high earnings per share. For Tootsie Roll, the forecast high price is $24.6 \times 2.10 = 51.7$.

USE JUDGEMENT

You do not have to stick rigidly to the average high P/E from the past. Instead, you may chose a P/E which feels more comfortable and which you can justify. A stock's P/E ratio represents investors' expectations for future growth rates and future earnings per share.

When you are working with historical P/Es, remember that as growth rates slow down, P/Es tend to decline as well. For example, if the EPS of a company had a historical growth rate of 20% and you are projecting 15% over the next five years, you may want to adjust your projected high P/E to something less than the historical high P/E. If you use a P/E ratio that is too high, you may be setting an unattainable future high price target.

What is too high for the projected high P/E? This is a judgment call, but a projected P/E significantly in excess of a future EPS growth rate may be unwise.

SECTION 4B: FORECAST A LOW PRICE

You want to select the **downside risk** or low price for the next five years. This section offers four methods for estimating how low the price might drop within the next 5 years.

FOUR METHODS

Line 4B(a) *This method is appropriate for companies that display consistent growth.* Compute the low price per share in the next five years by multiplying the average low P/E (E7 in Section 3) by the estimated low earnings per share. The most recent year's earnings (C5 in Section 3) are used for the low earnings per share estimate. This EPS should be a low figure relative to the projected EPS over the next 5 years. Again, apply your judgment to selecting the representative low P/E ratio. For Tootsie Roll, you have $16.4 \times 1.37 = 22.5$.

Line 4B(b) *This method is appropriate for estimating the future low price for cyclical companies where the price movement is dictated more by general economic conditions than by growth in the company.* These include companies in industries such as automobiles, chemicals, and paper. Simply use the average low stock price for the past five years (B7 in Section 3) as the estimated low price for the next five. For Tootsie Roll, use 16.9.

Line 4B(c) *Method (c), like (b), is a guide for selecting the low price for cyclical companies, where price movement is dictated more by general economic conditions than by growth in the company.* The severe market low price is not necessarily the lowest price in Section 3, column B. A severe market is a bear market, a significant downturn in the overall stock market. Recessions that bring severe market lows are noted in grayed columns within the graph at the top of the Value Line sheets. Notice in the Value Line for Tootsie Roll on page 207 there was a recession in 1990. S&P does not provide a severe market indicator. The severe market low is used to suggest how far a price might fall when the overall stock market is down significantly. Such a time often provides a buying opportunity for fundamentally strong stocks.

You must use your judgment in selecting the severe market low price. Ask yourself, "When was the last 20% to 25% drop in the market?" If you don't know, you can ask any broker for this information. How low did your stock go in that year? Use that number for the severe market low. In 1998 from July to October there was a 20% drop in the

Not all investments work out. Take Planet Hollywood International, a movie-theme restaurant. Its IPO (Initial Public Offering) was priced at $18 in April of 1996. It hit its all time high price of $28 that same month due to high demand. But the restaurant company was new, had no established track record, did not manage expenses well, started to lose money, and hence, filed for bankruptcy. By December 14, 1999, the stock price had fallen to $0.09 per share!

market, so for Tootsie Roll use the low price for 1998, 27.4. Of course you can use a lower number if you prefer.

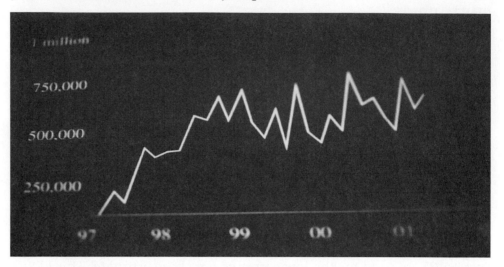

Cal-endar	GROSS QUARTERLY DIV'DS PAID c				Full Year
	Mar.31	Jun.30	Sep.30	Dec.31	
1995	.025	.03	.03	.03	.12
1996	.03	.035	.035	.035	.14
1997	.035	.04	.04	.04	.16
1998	.04	.05	.05	.05	.19
1999	.05	.05	.06		

Line 4B(d) *This approach to selecting a low price has more relevance for income (dividend) producing stocks than growth stocks.* You will find income stocks in industries such as utilities and banking and in mature large companies. This method is based on the fact that companies rarely decrease their dividend. Management likes to boast that they have maintained or raised their dividend for many years. This dividend yield acts as a buffer when a company's stock price may be declining. There is a point where the dividend will attract investors, and the dividend will support that particular price level.

To compute the price the dividend will support, first find the present annual dividend. If the dividend is paid quarterly, multiply the last quarter's dividend (from Value Line) by four to get the present annual dividend. For Tootsie Roll, the last dividend of 0.06 was in September 1999. So the present annual dividend is $4 \times 0.06 = 0.24$.

Find the highest number in the High Yield column H in Section 3. Remember to change the percent to a decimal (0.9% = 0.009). Then divide the present dividend by the high yield. For Tootsie Roll,

$$\frac{\text{Percent Dividend}}{\text{High Yield}} = \frac{0.24}{0.009} = 26.7$$

General economic conditions, rather than growth or changes by the company, govern the stock price of a cyclical company. Enter key words or phrases like *cyclical stock* to investigate companies in a cyclical industry.

Use Your Judgment From what you have learned by examining these four methods, you must select a low price for the next five years. The four methods are suited to different types of companies. Still, there are times when good judgment suggests a price somewhere in the middle of those prices. The low price of the last 52 weeks should be noted. If, for instance, the company is a good growth company where you would normally choose 4B(a), but the 52-week low price or current price is very close to the 4B(a) price, you may need a lower estimate. Certainly, you can never use a low price that is higher than the present price.

You should never just average the four methods. Doing so has no meaning. Many investors frequently select a low price that is around 20% to 25% below the current price of the stock under study—to acknowledge the possibility of a general stock market correction or normal volatility of the market and stock prices. You should use your own best judgment in estimating a low price or downside risk for the next five years.

SECTION 4C: ZONING

Next, establish three price zones—*buy*, *maybe* (or *hold*), and *sell*—between the high and low prices you have forecast.

In the first line of Section 4C, subtract the low forecast price (4B) from the high forecast price (4A) to determine the range. Then divide the range by 3 to determine one-third of the range. For Tootsie Roll,

Range High forecast – Low forecast = $51.70 – $22.50 = $29.20

One-third of Range $29.20 ÷ 3 = $9.70

PRICE ZONES

Buy Price Zone From the low forecast price to one-third of the range (4CD) plus the low forecast price.

low forecast + one-third of range = $22.50 + $9.70 = $32.20

Sell Price Zone From the high forecast price minus one-third of the range (4CD) to the high forecast price.

high forecast – one-third of range = $51.70 – $9.70 = $42.00

Maybe or Hold Price Zone From one-third of the range plus the low forecast price to the high forecast price minus one-third of the range.

For Tootsie Roll, it is a price between $32.20 and $42.00.

In the last line in Section 4C, write the present market price of the stock and indicate the zone (buy, maybe, or sell) it is in. For Tootsie Roll, the present price is $32.00, which is in the buy range.

SECTION 4D: UPSIDE/DOWNSIDE RATIO

If your high and low price forecasts are reasonably accurate, the upside/downside ratio will help you get a feel for whether the risks are worth taking. Ideally, you want to buy a significantly higher reward potential than level of risk. The upside/downside ratio attempts to estimate this relationship. NAIC recommends looking for at least a 3 to 1 upside/downside ratio to make your decision a prudent one. After all, you want to buy towards the lower end of the buy range, not the high end (buy low, sell high).

$$\text{Upside/Downside Ratio} = \frac{\text{High Price} - \text{Present Price}}{\text{Present Price} - \text{Low Price}}$$

For Tootsie Roll, $\frac{51.70 - 32}{32 - 22.50} = \frac{19.70}{9.50} = 2.07$.

The Tootsie Roll calculations do not show a 3 to 1 upside/downside ratio. However, the stock price is in the upper range of the buy zone, which is a positive factor.

ABNORMALLY HIGH UPSIDE/ DOWNSIDE RATIOS

You should be careful if you have an abnormally high upside/downside ratio. Ratios of 10 to 1 or higher should be questioned. Re-check the high and low forecast prices for accuracy.

Have you used a sufficiently conservative estimated low price? The estimated low price greatly affects the upside/downside ratio.

For example, if you chose 15.5 for the low price, the upside/downside ratio is:

$$\frac{51.70 - 32}{32 - 15.50} = \frac{19.70}{16.50} = 1.19$$

For example, if you chose 27.4 for the low price, the upside/downside ratio is:

$$\frac{51.70 - 32}{32 - 27.40} = \frac{19.70}{4.60} = 4.28$$

A lower low price decreases the upside/downside ratio and a higher low price increases the upside/downside ratio.

An abnormally high upside/downside ratio indicates that the stock is currently selling at or near its projected low for the next 5 years.

The upside/downside ratio is an indicator of the attractiveness of an investment. It is another tool for making a rational decision. Be honest with yourself and never force estimated high or low prices by manipulating the figures. They must be reasonable.

2 EVALUATING MANAGEMENT   Company _Tootsie Roll_

	19_89_	19_90_	19_91_	19_92_	19_93_	19_94_	19_95_	19_96_	19_97_	19_98_	LAST 5 YEAR AVG.	TREND UP	TREND DOWN
A % Pre-tax Profits on Sales (Net Before Taxed ÷ Sales)	18.5	19.1	21.2	21.1	22.2	20.6	20.5	22.0	25.4	27.3	23.2	↑	
B % Earned on Equity (E/S ÷ Book Value)	18.4	17.4	17.4	17.6	16.7	15.8	14.8	15.1	17.3	17.0	16.0	↑	

3 PRICE-EARNING HISTORY as an indication of the future

This shows how stock prices have fluctuated with earnings and dividends. It is a building block for translating earnings into future stock prices.

PRESENT PRICE ___32___   HIGH THIS YEAR ___46 15/16___   LOW THIS YEAR ___29 3/8___

	Year	A PRICE HIGH	B PRICE LOW	C Earnings Per Share	D Price Earnings Ratio HIGH A÷C	E Price Earnings Ratio LOW B÷C	F Dividend Per Share	G % Payout F÷C×100	H % High Yield F÷B×100
1	94	16.2	11.6	0.75	21.6	15.5	0.09	12.0	0.8
2	95	18.2	12.9	0.80	22.8	16.1	0.12	15.0	0.9
3	96	18.5	15.5	0.94	19.7	16.5	0.14	14.9	0.9
4	97	30.8	17.0	1.22	25.2	13.9	0.16	13.1	0.9
5	98	46.5	27.4	1.37	33.9	20.0	0.19	13.9	0.7
6	TOTAL		84.4		123.2	82.0		68.9	
7	AVERAGE		16.9		24.6	16.4		13.8	
8	AVERAGE PRICE EARNINGS RATIO 20.5				9 CURRENT PRICE EARNINGS RATIO 22.7				

4 EVALUATING RISK and REWARD over the next 5 years

Assuming one recession and one business boom every 5 years, calculations are made of how high and how low the stock might sell. The upside-downside ratio is the key to evaluating risk and reward.

A HIGH PRICE — NEXT 5 YEARS

Avg. High P/E ___24.6___ (3D7 as adj.) × Estimated High Earnings Per Share ___2.10___ = Forecast High Price $ ___51.7___ (4A1)

B LOW PRICE — NEXT 5 YEARS

(a) Avg Low P/E ___16.4___ (3E7 as adj.) × Estimated Low Earnings Per Share ___1.37___ = Forecast Low Price $ ___22.5___

(b) Avg Low Price of Last 5 Years = ___16.9___ (3B7)

(c) Recent Severe Market Low Price = ___27.4___ (3B7)

(d) Price Dividend Will Support   Present Divd. / High Yield (H) = ___0.24___ / ___0.009___ = ___26.7___

Selected Estimated Low Price _____ = $ ___22.5___

C ZONING

___51.70___ (4A1) High Forecast Price   Minus   ___22.50___ (4B1) Low Forecast Price   Equals   ___29.20___ (C)   Range. 1/3 of Range = ___9.70___ (4CD)

(4C2) Lower 1/3 = (4B1) ___22.50___ to ___32.20___ (Buy)

(4C3) Middle 1/3 = ___32.20___ to ___42.00___ (Maybe)

(4C3) Upper 1/3 = ___42.00___ to ___51.70___ (4A1) (Sell)

Present Market Price of ___$32.00___ is in the ___buy___ (4C5) Range

D UPSIDE DOWNSIDE RATIO (Potential Gain vs. Risk of Loss)

High Price (4A1) ___51.70___ Minus Present Price ___32___ / Present Price ___32___ Minus Low Price (4B1) ___22.50___ = ___19.70___ / ___9.50___ = ___2.07___ (4D) To 1

E PRICE TARGET (Note: This shows the potential market price appreciation over the next five years in simple interest terms.)

High Price (4A1) ___51.70___ / Present Market Price ___32___ = (___1.62___) × 100 = (___162___) − 100 = ___62___ (4E) % Appreciation

5 5-YEAR POTENTIAL *This combines price appreciation with dividend yield to get an estimate of total return. It provides a standard for comparing income and growth stocks.*

A Present Full Year's Dividend $ _____ / Present Price of Stock $ _____ = _____ × 100 = _____ (5A) Present Yield or % Returned on Purchase Price

B AVERAGE YIELD OVER NEXT FIVE YEARS

Avg. Earnings Per Share Next 5 Years _____ × Avg. % Payout (3G7) _____ = _____ / Present Price $ _____ = _____ % (5B)

C ESTIMATED AVERAGE ANNUAL RETURN OVER NEXT 5 YEARS

5-Year Appreciation Potential (4E) _____ / 5 = _____ %

Average Yield (5B) .... _____ %

Average Total Return Over The Next 5 Years (5C) _____ %

Table to Convert From Simple to Compound Rate

Simple Rate   2 4 6 8 10 12 14 16 18 20 22 24 26 28 30 32 34 36 38 40

Compound Rate   2 4 6 8 10 12 14 16 18 20 22 24

SECTION 4E: PRICE APPRECIATION

This section provides a way of using your estimated high price to determine whether the stock you are studying could double in price (or grow by 100%) in the next five years. Here's the formula:

$$\text{Potential 5-Year Appreciation} = \left(\frac{\text{High Price}}{\text{Present Price}} \times 100\right) - 100\%$$

You multiply by 100 to change the decimal to a percent. Then subtract 100% to obtain the percent of appreciation. The target should be at least double the present stock price, or 100% appreciation. Thus, the answer to Section 4E should be 100% or better. Note: If there is a dividend, the average annual dividend may be added to the price appreciation to estimate the total return.

For Tootsie Roll, the potential 5-year appreciation is

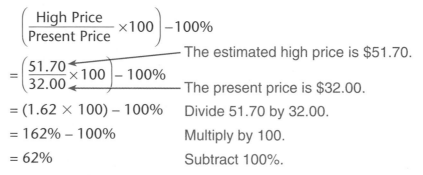

$$\left(\frac{\text{High Price}}{\text{Present Price}} \times 100\right) - 100\%$$

$$= \left(\frac{51.70}{32.00} \times 100\right) - 100\%$$

The estimated high price is $51.70.

The present price is $32.00.

$$= (1.62 \times 100) - 100\%$$ Divide 51.70 by 32.00.

$$= 162\% - 100\%$$ Multiply by 100.

$$= 62\%$$ Subtract 100%.

At 62% appreciation, this example does not meet the NAIC goal of doubling within the next 5 years, however, other criteria should also be taken into consideration. A buy is not based only on one portion of the study. All factors must be considered.

SUMMARY

The estimated high price in the next five years is determined by multiplying the average high P/E (after adjustments) by the estimated high earnings per share. There are four ways to estimate where the low price may fall within the next five years. There may be situations that call for choosing a low price somewhere in the middle of the calculated low prices. Buy, maybe, and sell ranges are determined by dividing the difference between the estimated high and low prices into thirds. When you buy a stock, it is important to estimate the risk/reward ratio. If you think a stock you own has reached its potential, do a new set of SSG calculations before selling it. Remember your goal: the stock price should double in the next five years.

UNDERSTAND TERMS AND IDEAS

1. On your SSG, calculate the estimated high price asked for on 4A.

2. For the stock you are studying, calculate the four methods for estimating a possible low price asked for in 4B(a), 4B(b), 4B(c) and 4B(d).

3. Explain when it is best to use each of the four methods for estimating future low price.

_____

_____

_____

_____

4. What situations may cause you to choose a price other than those shown by the four low prices calculated?

_____

_____

_____

_____

5. Choose an estimated low price for your study. Explain your choice.

_____

6. Explain how to find the buy, maybe, and sell zones.

_____

7. Calculate the buy, maybe and sell zones on your stock study.

_____

8. Explain the upside/downside ratio.

_____

_____

_____

9. Calculate the upside/downside ratio for the stock you are studying. Complete Section 4D.

_____

10. Complete Section 4E for the stock you are studying.

_____

11. Does your stock have an upside/downside ratio that meets the NAIC goal?

_____

Chapter 7 REVIEW

SUMMARY

LESSON 7.1 EVALUATE MANAGEMENT

Section 2 of the SSG identifies financial data that is helpful in evaluating a company's management. A well-managed company will have a good profit margin and a good return on equity capital.

LESSON 7.2 ESTIMATE FUTURE GROWTH RATES

Once you have calculated a company's historical growth rate, you must use your judgment about the company, the management, and the product to predict a company's future growth.

LESSON 7.3 PRICE-EARNINGS HISTORY

Section 3 of the SSG examines the company's five-year price/earnings history as an indicator of the future. The company's financial earnings data are crucial to your evaluation of the stock price.

LESSON 7.4 EVALUATE RISK AND REWARD

In Section 4, you estimate high and low prices for the next five years to establish buy, sell, and maybe price ranges. This helps you weigh the risk involved in making the stock purchase.

REVIEW INVESTING TERMS

Write the letter of the term that matches each definition.

1. _____ pre-tax profit divided by sales or profit margin

2. _____ the percentage of earnings that a company pays to shareholders in the form of cash dividends

3. _____ the dollar amount of earnings that a company pays to shareholders

4. _____ return on the capital supplied by common stockholders (through their stock purchases and through net profits plowed back into the company)

5. _____ the dividend as a ratio to the price

6. _____ low price for the next five years

a. dividend
b. downside risk
c. payout
d. percent earned on equity
e. price/earnings ratio (P/E)
f. profit margin trend
g. ratio of pre-tax profit to sales
h. yield

UNDERSTAND TERMS AND IDEAS

7. What time period in a company's history is the most important?

8. When making future projections of sales and earnings, which should you project first? Explain.

9. How does a P/E ratio help you set expectations for growth and compare the value of stocks? Explain the meaning of a high P/E ratio and a low P/E ratio.

10. Company A paid dividends last year. Company B did not. Both companies are well managed. What does this tell you about the companies?

11. What are the three price zones? How is each one calculated?

SHARPEN YOUR RESEARCH SKILLS

12. Analysts often issue buy, sell, and hold recommendations. They usually support these recommendations with some comments. List the comments analysts used to support the three different buy recommendations.

_____

_____

_____

13. How would you locate the recommendations? Describe another way you could have found the same type of information.

_____

_____

_____

THINK CRITICALLY

14. Your friend Alex is excited about a company he has been researching. All the numbers on the Stock Selection Guide he is filling out look good. However, you heard on *Wall Street Week* that the company has experienced major management changes in the last six months. What advice do you give him? Why?

_____

_____

_____

15. A local company sells special coffeepots used in military airplanes. They have been selling these successfully for 8 years, but have never developed any other customers. Their numbers look good on the Stock Selection Guide. What other information should you locate to evaluate them as an investment?

_____

_____

_____

_____

PROSPECTIVE PORTFOLIO PROJECT

In this chapter, you learned more about using the Stock Selection Guide to evaluate potential investments. Analyze your current portfolio. Continue the SSG you started for each of the stocks in your portfolio. As you fill in the data for Sections 2, 3, and 4 of the SSG, write comments in each column below for every stock in your portfolio. This will help you rate the stocks against each other. This is more detailed financial information. Some companies may move up in your portfolio. Others may be eliminated.

Company	Profit Margin Trend	Percent Earned on Equity Trend	Projections for Sales and EPS	Price Trend and Volatility	Price Zone	Price Appreciation

Compare the financial data and trends for the stocks in your portfolio. Is one of the companies starting to stand out in the ratings?

Chapter 8

THE BOTTOM LINE

LESSON 8.1 THE FIVE-YEAR POTENTIAL

LESSON 8.2 MAKE YOUR DECISION

INDUSTRY INDICATORS
BANKS

Republic Bancorp
Founded in 1986

Republic Bancorp became an incorporated bank holding company in Michigan in 1986. Its offices offer various financial services for individual customers, small businesses, and commercial developers. Through its 134 offices in 21 states, Republic Bancorp provides home equity, commercial, and consumer loans, as well as residential mortgage loans and construction loans for home buyers. In addition to offering loans, Republic Bancorp supplies retail banking services to customers in Michigan, Ohio, and Indiana through 40 retail bank branches.

Beginning as a Michigan bank holding company, Republic Bancorp greatly expanded its number of bank offices in the United States to become the 21st-largest retail mortgage lender in the country by 1998. It was also named the number one Small Business Administration lender in the state of Michigan, approving more small-business loans than any other lender in that state. The success of Republic Bancorp may be attributed to its policy of providing its customers with expertise, good service, and fast loan approvals. The volume of commercial loan closings by Republic Bancorp increased by 50% in 1998, due in part to its commitment to customer service.

Republic Bancorp merged with D&N Financial Corporation in 1999. As a result of this merger, Republic Bancorp became the 100th-largest bank in the United States, as well as the 19th-largest retail mortgage lender. It has 187 offices in 21 states and continues to open retail and mortgage business offices in growth-oriented markets.

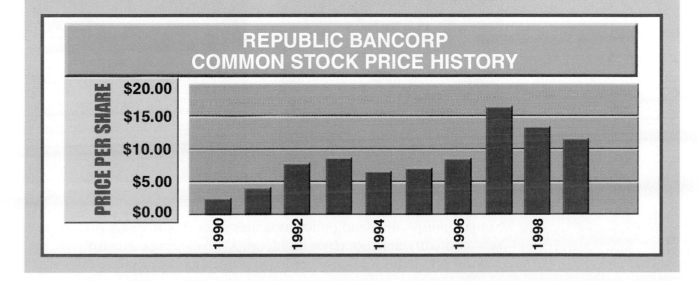

REPUBLIC BANCORP
COMMON STOCK PRICE HISTORY

The Five-Year Potential

T he last step in completing the SSG is Section 5, "5-Year Potential." In this section, you will estimate the annual total return for the stock you are studying. Remember that total return includes your return from the stock's price appreciation and from the dividend yield. This calculation is not intended to be precise, but is rather an estimate. This number is not a compound growth rate. It is a simple interest growth rate and must be 20% to double your investment in 5 years.

GOALS

■ Calculate dividend yield.

■ Find the estimated annual total return for the next 5 years.

DETERMINE THE TOTAL RETURN

As an investor, you have two basic ways to make money from investing in stocks:

Price Appreciation Buying at the present price and having the stock price increase.

Dividend Yield Receiving cash dividends for your shares of stock.

The **annual total return** you receive is a combination of both of these. If a company pays no dividend, the only gain comes from price appreciation. If a company does pay a dividend, then that is an additional source of gain. Although some companies do not pay a dividend, you need to be sure to include the dividend yield in your calculation of total return for those companies that do pay a dividend.

DIVIDEND POLICY FOR COMPANIES

Management's dividend policy indicates the company's growth stage. A new company may not pay a dividend. A developing company may pay a small dividend. A mature company typically pays a larger dividend.

The smaller the company the greater the need to retain earnings to help the company to grow, so smaller companies do not typically pay dividends. Larger companies can afford to share a portion of their earnings. The earnings per share growth rate of a larger company is usually less than that of a small company. The total annual return may be similar, however, since what the company lacks in price appreciation can be made up in dividend yield. For example, Tootsie Roll pays dividends that increase the total return.

SECTION 5A: CALCULATE PRESENT YIELD

The **present yield** (or current yield) of a common stock tells you how much of your annual return is from dividend income. You should be aware of this information, but remember that this figure is only your present yield and does not reflect future (potential) dividend increases or decreases. You calculate the present yield of your stock in Section 5A as shown on page 227.

General Electric Company is the only stock of the original 12 in the 1896 Dow Jones Industrial Average that is in the average today. Its stock closed at $108 its first day of trading in 1892. With dividend reinvestment and stock splits, that one share would have grown to about 60,000 shares worth about $9 million by December 1999! GE has had 8 stock splits in its history, and another one is planned in 2000. GE's dividends have increased every year for 24 consecutive years.

FIND THE FULL YEAR DIVIDEND

First, find the most recent quarterly dividend on the bottom left of the Value Line Report. Then, multiply the most recent quarterly dividend by four to determine the present full year dividend.

Cal-endar	GROSS QUARTERLY DIV'DS PAID c				Full Year
	Mar.31	Jun.30	Sep.30	Dec.31	
1995	.025	.03	.03	.03	.12
1996	.03	.035	.035	.035	.14
1997	.035	.04	.04	.04	.16
1998	.04	.05	.05	.05	.19
1999	.05	.05	.06		

Present full year dividend = Most recent quarterly dividend $\times$ 4

For Tootsie Roll, the most recent quarterly dividend is 0.06 for September 30, 1999. So, for Tootsie Roll, the present full year dividend is:

$$0.06 \times 4 = 0.24$$

Some companies pay an annual dividend rather than an quarterly dividend. For those companies, just use the annual dividend.

FIND THE PRESENT YIELD

To determine the present yield, which is the percentage returned on the purchase price, divide the present full year's dividend by the present price of the stock, and multiply by 100.

$$\text{Present Yield} = \frac{\text{Present full year's dividend}}{\text{Present price of stock}} \times 100$$

For Tootsie Roll, the present price is $32. So, the present yield is:

$$\text{Present Yield} = \frac{0.24}{32} \times 100 = 0.0075 \times 100 = 0.75\%$$

This means that no matter how the price of the stock varies, you will still get the dividend yield of 0.75%.

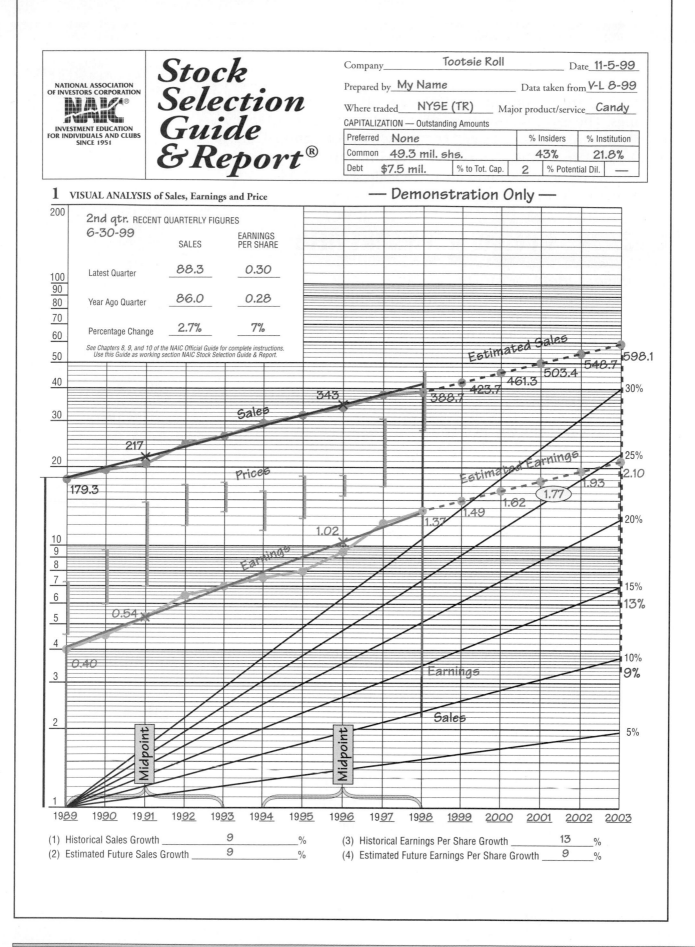

Stock Selection Guide & Report®

NATIONAL ASSOCIATION OF INVESTORS CORPORATION
NAIC®
INVESTMENT EDUCATION FOR INDIVIDUALS AND CLUBS SINCE 1951

Company	Tootsie Roll	Date	11-5-99
Prepared by	My Name	Data taken from	V-L 8-99
Where traded	NYSE (TR)	Major product/service	Candy

CAPITALIZATION — Outstanding Amounts

Preferred	None		% Insiders	% Institution
Common	49.3 mil. shs.		43%	21.8%
Debt	$7.5 mil.	% to Tot. Cap. 2	% Potential Dil.	—

1 VISUAL ANALYSIS of Sales, Earnings and Price

— Demonstration Only —

2nd qtr. RECENT QUARTERLY FIGURES
6-30-99

	SALES	EARNINGS PER SHARE
Latest Quarter	88.3	0.30
Year Ago Quarter	86.0	0.28
Percentage Change	2.7%	7%

See Chapters 8, 9, and 10 of the NAIC Official Guide for complete instructions.
Use this Guide as working section NAIC Stock Selection Guide & Report.

Estimated Sales

Estimated Earnings

Sales

Prices

Earnings

Sales

Earnings

Midpoint   Midpoint

598.1
548.7
503.4
461.3
423.7
388.7
343
217
179.3
2.10
1.93
1.77
1.62
1.49
1.37
1.02
0.54
0.40

30% 25% 20% 15% 13% 10% 9% 5%

1989 1990 1991 1992 1993 1994 1995 1996 1997 1998 1999 2000 2001 2002 2003

(1) Historical Sales Growth _____9_____ %
(2) Estimated Future Sales Growth _____9_____ %
(3) Historical Earnings Per Share Growth _____13_____ %
(4) Estimated Future Earnings Per Share Growth _____9_____ %

2 EVALUATING MANAGEMENT   Company _Tootsie Roll_

	19_89_	19_90_	19_91_	19_92_	19_93_	19_94_	19_95_	19_96_	19_97_	19_98_	LAST 5 YEAR AVG.	TREND UP	TREND DOWN
A % Pre-tax Profits on Sales (Net Before Taxed ÷ Sales)	18.5	19.1	21.2	21.1	22.2	20.6	20.5	22.0	25.4	27.3	23.2	↑	
B % Earned on Equity (E/S ÷ Book Value)	18.4	17.4	17.4	17.6	16.7	15.8	14.8	15.1	17.3	17.0	16.0	↑	

3 PRICE-EARNING HISTORY as an indication of the future

This shows how stock prices have fluctuated with earnings and dividends. It is a building block for translating earnings into future stock prices.

PRESENT PRICE ___32___   HIGH THIS YEAR ___46 15/16___   LOW THIS YEAR ___29 3/8___

	Year	A PRICE HIGH	B PRICE LOW	C Earnings Per Share	D Price Earnings Ratio HIGH A÷C	E Price Earnings Ratio LOW B÷C	F Dividend Per Share	G % Payout F÷C×100	H % High Yield F÷B×100
1	94	16.2	11.6	0.75	21.6	15.5	0.09	12.0	0.8
2	95	18.2	12.9	0.80	22.8	16.1	0.12	15.0	0.9
3	96	18.5	15.5	0.94	19.7	16.5	0.14	14.9	0.9
4	97	30.8	17.0	1.22	25.2	13.9	0.16	13.1	0.9
5	98	46.5	27.4	1.37	33.9	20.0	0.19	13.9	0.7
6	TOTAL		84.4		123.2	82.0		68.9	
7	AVERAGE		16.9		24.6	16.4		13.8	
8	AVERAGE PRICE EARNINGS RATIO 20.5				9	CURRENT PRICE EARNINGS RATIO 22.6			

4 EVALUATING RISK and REWARD over the next 5 years

Assuming one recession and one business boom every 5 years, calculations are made of how high and how low the stock might sell. The upside-downside ratio is the key to evaluating risk and reward.

A HIGH PRICE — NEXT 5 YEARS

Avg. High P/E ___24.6___ (3D7 as adj.) × Estimated High Earnings Per Share ___2.10___ (4A1) = Forecast High Price $ ___51.7___

B LOW PRICE — NEXT 5 YEARS

(a) Avg Low P/E ___16.4___ (3E7 as adj.) × Estimated Low Earnings Per Share ___1.37___ = Forecast Low Price $ ___22.5___

(b) Avg Low Price of Last 5 Years = ___16.9___ (3B7)

(c) Recent Severe Market Low Price = ___27.4___ (3B7)

(d) Price Dividend Will Support $\frac{\text{Present Divd.}}{\text{High Yield (H)}}$ = $\frac{0.24}{0.009}$ = ___26.7___

Selected Estimated Low Price _____ = $ ___22.5___

C ZONING

___51.70___ (4A1) High Forecast Price Minus ___22.50___ (4B1) Low Forecast Price Equals ___29.20___ (C) Range. 1/3 of Range = ___9.70___ (4CD)

(4C2) Lower 1/3 = (4B1) ___22.50___ to ___32.20___ (Buy)

(4C3) Middle 1/3 = ___32.20___ to ___42.00___ (Maybe)

(4C3) Upper 1/3 = ___42.00___ to ___51.70___ (4A1) (Sell)

Present Market Price of ___$32.00___ is in the ___buy___ (4C5) Range

D UPSIDE DOWNSIDE RATIO (Potential Gain vs. Risk of Loss)

$\frac{\text{High Price (4A1) } 51.70 \text{ Minus Present Price } 32}{\text{Present Price } 32 \text{ Minus Low Price (4B1) } 22.50}$ = $\frac{19.70}{9.50}$ = ___2.07___ (4D) To 1

E PRICE TARGET (Note: This shows the potential market price appreciation over the next five years in simple interest terms.)

$\frac{\text{High Price (4A1) } 51.70}{\text{Present Market Price } 32}$ = (___1.62___) × 100 = (___162___) - 100 = ___62___ (4E) % Appreciation

5 5-YEAR POTENTIAL   This combines price appreciation with dividend yield to get an estimate of total return. It provides a standard for comparing income and growth stocks.

A $\frac{\text{Present Full Year's Dividend \$ } 0.24}{\text{Present Price of Stock \$ } 32}$ = ___0.0075___ × 100 = ___0.75___ (5A) Present Yield or % Returned on Purchase Price

B AVERAGE YIELD OVER NEXT FIVE YEARS

Avg. Earnings Per Share Next 5 Years ___1.77___ × Avg. % Payout (3G7) ___0.138___ = $\frac{0.244}{32}$ Present Price $ = ___0.8___ (5B) %

C ESTIMATED AVERAGE ANNUAL RETURN OVER NEXT 5 YEARS

$\frac{\text{5-Year Appreciation Potential (4E) } 62}{5}$ = ___12.4___ %

Average Yield (5B) ___0.8___ %

Average Total Return Over The Next 5 Years (5C) ___13.2___ %

Table to Convert From Simple to Compound Rate

Simple Rate: 2 4 6 8 10 12 14 16 18 20 22 24 26 28 30 32 34 36 38 40

Compound Rate: 2 4 6 8 10 12 14 16 18 20 22 24

10.7%

SECTION 5B: AVERAGE YIELD OVER NEXT 5 YEARS

In Section 5B, you calculate your estimated (projected) average dividend yield. As earnings per share grow, dividends will also grow. You use the projected average annual earnings per share and the average percent of payout to figure out your projected dividend yield.

> ### DOLLAR SENSE
> **If the job has been correctly done when a common stock is purchased, the time to sell it is—almost never.**
>
> —*Philip Fisher*

FIND THE AVERAGE EARNINGS PER SHARE OVER NEXT 5 YEARS

Use the graph on page 1 of the Stock Selection Guide. The average earnings per share (EPS) over the next 5 years is on the earnings per share projection line. Simply look at the SSG Visual Analysis (graph) and read where the earning per share projection line crosses the middle (3rd) year of the 5 projected years. The right margin is the 5th year. For Tootsie Roll, this is $1.77 as shown on page 226.

FIND THE AVERAGE PERCENT OF PAYOUT

You calculated the average percent of payout in Section 3, column G, row 7. For Tootsie Roll, this is 13.8%.

ESTIMATE THE AVERAGE ANNUAL DIVIDEND PER SHARE

Next, multiply the average EPS over the next 5 years by the average payout ratio (percent converted to decimal by dividing by 100).

Average EPS next 5 years × average payout ratio

$$\$1.77 \times 0.138 = 0.224$$

Then divide the average dividend per share by the present price of the common stock, to obtain the estimated average annual dividend yield over the next 5 years. For Tootsie Roll, the present stock price per share is $32. So, the estimated average annual dividend yield over the next 5 years is

$$0.244 \div 32 = 0.007625 = 0.8\%$$

SECTION 5C: ESTIMATED ANNUAL TOTAL RETURN

The estimated annual total return over the next five years is the average annual price gain plus the average annual dividend yield. This is computed as follows:

Step 1 Divide the five-year percent of price appreciation from Section 4, box 4E by five to get the average annual price appreciation.

$$\text{Average annual price appreciation} = \frac{\text{5-year appreciation potential}}{5} = \frac{62\%}{5} = 12.4\%$$

Step 2 If a dividend is paid, add the average dividend yield from Section 5, box 5B to the annual price appreciation to get the average total return for the next 5 years.

Average annual price appreciation	+	Average yield over next 5 years	=	Average total return for the next 5 years
12.4%	+	0.8%	=	13.2%

This average total return is a simple interest rate. So, in order for you to double your money in 5 years, this rate would need to be 20%.

CONVERT TO COMPOUND RATE

You can convert the figure for the simple average annual total return to a compound rate of return. In the bottom right corner of page 2 of the SSG shown on page 227 you will find a table to convert from the simple rate to a compound rate of growth. For Tootsie Roll, the 13.2% simple rate converts to approximately a 10.7% compound rate.

WHAT DOES SECTION 5 MEAN?

Remember that the SSG is best suited for growth-oriented stocks. This section is important because it shows how to calculate total return and what the dividend yield contributes. Your goal is a doubling of the value of your investment in 5 years. Some stocks may yield 2% in dividends, and the appreciation may be 13%. That reaches our goal of 15% total annual return. Common stocks that pay a dividend tend to have less volatility in their prices than stocks where the total return is derived entirely from price appreciation. More cautious investors may prefer to choose stocks where some of the total annual return is from dividends.

inve$tor profile

Thomas O'Hara

Thomas O'Hara had a modest goal when he began to invest. He wanted to support a wife and family one day. He and a friend started an investment club in 1940, the year that most of the members were drafted into fighting World War II. February 2000 will be the 60th anniversary of the club. It now has a total of $6.5 million, despite considerable withdrawals from retiring members. Over the club's lifetime, the average annual return was 13.5%.

Thomas enjoyed investing and thought that if more people understood the benefit of investing, more people would do it. He was one of the three founders of the NAIC in 1951. He started by investing $10 a month in his investment club. Eventually, he invested 10% of his income each month. Now, he estimates that he invests close to 50% of his income in investment clubs and his own investments. His average annual return has been approximately 14%.

Thomas has raised his family and has enough money for a very comfortable retirement. He still enjoys spreading the NAIC message of the time value of money and sound investing principles. His children are all involved with the NAIC or investing. His wife has even joined a few investment clubs. She has used some of her profits to take her husband to China twice. Their investment goals have changed. Now they enjoy giving generously to their favorite charities.

UNDERSTAND TERMS AND IDEAS

1. Explain what the dividend policy may tell you about the company's growth stage.

2. Calculate the yield on the present purchase price for the stock you are studying.

3. Locate the average earnings per share for the next 5 years for your stock.

4. Calculate your stock's average yield over the next five years.

5. Calculate your stock's average annual return over the next five years.

6. Convert your stock's simple growth rate to a compound growth rate.

Make Your Decision

After completing pages 1 and 2 of the SSG for the stock you are studying, you are ready for a final decision. On SSG pages 3 and 4 you will answer a set of eight questions designed to help you reach a decision based on the data and calculations in the first two pages of the Stock Selection Guide and on several other important considerations.

SSG REPORT CARD

Pages 3 and 4 of the Stock Selection Guide are shown on pages 233 and 234. At the top of page 3 of the SSG is a "report card" for the stock you have just analyzed. You can grade the company (good, average, poor) in three main categories—judging management, evaluating price, and weighing other considerations. You can write your conclusion in the box provided.

The eight questions on SSG pages 3 and 4 deal with the same areas you are asked to judge on your report card. They provide a concise review of the work you have done so far. You may find it more natural to respond to the eight questions first, and then to complete the stock selection process by filling in the report card and writing your conclusion.

Other questions you may want to ask yourself as you conclude your study of a particular stock include:

- Is the stock in the buy zone?
- Is there at least a 3-to-1 upside/downside ratio?
- Is the current P/E equal to or less than the 5-year average P/E?
- Is the company growth rate acceptable?
- Are there signs of quality management?

Keep your goals and your tolerance for risk in mind. Remember, it's your money and your decision what investment is the best choice for you.

GOALS

- **Understand the relevance of each of the eight questions to your stock selection decision.**

- **Determine whether a stock qualifies as a growth stock and meets your investment needs.**

THE RULE OF FIVE

Keep in mind that the Stock Selection Guide (SSG) is just that, a guide with no guarantees attached to it. George Nicholson, Jr. was one of the founders of the NAIC, and the man who developed the Stock Selection Guide. He cautioned that, for every five stocks you select with the SSG, one is likely to have unexpected trouble, three will probably meet your expectations, and one may well perform decidedly better than you predicted. It is the average performance of your portfolio that will help you achieve your goal of doubling value every five years.

NAIC CLASSIC

Once you have mastered completing the Stock Selection Guide and have an understanding of what the figures tell you and how much you must rely on your own judgment, you may want to begin using NAIC Classic, a stock evaluation software program. This text includes a CD containing NAIC Classic, Student Edition. This program will save you time in completing the Stock Selection Guide. For those of you who sometimes feel lost around computers, the program features an animated wizard. He'll give you hints on the different procedures as you work, and you can summon him instantly with a single mouse click.

Rachel used the SSG to select five stocks. How well is her portfolio performing at the end of the first year? Is she on track to double her investment in five years?

Solution Use the Rule of Five to evaluate the portfolio. Her stocks performed as follows:

Stock	A	B	C	D	E
Gain	10%	28%	17%	41%	−23%

Add the performance of the 5 stocks to calculate the total gain or loss this year.

$$10\% + 28\% + 17\% + 41\% + (-23\%) = 73\%$$

To calculate the average gain or loss this year, divide the total gain by the number of stocks.

$$73\% \div 5 = 14.6\%$$

The average increase in her portfolio was 14.6%. In order to double her value in five years, her portfolio should grow about 15% every year. She seems to be on her way. Perhaps she should take a look at her fifth stock. It seems to be the one that did not meet expectations!

GOALS IN SELECTING A STOCK

You want to look ahead five years by **judging** Management capability and **evaluating** the Price you should pay for a stock. You should also look at **Other Considerations** and reach a **Conclusion. Your findings are registered in the table at the right and your Conclusion below.**

Novice and professional investors to varying degrees may act hastily on new products, tips, technical clues and short term factors rather than being methodical in their decisions. Thirty years of experience with this type of report tends to show that there is a RULE OF FIVE, which is this: If five companies are analyzed for their five year future, one may have unforeseeable trouble, three may be on target, and one may have unpredictable good fortune.

CONCLUSION: _____

_____

_____

_____

(1) Our goal is to find a company with **able** MANAGEMENT; and (2) to buy a stock at a **good** PRICE.

	Page	Good	Average	Poor
Judging Management				
Driving Force	3			
Earned on Sales	3			
Earned on Equity	3			
Evaluating Price				
High in 5 Years	4			
Low in 5 Years	4			
Upside-Downside Ratio	4			
Yield Current	4			
Total Return	4			
Other Considerations				
Industry Potentials	4			
State of Business Cycle	4			
Stock Price Trends	4			
Quality of Stock	4			
Capitalization and Finance	2			

METHOD-DATA-INSTRUCTIONS

This report organizes data presentation in a concise professional manner, avoiding among other things the agony of deciding what factors to cover. Because writing is a chore, the cross-out-method lets you report your judgments with ease. The data used comes from Value Line and Standard and Poor's Reports that are available on many listed and unlisted companies. You may wish to check your 5 year "high estimate" with Value Line's estimated Target Price Range for 3 to 5 years

hence. Instructions for completing pages 3 and 4 of this report are in the NAIC Official Guide obtainable from the National Association of Investors Corporation, P.O. Box 220, Royal Oak, Michigan 48068. Other sources of data are annual and quarterly reports from companies, brokers reports and visits to company annual meetings. You may learn by yourself, or with several friends, or by actually investing $20 or $50 a month through an investment club you have formed with friends.

1 WHAT DOES THE VISUAL ANALYSIS SHOW?

The trend of (sales) (revenues) is (up) (down) (sideways).

The trend of earnings per share is (up) (down) (sideways).

The price trend of the stock is (up) (down) (sideways).

If sales trend is up, the increase seems to have come from (taking a greater share of the market) (mergers and acquisitions) (new products or new product applications produced by research).

In my opinion, the stock should be (investigated) (discarded) because the trend of sales is (favorable) (neutral) (unfavorable); the trend of earnings per share is (favorable) (neutral) (unfavorable); the price is (favorable) (neutral) (unfavorable).

Also for other reasons as follows:

_____

_____

_____

_____

2 DOES THE COMPANY PASS THE THREE MANAGEMENT TESTS?

Investors lose money because of failing to test for good management. Instead they rely on outlook for the industry, new products, or a plausible story for protection and often lose.

TEST I: DRIVING FORCE OF MANAGEMENT
Management as indicated by the past record has the necessary ability to expand sales (yes) (no). The rate of sales expansion on the VISUAL ANALYSIS looks like _____ % annually. The rate of sales expansion is likely to be (better) (same) (worse) in the next five years.

TEST II: EARNED ON SALES
Management seems to have the ability to (maintain) (increase) profit margins (see 2A, Evaluating Management on page 2 at left). It shows the Pre-Tax Profit Margins for each of the last five years as follows in

chronological order:
_____ %, _____ %, _____ %, _____ %, _____ %.

TEST III: EARNED ON EQUITY
The company has earned on invested capital from _____ % to _____ %. See 2B, Evaluating Management on page 2 at left. Earnings on equity are (above) (below) 10%.

I conclude from these three tests that the company has (good) (average) (poor) management and will be (stronger) (same) (weaker) in five years.

Over a period of five years, a well-managed company will generally gain ground while a poor one loses its earning power. Remember this in making your decision.

continued . . .

3 WHAT IS THE PRICE RANGE LIKELY TO BE FOR THE NEXT FIVE YEARS?

Complete Section 3 of the Stock Selection Guide & Report (page 2). Two considerations are important: (1) It is usually better to project sales and apply profit margins and taxes than to project earnings per share on the chart because profit margins tend to have definite upside limits; and (2) it is well to pay less attention to, or discard the much higher price-earnings ratios existing in years of low earnings. Also, avoid being misled by sales increases in early years of a new product or attributable to government or other types of contracts that may not be renewed or are due entirely to the upswing of a business cycle.

Have price-earnings (P/E) ratios for the past five years been trending (downward) (level) (upward)? Is the P/E ratio (higher) (same) (lower) than its competitors? Have the average price earnings ratios of the past five years been influenced by years when the ratio was (unusually high) (unusually low)?

Over the next five years, the stock might be expected to reach a high price of _____ and also a low of _____ when the next depression comes. It now sells at _____ , indicating (little) (average) (great) risk. Its suggested buy prices should range from _____ to _____ , hold from _____ to _____ , and sell from _____ to _____ .

These are the zones calculated in the Stock Selection Guide & Report (Section 4C, page 2). Be a careful buyer.

4 HOW DOES THE STOCK MEET THE THREE SAFETY TESTS OF PRICE?

Unsuccessful investment clubs and investors make two mistakes; (1) selection of poorly managed companies, (2) pay too much for stocks. The second mistake is by far the most prevalent and most damaging, and is easily corrected. Big losses have been taken in high grade stocks because they were bought mainly, "because they were moving" or sold "because they went down" —not because of price. The best results have been obtained by investors that buy carefully.

TEST I: SHOWS PROBABILITY OF GETTING OUT EVEN
The stock under review has sold at its present price in (_____)* (none) of the last five years. The risk of loss seems (small) (average) (considerable) at the present price on the basis of price history.

* *Three of five is a good standard.*

TEST II: STACK THE ODDS IN THE INVESTORS FAVOR
The upside-downside ratio from Section 4D, page 2 of the Stock Selection Guide & Report is_____ to 1. This is (favorable) (average) (unfavorable), indicating that we need to pay attention to past price history (considerably) (some) (not much).

TEST III: THESE STANDARDS HELP INVESTORS AVOID LOSS
The pay-off test is whether at least 100% appreciation is possible in five years—or in the case of cyclical stocks, 20% a year for the number of years held. Analysis shows a high price of _____ is reasonable in _____ years, equal to _____ % a year.

In the case of cyclical stocks, comment should include the number of months the cycle has advanced and the dangers on this account.

5 WHAT ARE THE INVESTMENT CHARACTERISTICS OF THE COMPANY?

The Company is (well established) (new) and operates (internationally) (nationally) (regionally). The product line or service is (diversified) (narrow) and sold to (consumers) (manufacturers) (government). The business cycle affects sales and earnings (not much) (severely) (average). The company is (largest) (in top four) (a smaller factor) in its industry. The company and products are (well known) (average) (not known) to the investing public. Its common stock is listed on (New York) (American) (other exchange) (unlisted) and has price records covering (five years) (only _____ years). It has (a continuous dividend record dating from _____) (a spotty dividend record) (no dividend record). Investment characteristics are (good) (average) (poor).

6 WHAT ARE THE CHARACTERISTICS OF THE COMPANY'S MAJOR INDUSTRY?

The _____ industry is (established) (new) and has (exceptional) (average) (below average) potential. The potential is based on (population) (product development) (science) (international expansion). Sales, profit margins and earnings per share fluctuate with the business cycle (widely—like the steel industry) (narrowly—like food) (average—like oil). Capital investment per dollar of sales in the industry is (high—like chemicals) (low—like clothing manufacture) (average—like metal products manufacturing), making it (easy) (difficult) for new competition to enter the business. Price competition between companies is (no problem) (severe) (average).

In my opinion, the major industry, everything considered, is (favorable) (average) (unfavorable). The company being analyzed will be (aided by the trend of the industry) or (will have to take business from competitors to grow).

7 WHAT ABOUT THE BUSINESS CYCLE?

About 33 months is an average business cycle, though variations from this norm are wide.

A well-managed company gains on marginal competitors in a depression or inflation as a general rule. In a period of business recovery, high grade stocks advance first, second grade stocks next, and marginal stocks last, as a general rule. Also, non-growth cyclical stocks are good purchases when business turns up and should be sold in the later stages of the cycle because of exposure to substantial drops in price, earnings, and sometimes dividends.

The trend of business has been (up) (down) for _____ months. The current stage of the business cycle tends to (help) (not affect) (hurt) profits of the company. The present stage of the business cycle suggests (no concern) (caution) (daring) for the stock under review.

8 WHAT ABOUT THE STOCK MARKET AND YIELDS ON BONDS?

The price the stock is selling at is _____ and the Dow Jones Averages are at: Industrials _____ , Transportation _____ and Utilities _____ . This provides a reference in case of review of this stock in the future.

From the Value Line, it is seen that the stock under review has performed, as compared relatively (better) (same) (below).

You may also want to comment on the behavior of bond yields and Treasury Bill rates. Yields tend to rise in the later stages of a business cycle (attracting money from the stock market) and fall when business slows and investors want safety.

Bond yields may (attract) (not affect) (discourage) investment in this stock currently.

ST-1050

Data about the following companies has been included with the program: Abbott Laboratories, AFLAC Inc., Cisco Systems Inc., Coca-Cola Co., Dell Computer Corp, Johnson & Johnson, McDonald's Corp, Microsoft, Nautica Enterprises, Oracle Corp., RPM Inc.-Ohio, Schering-Plough, Wal-Mart Stores. You may update the information on these companies and/or enter information on other companies by using the keyboard. Detailed instructions are included in the program.

SUMMARY

The Stock Selection Guide can help you identify good, well-managed growth companies whose stocks are selling at reasonable prices today and have the potential to double in five years. The NAIC's goal is for you to start an investment program now while you are still young, and because of it, to achieve a better quality of life.

Now that you have learned to use the tools provided by the NAIC, perhaps you are ready to invest on your own, join an investment club, or start an investment club of your own. Start at the NAIC site, www.better-investing.org, or enter investment club at a web search site.

UNDERSTAND TERMS AND IDEAS

1. How does filling in pages 3 and 4 of the SSG relate to the work you did on the first two pages?

    _____

    _____

2. The SSG is a tool for analyzing the fundamentals of a stock and a guide for estimating the appropriate buy price range of that stock. (T or F) Why or why not?

    _____

    _____

3. Complete pages 3 and 4 for the Tootsie Roll and then reach your own conclusion. Would you buy this stock now, based on your analysis? Why or why not?

    _____

    _____

4. Complete pages 3 and 4 for the stock you are studying and then reach your own conclusion. Would you buy this stock now, based on your analysis? Why or why not?

    _____

    _____

SUMMARY

LESSON 8.1 **THE FIVE-YEAR POTENTIAL**
The annual total return includes your return from the stock's price appreciation and from the dividend yield. The earnings per share growth rate of a larger company is usually less than that of a small company. The total annual return may be similar, however, since what the company lacks in price appreciation can be made up in dividend yield.

LESSON 8.2 **MAKE YOUR DECISION**
After completing most of the information on the SSG, you will answer a set of eight questions designed to help you reach a decision based on the data and calculations in the first two pages of the SSG and on several other important considerations. You are ready for a final decision!

REVIEW INVESTING TERMS

Write the letter of the term that matches each definition. Some terms may not be used.

1. _____ receiving dividends for your shares of stock

2. _____ buying at the present price and having the stock price increase

3. _____ for a common stock, identifies how much of your annual return is from dividend income

4. _____ combination of price appreciation and dividend yield

a. annual total return

b. dividend yield

c. present yield

d. price appreciation

UNDERSTAND TERMS AND IDEAS

5. How does an investor make money from stocks?

_____

_____

_____

_____

6. What does the size of a company have to do with dividends?

_____

_____

_____

_____

7. Explain the Rule of Five.

_____

_____

_____

_____

8. What is the present yield and how do you calculate it?

_____

_____

_____

_____

9. What aspects of a company do you grade on the SSG?

_____

_____

_____

_____

SHARPEN YOUR RESEARCH SKILLS

10. Identify a company that recently paid dividends. Look at the company's history of paying dividends. Are there any trends or patterns?

_____

_____

_____

11. How did you locate the information about dividends? Describe another way you could have found the same type of information.

_____

_____

_____

THINK CRITICALLY

12. Your friend Janelle, a cautious investor, has completed studies on two different companies. One estimated 14% growth and pays dividends. The other estimated 18% growth without dividends. What advice do you give her? Why?

_____

_____

_____

_____

13. Sarah used the Stock Selection Guide to choose stocks in her portfolio. Her portfolio is performing pretty well, increasing an average of 13%. However, she worries that one of her stocks is pulling down her average. How would you explain this?

_____

_____

_____

_____

PROSPECTIVE PORTFOLIO PROJECT

This is it! In this chapter, you learned the final steps of completing the Stock Selection Guide. It's time to make your decisions about the stocks. Which ones would you select as investments?

Company	Present Yield	Average Yield Over Next 5 Years	Estimated Annual Total Return	Report Card	Decision

Compare your final portfolio with your initial list of stocks. Why did some stay on the list while others were removed?

Appendices

Mutual Funds Check List

SUMMARY OF DEFINITIONS

SECTION 1

 Investment Criteria The fund's objectives, strategies and policies are taken from the fund's prospectus and represent what a fund says it will invest in. If multiple classes of shares are offered, each class is listed, showing the length of time you should hold onto the fund to offset its fees for that class. If a fund's name or ownership has changed, such information is listed here.

 Portfolio Composition Composition percentages provide a breakdown of holdings into general investment classes. *Stocks* include straight common shares only. *Bonds* include fixed-income securities with maturities of more than one year. *Other* includes preferred stocks, convertible preferred, convertible bonds, warrants and options.

 Market Capitalization A fund's portfolio is broken down into five sizes of companies. The largest 1% of U.S. companies are called *Giant*, the next 4% *Large,* the next 15% *Medium*, the next 30% *Small*, and the bottom 50% *Micro*.

 Top 10 Company Holdings With this information you can clearly identify what drives the fund's performance. In the Portfolio Analysis Section on the Morningstar report the symbols to the left of the company name represent the buy and sell activity of the holdings. A plus sign means the fund has added shares to that holding; a minus sign indicates a reduction. New additions are noted with a star burst.

 Total Number of Stocks in Portfolio Indicates the total number of stock securities in a fund's portfolio. These do not simply refer to the stocks listed on the page; they represent all stocks in the portfolio.

SECTION 2

Net Asset Value The price per-share, computed at the end of each trading day. A fund's NAV is found by dividing the total net assets of the fund by the number of shares outstanding.

Annual Total Return Morningstar calculates total return by taking the change in a fund's NAV, assuming the reinvestment of all income and capital gain distributions during the period, and then dividing by the initial NAV. Unless marked as a load-adjusted return, Morningstar does not adjust total returns for sales charges or for redemption fees. Total returns do account for management, administrative and 12b-1 fees and other costs automatically deducted from fund assets.

+/– S&P 500 A statistic measuring the difference between a stock fund's total return and the total return of the S&P 500 index. A negative number indicates that the fund under-performed the index by the given amount; a positive number indicates that the fund out-performed the index by the given amount.

Turnover Rate Expressed as a percentage, Turnover Rate loosely indicates how much of a portfolio's holdings have changed over the past one year. It is calculated by the fund itself by dividing the lesser of purchases or sales by the fund's average monthly assets. The figure is helpful but somewhat vague, in that some of a fund's stocks may be held for long periods while others may be bought and sold with greater frequency.

Tax-Adjusted Return A fund's annualized after-tax total return for three-, five- and 10-year periods, excluding any capital-gains consequences as a result of selling at the end of the period. After-tax amounts are assumed to be reinvested in the fund. State and local taxes are not included.

3-Year Average Portfolio Earnings Growth Rate A measure of the trailing three-year annualized earnings-growth record of the stocks currently in the fund's portfolio. This number is weighted such that larger positions in the portfolio count proportionately more than lesser positions.

Average Price-to-Earnings Ratio The weighted average of the P/E ratios of the fund's stock holdings. The P/E ratio of a single company is calculated by dividing the trailing 12 months earnings per share by its price per share. This number is weighted such that larger positions in the portfolio count proportionately more than lesser positions.

SECTION 3

Management Fee The maximum percentage deducted from a fund's average net assets to pay an advisor or subadvisor. A portion of the management fee may also be charged in various forms. If these charges occur there will be a letter next to the figure shown that corresponds to the charge. For example, Management Fee: 0.40%A.

A Denotes an administrative fee, which is the fund's maximum allowable charge for its management fee structure, excluding advisor fees. Costs associated with SEC compliance may also be included under this label. Administrative fees often operate on a sliding scale and include the costs of basic fund operations, such as leasing office space.

G A charge in the form of a group fee. The fund family creates a sliding scale for the families total net assets and determines a percentage applied to each fund's asset base.

P Represents a performance fee, which raises or lowers the management fee based on the fund's returns related to an established index.

I Represents a gross income fee, which is a percentage based on the total amount of income generated by the investment portfolio.

 Expense Ratio The percentage of assets deducted each fiscal year for fund expenses including 12b-1 fees, management fees, administrative fees, operating costs and other costs incurred by the fund. The figure does not include portfolio transaction (brokerage) fees or sales charges.

Peer Group Average Expense Ratio Annual expense ratios of all funds in a given category divided by the number of funds in that category.

Average Brokerage Commission The dollar amount charged per share traded in the previous 12-month period. This information is reported in each equity fund's annual report.

Sales Fees (also known as "loads"). The following represent the various types of loads a fund can charge. If these charges occur there will be a letter next to the figure shown that corresponds to the charge. For example, Sales Fee: 0.05%B.

B 12b-1 fee represents the maximum annual charge deducted from fund assets to pay for distribution and marketing costs.

D Deferred load Also called a contingent deferred sales charge or back-end load. A deferred load is an alternative to the traditional front-end sales charge. The deferred load structure commonly decreases to zero over a period of time.

L Front-end load A deduction made from each investment in the fund.

N No-Load This label denotes the fund as a true no-load fund, charging no sales or 12b-1 fees.

R Redemption fee An amount charged when money is withdrawn from the fund. These fees typically operate only in specific time clauses. Charges are not imposed after the stated time has passed. The fees are typically imposed to discourage market timers, whose quick movements into and out of funds can be disruptive.

S Service fee Part of the 12b-1 fee and is deducted to compensate financial planners or brokers for ongoing shareholder-liaison services.

W Waived Indicates that the fund is waiving sales fees at the time of publication. A fund may do this to attract new shareholders.

NATIONAL ASSOCIATION OF INVESTORS CORPORATION

NAIC

INVESTMENT EDUCATION FOR INDIVIDUALS AND CLUBS SINCE 1951

EQUITY MUTUAL FUND
Check List®

(A) Fund Name _____

(B) Fund Ticker Symbol _____

(C) Fund Category _____

(D) Minimum Purchase($) _____ (E) Add ($) _____

(F) Min Auto Inv Plan($) _____ (G) Add ($) _____

(H) IRA($) _____

(I) Data Reference _____ (J) Page No._____

(K) Portfolio Analysis Date _____

(L) Current NAV($) _____

Prepared by _____ Date _____

Taxable Account _____ Tax-Deferred Account ____ 401(k)
IRA
Other

1. FUND INVESTMENT CHARACTERISTICS

(A) Stated Investment Objective _____

- What are the fund's investment criteria & investment policies?

(B) Portfolio Composition

	Cash	Stocks	Bonds	Other	Foreign
	%	%	%	%	%

- Does this composition reflect the fund's stated investment policies? _____
- A cash holding of 20% or more may indicate the manager is trying to time the market...very risky!

(C) Market Capitalization

	Giant	Large	Medium	Small	Micro
	%	%	%	%	%

- Are the assets concentrated accorcing to the stated objective? _____
- Does this provide you with the diversification you are looking for? _____

(D) Top 10 Company Holdings

No.	Company Name	Sector	Assets
1			%
2			%
3			%
4			%
5			%
6			%
7			%
8			%
9			%
10			%
			% Total

- Does any one holding make up a far greater % of assets than the other holdings? _____
- How many differeny sectors do the top ten holdings cover? _____
- The fewer number of holdings and sectors that the fund's assets are spread over the greater likelihood for volatility within the portfolio.

(E) Total Number of Stocks in Portfolio _____

- It becomes more difficult to perform better than the market as a whole, the more stocks held by the fund.
- A fund is likely to become more volatile over the short term, the fewer (less than 50) stocks it holds.

2. FUND MANAGEMENT CHARACTERISTICS

(A) (1) Fund Manager _____ **Years** _____ **(2) Date Fund Started** _____

Fund Manager #2 _____ **Years** _____

If manager has been with fund five years or less, give name of previous fund managed, length of service, and investment style.

_____

- Fund reports do not always include previous employment information, to get this you may have to call the fund directly.

(B) Management Record   Initial Year   (shade in blocks above years pertaining to current manager)

enter all years ⇒		1989	1990	1991	1992	1993	1994	1995	1996	1997	1998
(1)	Current Management Period										
(2)	Net Asset Value (NAV)										
(3)	Annual Total Return %—Subject Fund										
(4)	+/– Total Return %—S&P 500 Index										

- Has the current manager consistently out-performed the index? _____
- Has the NAV increased in value over the years? _____

(C) Turnover Rate (%)   Initial Year
(Most recent five years)

Years	1994	1995	1996	1997	1998	Total	Average
Turnover Rate							

Average = $\dfrac{\text{total of all turnover rates}}{\text{\# of years entered}}$

- Turnover rated in excess of 20% indicate that a buy and hold investment style is not being implemented.
- Higher turnover rates can cause high capital gains and brokerage fees.

(D) Tax Analysis   3 Yr.   5 Yr.   10 Yr.

Fund Total Return %   _____   _____   _____   (line 1)

Fund Tax-Adjusted Return %   – _____   – _____   – _____   (line 2)

Taxes (%) (subtract line 2 from line 1)   _____   _____   _____   (line 3)

- The lower the number on line 3 the more tax-efficient the fund is.
- The higher the number the more tax liability you will incur.

(E) (3-Year) Average Portfolio Earnings Growth Rate _____ %

- Earnings Growth leads to Higher Stock Prices which leads to increase in Fund Value.

(F) Average Price-to-Earnings (P/E) Ratio of Stocks in Portfolio _____

- High P/E ratios may indicate that stocks are being bought at high prices or that the current holdings may not produce gains in the near future

3. COST CONSIDERATIONS

(A) Management Fee.............................._____ %

          Fund   Peer Group Avg.   (listed on
          Expense Ratio   Expense Ratio   overview sheet)

(B) Expense Ratios.._____ %   (C) _____ %

(D) Avg. Broker Commission (if applicable).._____ %

(E) 12b-1 Charges (if any)........................._____ %

(F) Load / No Load................._____ %   (G) Deferred Sales Charge or Redemption Fee (if any) _____ %

- High costs will greatly impact your return on investment.

4. REVIEW (Read Check List Summary prior to answering questions)

(a) Is it clear to you how the fund invests?   Yes _____ No _____
(b) Are you familiar with the types of companies the fund manager invests in?   Yes _____ No _____
(c) Are these growth companies? (What does Value Line say?)   Yes _____ No _____
(d) Does the average earnings growth rate indicate growth companies?   Yes _____ No _____
(e) Does the fund manager appear to follow a buy and hold method for investing in stocks?   Yes _____ No _____
(f) Has the fund manager been with the fund for at least five years?   Yes _____ No _____
(g) Has the manager's record shown consistency in outperforming the S&P 500 index?   Yes _____ No _____
(h) Are the taxes being generated so high that the fund belongs in a tax-deferred account?   Yes _____ No _____
(i) Are the costs of the fund reasonable to you?   Yes _____ No _____

Completing this checklist will provide you with a better understanding of how this mutual fund invests, what it invests in, how long and how effective the current management tenure has been, and what percentage of your investment dollars will be used to pay the fund's expenses.

NATIONAL ASSOCIATION
OF INVESTORS CORPORATION

NAIC

INVESTMENT EDUCATION
FOR INDIVIDUALS AND CLUBS
SINCE 1951

EQUITY
MUTUAL FUND
Check List®

(A) Fund Name _____

(B) Fund Ticker Symbol _____

(C) Fund Category _____

(D) Minimum Purchase($) _____ (E) Add ($) _____

(F) Min Auto Inv Plan($) _____ (G) Add ($) _____

(H) IRA($) _____

(I) Data Reference _____ (J) Page No._____

(K) Portfolio Analysis Date _____

(L) Current NAV($) _____

Prepared by _____ Date _____

Taxable Account _____ Tax-Deferred Account _____ 401(k)
IRA
Other

1. FUND INVESTMENT CHARACTERISTICS

(A) **Stated Investment Objective** _____

- What are the fund's investment criteria & investment policies?

(B) **Portfolio Composition**

Cash	Stocks	Bonds	Other	Foreign
%	%	%	%	%

- Does this composition reflect the fund's stated investment policies? _____
- A cash holding of 20% or more may indicate the manager is trying to time the market...very risky!

(C) **Market Capitalization**

Giant	Large	Medium	Small	Micro
%	%	%	%	%

- Are the assets concentrated accorcing to the stated objective? _____
- Does this provide you with the diversification you are looking for? _____

(D) **Top 10 Company Holdings**

No.	Company Name	Sector	Assets
1			%
2			%
3			%
4			%
5			%
6			%
7			%
8			%
9			%
10			%
			% Total

- Does any one holding make up a far greater % of assets than the other holdings? _____
- How many differeny sectors do the top ten holdings cover? _____
- The fewer number of holdings and sectors that the fund's assets are spread over the greater likelihood for volatility within the portfolio

(E) **Total Number of Stocks in Portfolio** _____

- It becomes more difficult to perform better than the market as a whole, the more stocks held by the fund.
- A fund is likely to become more volatile over the short term, the fewer (less than 50) stocks it holds.

2. FUND MANAGEMENT CHARACTERISTICS

(A) (1) Fund Manager _____ **Years** _____ **(2) Date Fund Started** _____
Fund Manager #2 _____ **Years** _____
If manager has been with fund five years or less, give name of previous fund managed, length of service, and investment style.

_____

- Fund reports do not always include previous employment information, to get this you may have to call the fund directly.

(B) Management Record   Initial Year   (shade in blocks above years pertaining to current manager)

enter all years ⇒										
(1) Current Management Period										
(2) Net Asset Value (NAV)										
(3) Annual Total Return %—Subject Fund										
(4) +/- Total Return %—S&P 500 Index										

- Has the current manager consistently out-performed the index? _____
- Has the NAV increased in value over the years? _____

(C) Turnover Rate (%)   Initial Year
(Most recent five years)

Years					Total	Average
Turnover Rate						

$$\text{Average} = \frac{\text{total of all turnover rates}}{\text{\# of years entered}}$$

- Turnover rated in excess of 20% indicate that a buy and hold investment style is not being implemented.
- Higher turnover rates can cause high capital gains and brokerage fees.

(D) Tax Analysis

	3 Yr.	5 Yr.	10 Yr.	
Fund Total Return %	_____	_____	_____	(line 1)
Fund Tax-Adjusted Return %	– _____	– _____	– _____	(line 2)
Taxes (%) (subtract line 2 from line 1)	_____	_____	_____	(line 3)

- The lower the number on line 3 the more tax-efficient the fund is.
- The higher the number the more tax liability you will incur.

(E) (3-Year) Average Portfolio Earnings Growth Rate _____%

- Earnings Growth leads to Higher Stock Prices which leads to increase in Fund Value.

(F) Average Price-to-Earnings(P/E) Ratio of Stocks in Portfolio _____

- High P/E ratios may indicate that stocks are being bought at high prices or that the current holdings may not produce gains in the near future

3. COST CONSIDERATIONS

(A) Management Fee............................. _____ %

      Fund   Peer Group Avg.   (listed on
      Expense Ratio   Expense Ratio   overview sheet)

(B) Expense Ratios..._____% **(C)** _____%

(D) Avg. Broker Commission (if applicable).._____%

(E) 12b-1 Charges (if any)........................._____%

(F) Load / No Load................._____% **(G) Deferred Sales Charge or Redemption Fee** (if any) _____%

- High costs will greatly impact your return on investment.

4. REVIEW (Read Check List Summary prior to answering questions)

(a) Is it clear to you how the fund invests?   Yes _____ No _____
(b) Are you familiar with the types of companies the fund manager invests in?   Yes _____ No _____
(c) Are these growth companies? (What does Value Line say?)   Yes _____ No _____
(d) Does the average earnings growth rate indicate growth companies?   Yes _____ No _____
(e) Does the fund manager appear to follow a buy and hold method for investing in stocks?   Yes _____ No _____
(f) Has the fund manager been with the fund for at least five years?   Yes _____ No _____
(g) Has the manager's record shown consistency in outperforming the S&P 500 index?   Yes _____ No _____
(h) Are the taxes being generated so high that the fund belongs in a tax-deferred account?   Yes _____ No _____
(i) Are the costs of the fund reasonable to you?   Yes _____ No _____

Completing this checklist will provide you with a better understanding of how this mutual fund invests, what it invests in, how long and how effective the current management tenure has been, and what percentage of your investment dollars will be used to pay the fund's expenses.

volume 35, Issue 3, June 6, 1999.

Harbor Capital Appreciation

	Ticker	Load	NAV	Yield	SEC Yield	Total Assets	Mstar Category
	HACAX	None	$42.25	0.1%	—	$5,599.4 mil	Large Growth

Prospectus Objective: Growth

Harbor Capital Appreciation Fund seeks long-term growth of capital; dividend income is secondary.

The fund normally invests at least 65% of assets in equity securities of established companies, typically those with market capitalizations of at least $1 billion. To select securities, the advisor seeks companies exhibiting superior sales growth, high returns on equity, strong balance sheets, excellent management capability, strong R&D, and unique marketing competence. The fund may also invest in short-term obligations and foreign securities in the form of depositary receipts.

Prior to May 1, 1990, the fund was named Harbor U.S. Equities Fund.

Historical Profile

Return High
Risk Above Avg
Rating ★★★★ Highest

Investment Style
Equity
Average Stock %

▼ Manager Change
▽ Partial Manager Change
► Mgr Unknown After
◄ Mgr Unknown Before

Fund Performance vs. Category Average

▓ Quarterly Fund Return
+/– Category Average
— Category Baseline

Performance Quartile (within Category)

	1988	1989	1990	1991	1992	1993	1994	1995	1996	1997	1998	04-99	History
	11.05	12.31	11.09	16.11	15.65	16.37	16.71	22.69	26.33	29.47	37.99	42.25	NAV
	15.37	24.21	−1.81	54.79	9.98	12.12	3.37	37.82	19.85	31.46	36.80	11.21	Total Return %
	−1.24	−7.48	1.31	24.30	2.36	2.06	2.06	0.29	−3.10	−1.90	8.23	2.17	+/– S&P 500
	4.50	−13.48	−3.18	15.38	6.09	12.19	−1.48	−0.83	−5.67	−2.29	−8.30	5.09	+/– Russ Top 200 Grt
	1.77	1.88	1.14	0.39	0.12	0.22	0.23	0.15	0.09	0.25	0.22	0.00	Income Return %
	13.60	22.33	−2.95	54.40	9.86	11.90	3.14	37.67	19.76	31.20	36.58	11.21	Capital Return %
	26	78	47	21	11	32	9	14	45	22	36	23	Total Rtn % Rank Cat
	0.18	0.21	0.14	0.04	0.02	0.03	0.04	0.03	0.02	0.07	0.07	0.00	Income $
	0.38	1.18	0.86	0.98	2.04	1.13	0.17	0.31	0.86	4.85	2.28	0.00	Capital Gains $
	0.99	0.92	0.88	0.89	0.91	0.86	0.81	0.75	0.75	0.70	0.68	—	Expense Ratio %
	1.48	1.77	1.18	0.47	0.12	0.24	0.24	0.23	0.11	0.23	0.24	—	Income Ratio %
		75	162	90	69	93	73	52	74	73	70	—	Turnover Rate %
	46.2	61.8	62.1	90.9	105.0	149.9	239.1	989.3	1,681.7	2,906.3	4,696.7	5,599.4	Net Assets $mil

Portfolio Manager(s)

Spiros Segalas. Since 5-90. BA'55 Princeton U. Segalas is the founding director and chief investment officer of Jennison Associates Capital Corporation. He began his investment career as a research analyst with Bankers Trust Company in 1960. He subsequently was promoted to vice president and manager. He served two years as a naval officer and has held several positions in the shipping industry. Other funds currently managed: Prudential Jennison Growth, Masters' Select Equity, Prudential 20/20 Focus, Style Select Focus.

Performance 04-30-99

	1st Qtr	2nd Qtr	3rd Qtr	4th Qtr	Total
1995	10.17	15.86	8.58	−0.56	37.82
1996	4.54	4.13	3.56	6.31	19.85
1997	−1.44	19.81	14.63	−2.88	31.46
1998	15.27	5.12	−13.16	30.01	36.80
1999	12.08				

Trailing	Total Return%	+/– S&P 500	+/– Russ Top 200 Grth	% Rank All	% Rank Cat	Growth of $10,000
3 Mo	0.57	−4.10	0.95	57	64	10,057
6 Mo	33.80	11.49	9.42	6	20	13,380
1 Yr	28.03	6.20	−2.64	4	32	12,803
3 Yr Avg	30.11	1.05	−4.24	2	16	22,028
5 Yr Avg	28.75	1.88	−2.69	1	9	35,381
10 Yr Avg	21.65	2.83	0.75	2	6	70,952
15 Yr Avg	—	—	—	—	—	—

Tax Analysis	Tax-Adj Ret%	%Rank Cat	%Pretax Ret	%Rank Cat
3 Yr Avg	27.90	16	92.6	33
5 Yr Avg	27.23	6	94.7	15
10 Yr Avg	19.32	6	89.3	23

Potential Capital Gain Exposure: 37% of assets

Analysis by Christopher Traulsen 05-14-99

If it's the golden age of indexing, nobody told Harbor Capital Appreciation Fund.

This fund is one of the few actively managed offerings to beat the S&P 500 index over all trailing periods of a year or more, and it hasn't slowed in 1999. Its year-to-date return through early May bests 75% of its large-cap growth peers and is easily ahead of the index. Its stake in big-cap drug names has been a drag, but other areas have boosted performance. Manager Sig Segalas has continued to build the fund's stake in CBS, for example, which has been one of the portfolio's stronger holdings for the year to date. Bellwether tech stocks such as Cisco and Microsoft and financials such as Citigroup, Schwab, and Morgan Stanley Dean Witter have further juiced returns. The fund also avoided much of Compaq's meltdown when Segalas sold it in the first quarter.

Despite the fund's hefty tech weighting, its results flow from a bottom-up strategy.

Segalas looks for companies that can grow faster than the S&P 500 index average and that have some competitive advantage that will help sustain that growth. He then tries to pick them up at reasonable prices. He bought CBS, for example, because he likes Mel Karmazin's focus on adding value for shareholders and sees a rosy picture ahead for its advertising revenues. In a nod to the importance of the Internet, he also took a 0.5% position in AOL earlier in 1999. Other plays are less glitzy—Gillette recently made it into the fund because he thinks its new blade system will fuel stronger growth.

With a 33% technology stake and a relatively concentrated portfolio, this fund isn't tame. Still, it has rarely disappointed, even in value-led years like 1993. To top it all off, it's one of the category's more tax-efficient funds, and its expense ratio is well below its average no-load peer's. Investors seeking a core growth holding won't find many that offer more.

Address:	One SeaGate
	Toledo, OH 43666
	800–422–1050 / 419–247–2477
Inception:	12-29-87
Advisor:	Harbor Capital Advisors
Subadvisor:	Jennison Associates Capital
Distributor:	HCA Securities
NTF Plans:	N/A

Minimum Purchase:	$2000	Add: $500	IRA: $500
Min Auto Inv Plan:	$500	Add: $100	
Sales Fees:	No–load		
Management Fee:	0.60%		
Actual Fees:	Mgt: 0.60%	Dist: —	
Expense Projections:	3Yr: $220*	5Yr: $385*	10Yr: $877*
Avg Brok Commission:	—	Income Distrib: Annually	

Total Cost (relative to category): —

Risk Analysis

Time Period	Load-Adj Return %	Risk %Rank[1] All	Cat	Morningstar Return Risk	Morningstar Risk-Adj Rating
1 Yr	28.03				
3 Yr	30.11	83	75	2.41 1.13	★★★★★
5 Yr	28.75	84	74	2.23 1.14	★★★★★
10 Yr	21.65	86	75	2.33 1.21	★★★★★

Average Historical Rating (101 months): 4.0★s

[1]=low, 100=high

Category Rating (3 Yr)	Other Measures	Standard Index S&P 500	Best Fit Index S&P 500
	Alpha	−3.6	−3.6
③④ Worst Best	Beta	1.26	1.26
	R-Squared	86	86
	Standard Deviation	29.10	
Return Above Avg	Mean	30.11	
Risk Above Avg	Sharpe Ratio	0.96	

Portfolio Analysis 03-31-99

Share change since 02-99 Total Stocks: 58

	Sector	PE	YTD Ret%	% Assets
⊖ MCI WorldCom	Services	—	14.55	5.01
⊕ Microsoft	Technology	64.3	17.26	4.13
⊕ Cisco Sys	Technology	NMF	22.90	3.25
Citigroup	Financials	29.5	51.60	3.20
⊕ General Elec	Industrials	36.6	3.67	3.08
⊖ Chase Manhattan	Financials	17.3	17.38	2.93
⊕ CBS	Services	92.9	38.66	2.92
⊕ Texas Instruments	Technology	NMF	19.47	2.68
Home Depot	Retail	56.4	−2.30	2.58
⊕ Intel	Technology	31.5	3.24	2.54
⊕ IBM	Technology	29.6	13.61	2.53
Morgan Stanley/Dean Witter	Financials	16.1	40.12	2.47
⊕ Schering–Plough	Health	39.0	−12.30	2.41
⊕ American Home Products	Health	38.1	8.63	2.29
⊕ McDonald's	Services	37.5	10.44	2.20
American Intl Grp	Financials	32.8	21.15	2.16
Clear Channel Comms	Services	NMF	27.52	2.04
⊕ Applied Matls	Technology	NMF	25.62	1.97
Kohl's	Retail	56.3	8.14	1.97
⊕ Pfizer	Health	43.6	−7.79	1.92
Merck	Health	31.7	−4.25	1.85
⊕ AirTouch Comms	Services	87.4	29.03	1.85
Omnicom Grp	Services	41.2	25.27	1.84
Gap	Retail	48.6	18.66	1.80
⊕ Warner–Lambert	Health	42.4	−9.56	1.71

Current Investment Style		Stock Port Avg	Relative S&P 500 Current	Hist	Rel Cat
Style: Value Blnd Growth	Price/Earnings Ratio	43.2	1.26	1.28	1.06
Size: Large Med Small	Price/Book Ratio	9.9	1.15	1.26	0.93
	Price/Cash Flow	30.8	1.29	1.38	1.08
	3 Yr Earnings Growth	18.8	1.12	1.34	0.84
	1 Yr Earnings Est%	26.3	1.57	—	1.16
	Debt % Total Cap	23.8	0.76	0.71	0.90
	Med Mkt Cap $mil	60,423	0.9	0.8	1.05

Special Securities	% of assets 03-31-99
○ Restricted/Illiquid Secs	0
○ Emerging-Markets Secs	0
○ Options/Futures/Warrants	No

Composition	% of assets 03-31-99		Market Cap	
Cash	3.2	Giant	55.2	
Stocks*	96.8	Large	36.7	
Bonds	0.0	Medium	7.5	
Other	0.0	Small	0.6	
*Foreign (% of stocks)	3.4	Micro	0.0	

Sector Weightings	% of Stocks	Rel S&P	5-Year High	Low
Utilities	0.0	0.0	4	0
Energy	0.0	0.0	6	0
Financials	17.9	1.1	22	3
Industrials	3.5	0.3	10	0
Durables	0.0	0.0	7	0
Staples	2.0	0.3	10	0
Services	19.5	1.3	31	12
Retail	9.7	1.5	17	4
Health	14.1	1.3	26	5
Technology	33.3	1.7	47	16

MORNINGSTAR Mutual Funds

HOME DEPOT NYSE-HD

RECENT PRICE **66**	P/E RATIO **48.9** (Trailing: 56.9 / Median: 33.0)	RELATIVE P/E RATIO **2.81**	DIV'D YLD **0.3%**	VALUE LINE **887**

TIMELINESS	**2**	Lowered 5/21/99
SAFETY	**2**	Raised 10/18/96
TECHNICAL	**2**	Lowered 4/2/99
BETA	1.30	(1.00 = Market)

High:	1.6	2.8	4.8	11.7	17.2	17.0	16.1	16.6	19.8	30.3	62.0	67.9
Low:	0.9	1.4	2.6	3.8	9.9	11.7	12.2	12.2	13.8	15.9	27.7	51.9

LEGENDS
- 21.0 x "Cash Flow" p sh
- .... Relative Price Strength
- 3-for-2 split 9/87
- 3-for-2 split 7/89
- 3-for-2 split 7/90
- 3-for-2 split 6/91
- 3-for-2 split 7/92
- 4-for-3 split 4/93
- 3-for-2 split 7/97
- 2-for-1 split 7/98
- Options: Yes
- Shaded area indicates recession

2002-04 PROJECTIONS

	Price	Gain	Ann'l Total Return
High	90	(+35%)	9%
Low	70	(+5%)	2%

Insider Decisions

	A	S	O	N	D	J	F	M	A
to Buy	0	0	0	0	0	0	0	0	0
Options	2	2	0	1	3	0	2	2	0
to Sell	2	3	0	4	5	0	2	4	0

Institutional Decisions

	3Q1998	4Q1998	1Q1999
to Buy	388	464	478
to Sell	368	347	385
Millions	921	942	-----

Percent shares traded: 18.0 / 12.0 / 6.0

Target Price Range 2002 | 2003 | 2004

% TOT. RETURN 6/99

	THIS STOCK	VL ARITH. INDEX
1 yr.	55.5	10.4
3 yr.	261.7	66.9
5 yr.	367.6	139.8

1983	1984	1985	1986	1987	1988	1989	1990	1991	1992	1993	1994	1995	1996	1997	1998	1999	2000	© VALUE LINE PUB., INC.	02-04
.34	.57	.92	1.17	1.45	1.97	2.66	3.51	4.06	5.37	6.85	9.17	10.81	13.55	16.50	20.48	25.10	30.60	Sales per sh A	52.75
.01	.02	.02	.04	.06	.09	.13	.18	.24	.33	.41	.54	.64	.81	.99	1.35	1.70	2.05	"Cash Flow" per sh	3.60
.01	.02	.01	.03	.06	.07	.11	.15	.20	.27	.34	.44	.51	.65	.78	1.06	1.35	1.65	Earnings per sh B	2.95
--	--	--	--	.00	.01	.01	.01	.02	.03	.04	.05	.06	.08	.10	.12	.15	.19	Div'ds Decl'd per sh C	.33
.09	.11	.12	.19	.32	.38	.49	.63	1.34	1.73	2.09	2.53	3.48	4.13	4.85	5.92	7.10	8.60	Book Value per sh	15.25
756.13	761.03	763.91	862.04	1000.5	1017.1	1036.6	1087.5	1266.6	1330.7	1348.1	1360.1	1431.3	1441.5	1464.2	1475.50	1473.00	1470.00	Common Shs Outst'g D	1460.00
57.0	31.7	48.5	19.8	18.1	17.8	21.4	25.4	40.9	47.1	42.3	33.0	27.9	26.5	30.8	40.1	Bold figures are Value Line estimates		Avg Ann'l P/E Ratio	27.0
4.82	2.95	3.94	1.34	1.21	1.48	1.62	1.89	2.61	2.86	2.50	2.16	1.87	1.66	1.78	2.86			Relative P/E Ratio	1.95
--	--	--	--	.3%	.4%	.4%	.3%	.2%	.2%	.3%	.3%	.4%	.4%	.4%	.3%			Avg Ann'l Div'd Yield	.4%

CAPITAL STRUCTURE as of 5/2/99

Total Debt $1327.0 mill. **Due in 5 Yrs** $42.0 mill.
LT Debt $1319.0 mill. **LT Interest** $65.0 mill.
(L-T int. earned, total int. coverage: More than 30x)
incl. $1104.0 mill. 3.25% subord. notes, conv. to
comm. at $23.042, due 10/01, redeemable 10/99.
(12% of Cap'l)
Leases, Uncapitalized Annual rentals $294.0 mill.
Pension Liability No defined benefit plan.

Pfd Stock None
Common Stock 1,475,000,000 shs. (88% of Cap'l)

MARKET CAP: $95 billion (Large Cap)

	2758.5	3815.4	5136.7	7148.4	9238.8	12477	15470	19536	24156	30219	37000	45000	Sales ($mill) A	77000
	28.6%	28.8%	29.1%	28.5%	28.6%	29.0%	28.9%	29.0%	29.2%	29.7%	30.0%	29.5%	Gross Margin	30.0%
	7.5%	7.9%	8.4%	8.7%	8.6%	9.0%	8.8%	9.0%	9.5%	10.0%	10.5%	10.0%	Operating Margin	10.0%
	118	145	174	214	214	340	422	512	624	761	924	1079	Number of Stores	1460
	112.0	163.4	249.2	362.9	457.4	604.5	731.5	937.7	1160.0	1614.0	2070	2535	Net Profit ($mill)	4515
	38.5%	37.1%	37.1%	37.0%	37.9%	38.3%	38.8%	38.9%	38.9%	39.2%	39.0%	39.0%	Income Tax Rate	39.0%
	4.1%	4.3%	4.9%	5.1%	5.0%	4.8%	4.7%	4.8%	4.8%	5.3%	5.6%	5.6%	Net Profit Margin	5.9%
	273.8	300.9	624.0	807.1	994.0	918.8	1255.5	1867.3	2004.0	2076.0	2540	3090	Working Cap'l ($mill)	5290
	302.9	530.8	270.6	843.7	842.0	983.4	720.1	1246.6	1303.0	1566.0	1490	1415	Long-Term Debt ($mill)	1210
	512.1	683.4	1691.2	2304.1	2814.1	3442.2	4987.8	5955.2	7098.0	8740.0	10490	12630	Shr. Equity ($mill)	22275
	14.9%	14.7%	13.3%	12.3%	13.1%	14.3%	13.0%	13.3%	14.2%	16.0%	17.5%	18.5%	Return on Total Cap'l	19.5%
	21.9%	23.9%	14.7%	15.7%	16.3%	17.6%	14.7%	15.7%	16.3%	18.5%	19.5%	20.0%	Return on Shr. Equity	20.5%
	20.2%	22.0%	13.4%	14.2%	14.5%	15.6%	12.9%	13.9%	14.4%	16.5%	17.5%	18.0%	Retained to Com Eq	18.0%
	7%	8%	9%	11%	12%	12%	12%	12%	12%	11%	11%	11%	All Div'ds to Net Prof	11%

CURRENT POSITION

($MILL.)	1997	1998	5/2/99
Cash Assets	174.0	62.0	604.0
Receivables	556.0	469.0	502.0
Inventory (LIFO)	3602.0	4293.0	4955.0
Other	128.0	109.0	150.0
Current Assets	4460.0	4933.0	6211.0
Accts Payable	1358.0	1586.0	2592.0
Debt Due	8.0	14.0	8.0
Other	1090.0	1257.0	1616.0
Current Liab.	2456.0	2857.0	4216.0

ANNUAL RATES

of change (per sh)	Past 10 Yrs.	Past 5 Yrs.	Est'd '95-'97 to '02-'04
Sales	27.5%	26.0%	21.0%
"Cash Flow"	35.5%	26.5%	23.0%
Earnings	35.0%	25.5%	24.0%
Dividends	--	32.5%	22.0%
Book Value	35.0%	27.5%	20.0%

QUARTERLY SALES ($ mill.) A

Fiscal Year Begins	Apr.30	Jul.31	Oct.31	Jan.31	Full Fiscal Year
1996	4362	5293	4922	4959	19536
1997	5657	6550	6217	5732	24156
1998	7123	8139	7699	7258	30219
1999	8952	9748	9300	9000	37000
2000	10600	11800	11600	11000	45000

EARNINGS PER SHARE A B

Fiscal Year Begins	Apr.30	Jul.31	Oct.31	Jan.31	Full Fiscal Year
1996	.14	.19	.15	.17	.65
1997	.18	.24	.16	.20	.78
1998	.23	.31	.26	.27	1.06
1999	.32	.37	.32	.34	1.35
2000	.34	.45	.42	.44	1.65

QUARTERLY DIVIDENDS PAID C

Calendar	Mar.31	Jun.30	Sep.30	Dec.31	Full Year
1995	.014	.017	.017	.017	.07
1996	.017	.02	.02	.02	.08
1997	.02	.025	.025	.025	.10
1998	.025	.03	.03	.03	.12
1999	.03	.03			

BUSINESS: The Home Depot, Inc. operates a chain of retail building supply/home improvement "warehouse" stores across the U.S. and in Canada. Acquired 75% interest in Aikenhead's (renamed Home Depot Canada) in 2/94. Avg. store size: 107,000 sq. ft. indoor plus 24,000 sq. ft. garden center; items stocked: 45,000. Product lines incl. building mat'ls, lumber, floor/wall coverings; plumbing, heating, and electrical; paint & furniture; seasonal and specialty items; hardware & tools. '98 deprec. rate: 4.5%. Has about 125,000 employees; 61,000 stkhldrs. Off. & Dir. own 9% of stock (4/99 Proxy). Chairman: Bernard Marcus. President and C.E.O.: Arthur M. Blank. Inc.: Del. Address: 2455 Paces Ferry Road N.W., Atlanta, GA 30339. Tel.: 770-433-8211. Internet: www.homedepot.com.

Home Depot is racking up big numbers. The company dominates the home improvement warehouse sector. Depot's stores are among the biggest in the industry. Moreover, the company has the most stores in the industry, and it achieves the highest per-store sales, at about $845,000 a week. The high sales levels and tight operations have enabled Depot to achieve consistent earnings growth. Through the first quarter of fiscal 1999, the retailer has posted 53 consecutive quarters—13 years plus—with year-over-year increases in earnings per share. The company is likely to maintain its better-than 20% earnings growth rate at least through fiscal 2000.

The retailer is expanding at a remarkable rate. Home Depot is essentially in two businesses: operating stores and building stores. The retailer is adding warehouse stores at a rate of more than two a week. Depot vaulted past the $30 billion sales level in fiscal 1998 (ended January 31, 1999), putting it on a par with Kmart and J.C. Penney and behind only Wal-Mart and Sears. But this stock carries a higher P/E multiple, reflecting Home Depot's higher growth.

Home Depot is striving to maintain its high growth. The retailer has picked the "low-hanging fruit"; it has already entered the most attractive markets. To avoid "cannibalization"—which occurs when duplicative stores are situated too close together—the company is developing complementary formats. For example, Depot is beginning to roll out its *Expo Design Center* chain, which offers one-stop sales and service for kitchen and bath and other remodeling and renovation work. Too, the company has created a new store format, *Villager's Hardware*, for downtown and Main Street locations. Depot has also made strategic acquisitions. The company bought Maintenance Warehouse/America Corp. in 1997, giving it entry to the institutional maintenance business; most recently, Depot acquired Georgia Lighting, a specialty lighting retailer.

This stock is timely for the year ahead. Home Depot's continuing growth and this stock's performance over the longer term will depend on the success of the company's new formats, which are still in the embryonic stage.
Ben Sharav, CFA   *July 16, 1999*

(A) Fiscal year ends Sunday closest to January 31 of the following year.
(B) Diluted earnings. Excluding extraord. gain: '85, 1¢. '98 quart's don't sum to full yr. due to change in shs. out. Next earnings report due early August.
(C) Next dividend meeting about August 20. Goes ex about Sept. 2. Approx. dividend payment dates: 24th of March, June, Sept., Dec.
(D) In millions, adjusted for stock splits.

Company's Financial Strength	A++
Stock's Price Stability	65
Price Growth Persistence	80
Earnings Predictability	95

Stock Selection Guide & Report ®

NATIONAL ASSOCIATION OF INVESTORS CORPORATION

NAIC ®

INVESTMENT EDUCATION FOR INDIVIDUALS AND CLUBS SINCE 1951

Company_____ Date_____

Prepared by_____ Data taken from_____

Where traded_____ Major product/service_____

CAPITALIZATION — Outstanding Amounts

Preferred		% Insiders	% Institution
Common			
Debt	% to Tot. Cap.	% Potential Dil.	

1 VISUAL ANALYSIS of Sales, Earnings and Price

RECENT QUARTERLY FIGURES

	SALES	EARNINGS PER SHARE
Latest Quarter	_____	_____
Year Ago Quarter	_____	_____
Percentage Change	_____	_____

See Chapters 8, 9, and 10 of the NAIC Official Guide for complete instructions. Use this Guide as working section NAIC Stock Selection Guide & Report.

(1) Historical Sales Growth _____%

(2) Estimated Future Sales Growth _____%

(3) Historical Earnings Per Share Growth _____%

(4) Estimated Future Earnings Per Share Growth _____%

2 EVALUATING MANAGEMENT   Company _____

		19__	19__	19__	19__	19__	19__	19__	19__	19__	19__	LAST 5 YEAR AVG.	TREND UP	TREND DOWN
A	% Pre-tax Profits on Sales (Net Before Taxed ÷ Sales)													
B	% Earned on Equity (E/S ÷ Book Value)													

3 PRICE-EARNING HISTORY as an indication of the future

This shows how stock prices have fluctuated with earnings and dividends. It is a building block for translating earnings into future stock prices.

PRESENT PRICE _____   HIGH THIS YEAR _____   LOW THIS YEAR _____

	Year	A PRICE HIGH	B PRICE LOW	C Earnings Per Share	D Price Earnings Ratio HIGH A ÷ C	E Price Earnings Ratio LOW B ÷ C	F Dividend Per Share	G % Payout F ÷ C × 100	H % High Yield F ÷ B × 100
1									
2									
3									
4									
5									
6	TOTAL								
7	AVERAGE								
8	AVERAGE PRICE EARNINGS RATIO				9	CURRENT PRICE EARNINGS RATIO			

4 EVALUATING RISK and REWARD over the next 5 years

Assuming one recession and one business boom every 5 years, calculations are made of how high and how low the stock might sell. The upside-downside ratio is the key to evaluating risk and reward.

A HIGH PRICE — NEXT 5 YEARS

Avg. High P/E _____ (3D7 as adj.) × Estimated High Earnings Per Share _____ = Forecast High Price $ _____ (4A1)

B LOW PRICE — NEXT 5 YEARS

(a) Avg Low P/E _____ (3E7 as adj.) × Estimated Low Earnings Per Share _____ = Forecast Low Price $ _____

(b) Avg Low Price of Last 5 Years = _____ (3B7)

(c) Recent Severe Market Low Price = _____ (3B7)

(d) Price Dividend Will Support $\frac{\text{Present Divd.}}{\text{High Yield (H)}}$ = _____ = _____

Selected Estimated Low Price _____ = $ _____

C ZONING

_____ (4A1) High Forecast Price Minus _____ (4B1) Low Forecast Price Equals _____ (C) Range. 1/3 of Range = _____ (4CD)

(4C2) Lower 1/3 = (4B1) _____ to _____ (Buy)

(4C3) Middle 1/3 = _____ to _____ (Maybe)

(4C3) Upper 1/3 = _____ to _____ (4A1) (Sell)

Present Market Price of _____ is in the _____ (4C5) Range

D UPSIDE DOWNSIDE RATIO (Potential Gain vs. Risk of Loss)

$\frac{\text{High Price (4A1) \_\_\_\_\_ Minus Present Price \_\_\_\_\_}}{\text{Present Price \_\_\_\_\_ Minus Low Price (4B1) \_\_\_\_\_}}$ = _____ = _____ To 1 (4D)

E PRICE TARGET   (Note: This shows the potential market price appreciation over the next five years in simple interest terms.)

$\frac{\text{High Price (4A1) \_\_\_\_\_}}{\text{Present Market Price \_\_\_\_\_}}$ = (_____) × 100 = (_____) − 100 = _____ % Appreciation (4E)

5 5-YEAR POTENTIAL   *This combines price appreciation with dividend yield to get an estimate of total return. It provides a standard for comparing income and growth stocks.*

A $\frac{\text{Present Full Year's Dividend \$ \_\_\_\_\_}}{\text{Present Price of Stock \$ \_\_\_\_\_}}$ = _____ × 100 = _____ (5A) Present Yield or % Returned on Purchase Price

B AVERAGE YIELD OVER NEXT FIVE YEARS

Avg. Earnings Per Share Next 5 Years _____ × Avg. % Payout (3G7) _____ = $\frac{\_\_\_\_\_}{\text{Present Price \$ \_\_\_\_\_}}$ = _____ (5B) %

C ESTIMATED AVERAGE ANNUAL RETURN OVER NEXT 5 YEARS

$\frac{\text{5-Year Appreciation Potential (4E) \_\_\_\_\_}}{5}$ = _____ %

Average Yield (5B) .... _____ %

Average Total Return Over The Next 5 Years (5C) _____ %

Table to Convert From Simple to Compound Rate

Simple Rate 2 4 6 8 10 12 14 16 18 20 22 24 26 28 30 32 34 36 38 40

Compound Rate 2 4 6 8 10 12 14 16 18 20 22 24

Stock Selection Guide & Report ®

NATIONAL ASSOCIATION OF INVESTORS CORPORATION

NAIC ®

INVESTMENT EDUCATION FOR INDIVIDUALS AND CLUBS SINCE 1951

Company_____ Date_____

Prepared by_____ Data taken from_____

Where traded_____ Major product/service_____

CAPITALIZATION — Outstanding Amounts

Preferred			% Insiders	% Institution
Common				
Debt	% to Tot. Cap.		% Potential Dil.	

1 VISUAL ANALYSIS of Sales, Earnings and Price

RECENT QUARTERLY FIGURES

	SALES	EARNINGS PER SHARE
Latest Quarter		
Year Ago Quarter		
Percentage Change		

See Chapters 8, 9, and 10 of the NAIC Official Guide for complete instructions. Use this Guide as working section of NAIC Stock Selection Guide & Report.

(1) Historical Sales Growth _____ %
(2) Estimated Future Sales Growth _____ %
(3) Historical Earnings Per Share Growth _____ %
(4) Estimated Future Earnings Per Share Growth _____ %

2 EVALUATING MANAGEMENT Company _____

	19__	19__	19__	19__	19__	19__	19__	19__	19__	19__	LAST 5 YEAR AVG.	TREND UP	TREND DOWN
A % Pre-tax Profit on Sales (Net Before Taxes ÷ Sales)													
B % Earned on Equity (E/S ÷ Book Value)													

3 PRICE-EARNINGS HISTORY as an indicator of the future

This shows how stock prices have fluctuated with earnings and dividends. It is a building block for translating earnings into future stock prices.

PRESENT PRICE _____ HIGH THIS YEAR _____ LOW THIS YEAR _____

Year	A PRICE HIGH	B PRICE LOW	C Earnings Per Share	D Price Earnings Ratio HIGH A ÷ C	E Price Earnings Ratio LOW B ÷ C	F Dividend Per Share	G % Payout F ÷ C X 100	H % High Yield F ÷ B X 100
1								
2								
3								
4								
5								
6 TOTAL								
7 AVERAGE								

8 AVERAGE PRICE EARNINGS RATIO	9 CURRENT PRICE EARNINGS RATIO

4 EVALUATING RISK and REWARD over the next 5 years

Assuming one recession and one business boom every 5 years, calculations are made of how high and how low the stock might sell. The upside-downside ratio is the key to evaluating risk and reward.

A HIGH PRICE — NEXT 5 YEARS

Avg. High P/E _____ (3D7 as adj.) X Estimate High Earnings/Share _____ = Forecast High Price $ _____ (4A1)

B LOW PRICE — NEXT 5 YEARS

(a) Avg. Low P/E _____ (3E7 as adj.) X Estimated Low Earnings/Share _____ = $ _____

(b) Avg. Low Price of Last 5 Years = _____ (3B7)

(c) Recent Severe Market Low Price = _____

(d) Price Dividend Will Support $\dfrac{\text{Present Divd.}}{\text{High Yield (H)}}$ = _____ = _____

Selected Estimated Low Price = $ _____ (4B1)

C ZONING

_____ High Forecast Price Minus _____ Low Forecast Price Equals _____ Range. 1/3 of Range = _____
(4A1) ... (4B1) ... (C) ... (4CD)

(4C2) Lower 1/3 = (4B1) _____ to _____ (Buy)

(4C3) Middle 1/3 = _____ to _____ (Maybe)

(4C4) Upper 1/3 = _____ to _____ (4A1) (Sell)

Present Market Price of _____ is in the _____ Range
(4C5)

D UP-SIDE DOWN-SIDE RATIO (Potential Gain vs. Risk of Loss)

$\dfrac{\text{High Price (4A1)} \_\_\_ \text{Minus Present Price} \_\_\_}{\text{Present Price} \_\_\_ \text{Minus Low Price (4B1)} \_\_\_}$ = _____ = _____ To 1
(4D)

E PRICE TARGET (Note: This shows the potential market price appreciation over the next five years in simple interest terms.)

$\dfrac{\text{High Price (4A1)} \_\_\_}{\text{Present Market Price} \_\_\_}$ = (_____) X 100 = (_____) − 100 = _____ % Appreciation
(4E)

5 5-YEAR POTENTIAL

This combines price appreciation with dividend yield to get an estimate of total return. It provides a standard for comparing income and growth stocks.

A $\dfrac{\text{Present Full Year's Dividend } \$ \_\_\_}{\text{Present Price of Stock } \$ \_\_\_}$

Note: Results are expressed as a simple rate; use the table below to convert to a compound rate.

= _____ X 100 = _____ Present Yield or % Returned on Purchase Price
(5A)

B AVERAGE YIELD OVER NEXT 5 YEARS

Avg. Earnings Per Share Next 5 Years _____ X Avg. % Payout (3G7) _____

= $\dfrac{_____}{\text{Present Price } \$ _____}$ = _____ %
(5B)

C ESTIMATED AVERAGE ANNUAL RETURN OVER NEXT FIVE YEARS

$\dfrac{\text{5 Year Appreciation Potential (4E)} \_\_\_}{5}$ = _____ %

Average Yield (5B) . . . . _____ %

Average Total Annual Return Over The Next 5 Years (5C) _____ %

Table to Convert From Simple to Compound Rate

Simple Rate: 2 4 6 8 10 12 14 16 18 20 22 24 26 28 30 32 34 36 38 40

Compound Rate: 2 4 6 8 10 12 14 16 18 20 22 24

Calculations for SSG Section 2A

APPENDIX F

Calculations for Section 2A Form

Year												
Net Profit (from Value Line)												
Tax Rate as a decimal (from Value Line)												
1 – Tax Rate												
Pre-Tax Profit = $\frac{\text{Net Profit}}{1 - \text{Tax Rate}}$												
Sales (from Value Line)												
$\frac{\text{Pre-Tax Profit}}{\text{Sales}}$												
Pre-Tax Profits as a Percent of Sales												

Calculations for Section 2A Form

Year												
Net Profit (from Value Line)												
Tax Rate as a decimal (from Value Line)												
1 – Tax Rate												
Pre-Tax Profit = $\frac{\text{Net Profit}}{1 - \text{Tax Rate}}$												
Sales (from Value Line)												
$\frac{\text{Pre-Tax Profit}}{\text{Sales}}$												
Pre-Tax Profits as a Percent of Sales												

SAMPLE BUDGET WORKSHEET

	Month 1	Month 2	Month 3	Average
Income Source				
Paycheck	1600	1600	1600	1600
Allowance				
Cash Gifts				
Interest on Savings				
Total Income	1600	1600	1600	1600
Fixed Expenses				
Housing	835	835	835	835
Utilities	42	60	90	64
Telephone	30	25	25	26.67
Car Payments				
Car Insurance				
Medical Insurance				
Savings				
Cable	69	80	72	73.67
Flexible Expenses				
Groceries	80	110	110	100
Dining Out				
Clothes	100	/	132	77.3
Laundry	4	6	20	
Transportation	10	10	10	10
Medical				
Entertainment				
Personal-Care Items				
Diapers	80	80	80	80
Total Expenses	1250	1206	1394	1266.67

GOALS IN SELECTING A STOCK

You want to look ahead five years by **judging** Management capability and **evaluating** the Price you should pay for a stock. You should also look at **Other Considerations** and reach a **Conclusion. Your findings are registered in the table at the right and your Conclusion below.**

Novice and professional investors to varying degrees may act hastily on new products, tips, technical clues and short term factors rather than being methodical in their decisions. Thirty years of experience with this type of report tends to show that there is a RULE OF FIVE, which is this: If five companies are analyzed for their five year future, one may have unforeseeable trouble, three may be on target, and one may have unpredictable good fortune.

CONCLUSION: _____

_____

_____

(1) Our goal is to find a company with **able** MANAGEMENT; and (2) to buy a stock at a **good** PRICE.

	Page	Good	Average	Poor
Judging Management				
Driving Force	3			
Earned on Sales	3			
Earned on Equity	3			
Evaluating Price				
High in 5 Years	4			
Low in 5 Years	4			
Upside-Downside Ratio	4			
Yield Current	4			
Total Return	4			
Other Considerations				
Industry Potentials	4			
State of Business Cycle	4			
Stock Price Trends	4			
Quality of Stock	4			
Capitalization and Finance	2			

METHOD-DATA-INSTRUCTIONS

This report organizes data presentation in a concise professional manner, avoiding among other things the agony of deciding what factors to cover. Because writing is a chore, the cross-out-method lets you report your judgments with ease. The data used comes from Value Line and Standard and Poor's Reports that are available on many listed and unlisted companies. You may wish to check your 5 year "high estimate" with Value Line's estimated Target Price Range for 3 to 5 years

hence. Instructions for completing pages 3 and 4 of this report are in the NAIC Official Guide obtainable from the National Association of Investors Corporation, P.O. Box 220, Royal Oak, Michigan 48068. Other sources of data are annual and quarterly reports from companies, brokers reports and visits to company annual meetings. You may learn by yourself, or with several friends, or by actually investing $20 or $50 a month through an investment club you have formed with friends.

1 WHAT DOES THE VISUAL ANALYSIS SHOW?

The trend of (sales) (revenues) is (up) (down) (sideways).

The trend of earnings per share is (up) (down) (sideways).

The price trend of the stock is (up) (down) (sideways).

If sales trend is up, the increase seems to have come from (taking a greater share of the market) (mergers and acquisitions) (new products or new product applications produced by research).

In my opinion, the stock should be (investigated) (discarded) because the trend of sales is (favorable) (neutral) (unfavorable); the trend of earnings per share is (favorable) (neutral) (unfavorable); the price is (favorable) (neutral) (unfavorable).

Also for other reasons as follows: _____

_____

_____

_____

2 DOES THE COMPANY PASS THE THREE MANAGEMENT TESTS?

Investors lose money because of failing to test for good management. Instead they rely on outlook for the industry, new products, or a plausible story for protection and often lose.

TEST I: DRIVING FORCE OF MANAGEMENT

Management as indicated by the past record has the necessary ability to expand sales (yes) (no). The rate of sales expansion on the VISUAL ANALYSIS looks like _____ % annually. The rate of sales expansion is likely to be (better) (same) (worse) in the next five years.

TEST II: EARNED ON SALES

Management seems to have the ability to (maintain) (increase) profit margins (see 2A, Evaluating Management on page 2 at left). It shows the Pre-Tax Profit Margins for each of the last five years as follows in

chronological order:

_____ %, _____ %, _____ %, _____ %, _____ %.

TEST III: EARNED ON EQUITY

The company has earned on invested capital from _____ % to _____ %. See 2B, Evaluating Management on page 2 at left. Earnings on equity are (above) (below) 10%.

I conclude from these three tests that the company has (good) (average) (poor) management and will be (stronger) (same) (weaker) in five years.

Over a period of five years, a well-managed company will generally gain ground while a poor one loses its earning power. Remember this in making your decision.

continued . . .

3 WHAT IS THE PRICE RANGE LIKELY TO BE FOR THE NEXT FIVE YEARS?

Complete Section 3 of the Stock Selection Guide & Report (page 2). Two considerations are important: (1) It is usually better to project sales and apply profit margins and taxes than to project earnings per share on the chart because profit margins tend to have definite upside limits; and (2) it is well to pay less attention to, or discard the much higher price-earnings ratios existing in years of low earnings. Also, avoid being misled by sales increases in early years of a new product or attributable to government or other types of contracts that may not be renewed or are due entirely to the upswing of a business cycle.

Have price-earnings (P/E) ratios for the past five years been trending (downward) (level) (upward)? Is the P/E ratio (higher) (same) (lower) than its competitors? Have the average price earnings ratios of the

past five years been influenced by years when the ratio was (unusually high) (unusually low)?

Over the next five years, the stock might be expected to reach a high price of _____ and also a low of _____ when the next depression comes. It now sells at _____, indicating (little) (average) (great) risk. Its suggested buy prices should range from _____ to _____, hold from _____ to _____, and sell from _____ to _____.

These are the zones calculated in the Stock Selection Guide & Report (Section 4C, page 2). Be a careful buyer.

4 HOW DOES THE STOCK MEET THE THREE SAFETY TESTS OF PRICE?

Unsuccessful investment clubs and investors make two mistakes; (1) selection of poorly managed companies, (2) pay too much for stocks. The second mistake is by far the most prevalent and most damaging, and is easily corrected. Big losses have been taken in high grade stocks because they were bought mainly, "because they were moving" or sold "because they went down" —not because of price. The best results have been obtained by investors that buy carefully.

TEST I: SHOWS PROBABILITY OF GETTING OUT EVEN
The stock under review has sold at its present price in (_____)* (none) of the last five years. The risk of loss seems (small) (average) (considerable) at the present price on the basis of price history.

* Three of five is a good standard.

TEST II: STACK THE ODDS IN THE INVESTORS FAVOR
The upside-downside ratio from Section 4D, page 2 of the Stock Selection Guide & Report is_____ to 1. This is (favorable) (average) (unfavorable), indicating that we need to pay attention to past price history (considerably) (some) (not much).

TEST III: THESE STANDARDS HELP INVESTORS AVOID LOSS
The pay-off test is whether at least 100% appreciation is possible in five years—or in the case of cyclical stocks, 20% a year for the number of years held. Analysis shows a high price of _____ is reasonable in _____ years, equal to _____ % a year.

In the case of cyclical stocks, comment should include the number of months the cycle has advanced and the dangers on this account.

5 WHAT ARE THE INVESTMENT CHARACTERISTICS OF THE COMPANY?

The Company is (well established) (new) and operates (internationally) (nationally) (regionally). The product line or service is (diversified) (narrow) and sold to (consumers) (manufacturers) (government). The business cycle affects sales and earnings (not much) (severely) (average). The company is (largest) (in top four) (a smaller factor) in its industry. The company and products are (well known) (average)

(not known) to the investing public. Its common stock is listed on (New York) (American) (other exchange) (unlisted) and has price records covering (five years) (only _____ years). It has (a continuous dividend record dating from _____) (a spotty dividend record) (no dividend record). Investment characteristics are (good) (average) (poor).

6 WHAT ARE THE CHARACTERISTICS OF THE COMPANY'S MAJOR INDUSTRY?

The _____ industry is (established) (new) and has (exceptional) (average) (below average) potential. The potential is based on (population) (product development) (science) (international expansion). Sales, profit margins and earnings per share fluctuate with the business cycle (widely—like the steel industry) (narrowly—like food) (average—like oil). Capital investment per dollar of sales in the industry is (high—like chemicals) (low—like clothing manufacture) (aver-

age—like metal products manufacturing), making it (easy) (difficult) for new competition to enter the business. Price competition between companies is (no problem) (severe) (average).

In my opinion, the major industry, everything considered, is (favorable) (average) (unfavorable). The company being analyzed will be (aided by the trend of the industry) or (will have to take business from competitors to grow).

7 WHAT ABOUT THE BUSINESS CYCLE?

About 33 months is an average business cycle, though variations from this norm are wide.

A well-managed company gains on marginal competitors in a depression or inflation as a general rule. In a period of business recovery, high grade stocks advance first, second grade stocks next, and marginal stocks last, as a general rule. Also, non-growth cyclical stocks are good purchases when business

turns up and should be sold in the later stages of the cycle because of exposure to substantial drops in price, earnings, and sometimes dividends.

The trend of business has been (up) (down) for _____ months. The current stage of the business cycle tends to (help) (not affect) (hurt) profits of the company. The present stage of the business cycle suggests (no concern) (caution) (daring) for the stock under review.

8 WHAT ABOUT THE STOCK MARKET AND YIELDS ON BONDS?

The price the stock is selling at is _____ and the Dow Jones Averages are at: Industrials _____, Transportation _____ and Utilities _____. This provides a reference in case of review of this stock in the future.

From the Value Line, it is seen that the stock under review has performed, as compared relatively (better) (same) (below).

You may also want to comment on the behavior of bond yields and Treasury Bill rates. Yields tend to rise in the later stages of a business cycle (attracting money from the stock market) and fall when business slows and investors want safety.

Bond yields may (attract) (not affect) (discourage) investment in this stock currently.

ST-1050

Index

INDEX

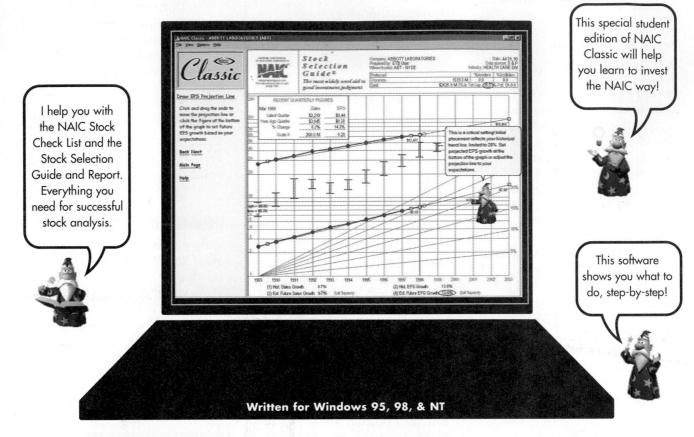